D0253302

IT'S A
WONDERFUL
LiE

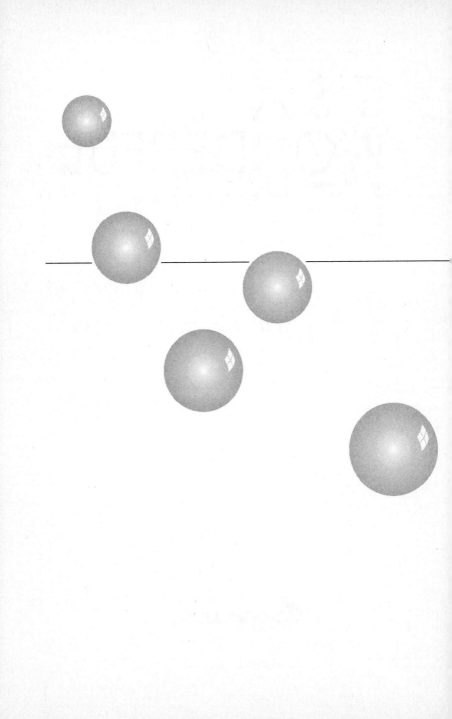

IT'S A
WONDERFUL
LiE

26 Truths About
Life in Your Twenties

Edited by Emily Franklin

FOREWORD BY ALEXANDRA ROBBINS

NEW YORK   BOSTON

Copyright page continues on page 282.

5 Spot

Warner Books
1271 Avenue of the Americas
New York, NY 10020

5 Spot and the 5 Spot logo are trademarks of Warner Books, Inc.

Printed in the United States of America

First Edition: January 2007
10 9 8 7 6 5 4 3 2 1

Library of Congress Cataloging-in-Publication Data

It's a wonderful lie : 26 truths about life in your twenties / edited by Emily Franklin.
—1st ed.
    p. cm
    Summary: "A collection of 26 original essays, ranging in tone from comedic to reflective, aims to empathize with, encourage, and inspire twentysomething women, addressing the overwhelming choices, new responsibilities, and freedoms they face every day"—Provided by the publisher.
    ISBN-13: 978-0-446-69777-4
    ISBN-10: 0-446-69777-X
1. Young women—Social conditions.   2. Young women—Psychology.   3. Young women—Economic conditions.   I. Franklin, Emily.
    HQ1229.I8   2007
    305.242'2—dc22   2006016566

For the friends
who saw me into and out of
my twenties

Acknowledgments

To Andie Avila; Faye Bender; everyone at Warner for help and enthusiasm; and to that wonderful, weird, crazy, demanding, lovely decade gone by—thank you.

Contents

LIE #5: "I'll be where I'm supposed to be, doing what I'm meant to be doing"

Foreword

Over the last several years, I've interviewed thousands of twenty-somethings, many of whom told me stories like this one: When Gail, a thirtysomething in New York City, was in her twenties, there was a period when she was crying every day. She hated her job, she knew her boyfriend of four years wasn't The One, she was sick of her roommates, and worst of all, she had an identical twin sister in medical school to whom she was constantly being compared. "[She was] on a track. Where was *my* track?" Gail recalled. "I was flipping out. I was reaching a dead end; I was miserable and lonely. It was like, 'Where do I go from here?' I felt I wasn't a real adult yet."

After several months, Gail decided to consult a psychiatrist for the first time. In the clichéd dim and dingy office, an older man with a notepad asked her what seemed to be the problem. Gail broke down in tears and explained her issues. She could think of only one way to describe them. "I'm having a midlife crisis," she said.

The doctor burst out laughing. "You don't look middle-aged to me," he said, guffawing, "so I don't think you're having a midlife crisis."

While the doctor's insensitive reaction left Gail feeling more depressed than before, he was right about one thing: Gail wasn't having a midlife crisis. She was having a *Quarterlife* Crisis.

I'm not one to label for the sake of labeling, and I don't think the rest of our generation is, either. In recent years, a new wave of classifications have been thrust upon those of us who happen to fall between the ages of eighteen and twenty-nine: We are, apparently, twixters, permanent adolescents, boomerangers, kidults, thresholders, and slackers, living in a "Peter Pan syndrome."

Peter Pan syndrome is so named because many researchers and reporters assume that twentysomethings "refuse to grow up." Similarly, the terms "twixters" and "thresholders" are based on the notion that the post-pubescent purgatory we occupy is one of our own choosing. Sociologist Terri Apter insisted recently, "They're on the threshold, the doorway to adulthood, and they're not going through it." It's as if, after sixteen or more years in a sheltered school setting, we pull over our graduation tassels and suddenly are expected to become equipped emotionally, pragmatically, and financially to make the major decisions associated with going through that door. But that's not the way it works.

The labels "permanent adolescents" and "boomerangers"—as in we listlessly boomerang back into our parents' homes—imply that, out of laziness, we would much prefer to waste our lives loafing while watching afternoon television and munching Fritos on our parents' couch. CNN has specifically accused twentysomethings of wanting merely to "lay around."

We don't languish in our state of limbo, however, as much as we battle it. Simply put, it is more difficult to be a twentysomething now than it was forty years ago. We face the most competitive hiring pool in history, with increasing numbers of college graduates. Furthermore, the age at which older generations expect us to succeed is rapidly plummeting; no longer is a thirty-year-old CEO deemed a whiz kid. With professional athletes drafted out of high school and A-list singer-actors in their teens, we're made to feel that if we haven't achieved something monumental by age twenty-five, then we're already over the hill. Regarding marriage, we are heavily influenced by that legendary 50 percent divorce rate. We do not want to make our parents' mistakes.

The truth is, we're not averse to growing up; we simply want to grow up responsibly. If "growing up" means attaining typically adult accoutrements, then it's not a question of won't, but can't. Generations before us could afford to support a marriage, house, and family in their early twenties because entry-level incomes could fund them. Today we wait until at least our late twenties, with good reason. We are the first generation in American history who won't do better financially than our parents. Add to that setback the crushing costs of student loans and lower incomes than previous twentysomethings had, and it's clear why taking our time is not just a preference but a necessity. Arguably, it is more adult of us to delay traditionally adult responsibilities until we financially and emotionally are able to support ourselves, let alone others.

When I first began using the phrase "Quarterlife Crisis" to describe a common experience occurring between the late teens and late thirties, it provoked derision from older adults. Contrary to a belief popular among older people, the Quarterlife Crisis is not the idle whining of a coddled, presumptuous post-adolescent. It is the response to reaching the turning point between young adulthood and adulthood; it is the amalgamation of doubt, confusion, and fear that comes with facing an overwhelming set of identity issues and societal expectations at once. The Quarterlife Crisis can spark a variety of reactions ranging from subtle self-doubt to issues as serious as clinical depression.

The biggest difference between my label and the condescending new catchphrases is that I identified an experience, not a generation. The term "Quarterlife Crisis" offers a category for those who wish to be reassured that their doubts are normal. Young adults can choose whether or not to associate with it.

I imagine if Gail's psychiatrist, whom she never went to again, heard me today, he would probably still laugh. Some adults—

usually those in a midlife crisis—roll their eyes when they hear "Quarterlife Crisis." "Twentysomethings can't be in crisis!" they say. "When you have your youth and freedom, you have nothing to complain about."

I try turning the tables. "If that's your reason for dismissing a Quarterlife Crisis," I reply, "then how can you complain about a midlife crisis when you have a spouse, a car, a savings account, and a backyard with a pool?" They are not amused. The generation gap grows fierce.

Gail, like many women in their thirties, is happy now and more at peace with herself. Over the years, she has taught herself strategies and coping mechanisms to help her figure out who she is and who she wants to be. I believe her success in conquering these issues means that for her, middle age will be a breeze. Because we in Gail's generation are confronting our identity demons in our twenties rather than waiting until our forties or fifties, I don't think we're going to *have* a midlife crisis. And then older doctors who dismissed our doubts will see who has the last laugh.

—Alexandra Robbins

Introduction

This collection came about through a universal feeling: the disillusionment of being twentysomething. We start the decade full of hope, curiosity, and images of what will be, and yet, once we're there, we're often left wondering if this is it.

After all, the movie version of being in your twenties seems ideal: You're free of parental control, living the good life with friends, fun, and a fabulous job. Love interests appear when you want them, and if they don't, well, the single, sexy life holds its own magic.

Yet the reality of life in your twenties is much more complex. Yes, you're free to move about the cabin as you wish, but what about that job satisfaction? What about that post-college relationship that falls flat once put to the test of the real world? What about feeling lonely?

This book explores the highs and lows of the exciting, frustrating, challenging decade between twenty and thirty, when everything is simultaneously at your feet and just out of reach.

When I graduated from college, I had only one item on my key chain: the key to my car. I had no apartment, no job, no relationship, and though I had secured a spot at a top graduate school, I suspected my reasons for going were more out of avoidance than out of wanting to continue my education. Looking back, I can tidy my path so it seems streamlined; I finished college, worked a bit, fell in love, and got married. But that's the simple version. The truth is, as with most of my friends, the path that got me to where I am now has a varied geographical and emotional topography.

I envisioned my twenties as a steady climb toward a constant work goal, but instead: I worked as a sous chef on a yacht, I wrote medical verbiage, I edited travel brochures, I labored in construction, I taught high school English and first grade, and—when money got really tight—I was a substitute gym and home ec teacher.

Where love was concerned, my parents met in high school, my brother met his wife in college, surely the love of my life would present himself to me shortly thereafter, right? Wrong. Right after college, I embarked on a summer fling that transformed into a live-in relationship that culminated in money owed (him), a wounded if not entirely broken heart (me), and tons of photographs from our travels (both), bookshelves we'd built together and faux-finished in a fit of domesticity, recipes I'd created while cooking for him every night (groan).

The vision I'd had of moving through the decade armed with my closest friends had to shift, too. One friend moved to London, another to Chicago, and I suddenly had to figure out what it was like to make friends without the commonality of classes or dorms. One old friendship finally crumbled, while new ones started to form from activities like book group, running, and knitting. Also, I reconnected with childhood friends or linked up with friends of friends.

Like everyone, I wanted an easy path—I wanted to be sure of where I was headed—but here's what I didn't know: It takes time. And within that time, I reexamined what it was I thought I wanted, otherwise known as learning from my experiences. So I didn't want to be a chef, a medical writer, in love with the wrong guy. But how to proceed?

For me, the answer was in the journal I constantly kept in my bag as I moved towns or apartments. One simple line helped to shape the rest of my life: *I need to write*. In a moment of truth with myself, I'd admitted my dream. So I left behind the odd jobs and bad boy and went back to graduate school (where I met more friends), complete with real-world knowledge that would ironically help me in crafting the novel I longed to write. I wrote and traveled and earned my master's, and a few years later, right when I was set to trek across India and Nepal (read: the *least* convenient time possible), I met the man of my dreams and the rest—as is often written—is history. But it's not general history, it's only *my* history.

And that's what is at the heart of being twentysomething: creating your own history, your memories, your own path to a job, financial independence, love, lust, and—finally—a life you can call your own.

The wonderful contributors in this collection reveal themselves (and some universal truths) and are grouped into sections that touch on the categories of twentysomething life (and lies).

"I'll have an amazing apartment and love my job" brings us inside first apartments and first flings with careers. With humor and vivid detail, Jill Kargman shows us the dingy, high-rent, low-frills flat she wanted to call home, while Donna Freitas lets us in on the doubts that plague her as she balances the phenomenal apartment that comes with a soul-sucking job. Leanne Shear and Tracey Toomey trace their path from being girls who were told they could achieve anything—as long as they achieved what other people wanted—to finding their places tending bar, raking in cash, and making the most of life. By exploring her wardrobe and the jobs that cling to each shirt or skirt, Alison Pace maps her employment history and her road to what she wants. Megan McCafferty takes a brave step and opens her personal journals to the world as she looks back on the wantings and what-ifs of her twentysomething mind.

"I'll have everything I need to live the life I've always wanted" leads with Cara Lockwood's all-too-true affair with her credit card, and the highs and lows of overspending. On the opposite end of the financial spectrum, Laura Caldwell lived on ramen noodles while earning her law degree; details her experience being left out of lavish nights on the town with friends and how the wait for solvency was worth it. Erica Kennedy floundered her way through a variety of jobs, surviving homelessness and near poverty, until she was able to forge a career as a writer in her late twenties and create the life she assumed she'd have straight out of college. Meanwhile, Megan Crane, like so many of us, couldn't figure out what to do when a job or a place didn't seem right, so she found her solace in graduate school.

"I'll know myself and what I want." Growing through the twenties doesn't come without humility, as we see from reading Anna Maxted's essay—haven't we all felt we're "too good" to be doing a certain level of work? With a surprising slant, Melissa Senate flip-flops the age-old "guy who couldn't commit" tale; she's the one who couldn't say yes to Mr. Right, and she learned more than she thought she would when tragedy struck. Shannon O'Keefe comes to terms with how your current age never feels like you thought it would. We're taught to say no as a means of self-preservation, but much of Beth Lisick's pleasure in life has come from saying yes. Rebecca Traister explores the need other people—particularly parents—have to see the twentysomething daughter, son, or friend as stunningly happy; she delves into how we make peace with that need ourselves.

"I'll have satisfying relationships, great sex, and fabulous friends." Love, sex, friendship, lust—juicy words in and of themselves, but what about when they're combined? With high expectations, Jennifer O'Connell moved in with her college boyfriend only to find that post-dorm domesticity wasn't all it's cracked up to be; she explains that moving to the next stage of life sometimes means dropping off luggage. Married in her early twenties, Pamela Ribon wonders about the sex she didn't have, and about what she might have gained (or lost) as a result. Female friendship can be as easy as a roommate assignment in college, but in the working world, friends can be hard to come by, as Leah Stewart notes. On the other side of friendship, Caprice Crane's words touch on the male-female friendship and its role in the twentysomething life. Deanna Kizis has plenty of guy friends—after the romance ended—and digs around at the post-breakup friendship phenomenon. Hollis Gillespie's comedic take on that forbidden-yet-inevitable work fling shows us the risks and rewards that come with the territory. For those of us who can't let go of Carrie Bradshaw as the image of single life, Kristen Harmel takes on her own Mr. Big and lives to tell the tale. Laurie Graff looks at the men in her life and concludes a hugely important twentysomething lesson: that life is continually evolving, and that the search for self rarely culminates in a tidy, perfect bow.

Without a doubt, part of the years between twenty-one and twenty-nine involve movement: apartment swapping, trekking uptown or down, retreating home, or venturing to places as yet unseen, as demonstrated in **"I'll be where I'm supposed to be, doing what I'm meant to be doing."** When Heather Swain left the safety of her midwestern life for a small town in Japan, she tested her new marriage and herself and gained more than she imagined she would. Anna Jane Grossman compels us to look at those "almost" points in life when one step in either direction seems like it will change the course of everything. Julianna Baggott's emotional real estate investment demonstrates that sometimes home is found within another person. We conclude the book with Giselle Zado Wasfie's relatable essay about the nomadic existence so common among twentysomethings—and how the search for self, committing to your own development, and finding completion can often involve staying put in one place long enough to take root.

I am now in my early thirties and still collecting moments, synthesizing my daily encounters to figure out where I want to go next. What I value most from my twenties—even though it was the hardest to deal with then—is the variety of jobs, dates, towns, and feelings I experienced. The recipes I made for the bad boy now help me to cook interesting dishes for my young children. The old friendship that dissolved keeps me mindful of the good friends I have now. The difficult dates make for great story fodder. Memories of the travel sustain me in months when I'm stuck treading the same path from preschool to home and back. The construction job gave me the confidence to paint, retile, and refinish a house myself. I may not have loved every minute of my twenties, but I love what I learned from those days, months, and seasons: mainly, the knowledge of who I am—or who I could be.

May the essays in this book provide you with humor, solace, food for thought, enlightenment, and entertainment as you look forward to or relive your twenties.

—Emily Franklin

Lie #1

"I'll have an amazing apartment and love my job"

A Letter to My Crappy One-Bedroom

By Jill Kargman

Dearest Apartment No. 5,

Some girls chart the chapters of their lives with jobs or guys or haircuts; I do it with real estate. You, No. 5, are inextricably linked to every memory I have from the mostly heinous four years we spent together, but in the end, you were the one that built me back up from lonely twenty-four-year-old whimpering kvetch subsumed with worries about The Future. I arrived scarred and feeble and left happy, relieved, and whole. But we both know it wasn't easy.

When we met, I was as maudlin as tattered Cosette in the *Les Miz* poster. You were way more charming than other shitboxes I'd seen on my Tasmanian Devil whirlwind tour of way too expensive hovels, but your exposed brick and dreamy location near Central Park didn't soothe my weary bones and battered emotions. I was from New York and had never thought anyone could be lonely there until the moment I signed your lease.

The Hot Israeli Movers came to pack me up from my downtown abode, a hipster gigantor luminous loft compared to you, my dark third floor-walkup. Let's face it, my sweet, you were definitely a downgrade. The movers found me tear-stained, sitting on a cardboard box, refugee-style.

"Breakup move?" one asked with a sympathetic look.

Whoa. ESP? "Mm-hmm." I sniffled, wiping a hot errant tear.

"Don't worry, honey, we do this all the time. You're gonna be just fine."

Then boom-chicka-boom porno music came on, and he banged me in the back of the Schlepper's truck. Just lying. Actually, I was beginning a long and heinous dry spell *sans saucisson*.

I realized this when my sitcom-style reverie of hot-neighbor sexual tension was dashed instantly: of the ten apartments, eight were occupied by single women. Of the remaining two tenants, one was a family with three kids (did I mention all the apartments were one-bedrooms?), and the other was a buzzer that read "Erlichman." I held out hope for an NJB (Nice Jewish Boy), but Erlichman turned out to be an AARP card carrier who told me his rent control had him paying $300 a month, compared to my nightmarish monthly ka-ching that was over six times that. "The landlord would love to see me go, but I got news for him," he told me in the staircase, which was adorned with pheasant-covered wallpaper. "They'll be taking me outta here in my coffin." Good times!

Then the gal directly upstairs moved out (got married, migrated to the 'burbs), and in came cocaine-snorting, Moby-blaring Michelle, the town bicycle—and I mean every guy in New York had a ride. I didn't know which was worse, the song "Body Rock" playing on a loop, like seriously eleventy times in a row, or the humping and bumping from her iron bed. Most mornings a different guy would emerge, each looking like he should have the word "disease" stamped across his forehead. The big twist here? Cokehead ho worked on Wall Street and donned hose and lady suits every day, weird.

Meanwhile, for normal non-druggie moi, there was pas d'action in the sack for a while. While I loved being out of a high-rise and into your intimate cozier perch, the views of hand-holding couples squoze lemon juice on the wound of my singledom. The nights with you were very lonely, sitting on an explosion of Pottery Barn, listening not only to the symphony of bangage upstairs but also to my racing thoughts that stomped on top of one another, collage-like, inside my head. Would I die in this apartment alone? Would they carry my lifeless bod down the walk-up steps, like the dude upstairs? Would I grow so lonely that I, too, would drag grody suitors up for a role in the hay to get rid of the forming cobwebs in my vag? No, no, I have never been able to do that.

I would turn on my el cheapo crappy TV that was so small, I might as well have been watching the yuppie across the street's giant plasma flatscreen. Nothing I wanted to watch was ever on. That's when I learned that 4:00 A.M. is the loneliest hour. Why do they show so many upsetting movies in the middle of the night? I mean, nervous-breakdown central. I remember watching *Jagged Edge* and *Single White Female* alone, and somewhere around the time Jennifer Jason Leigh jammed her stiletto through the guy's eyeball socket into his brain and killed him, I thought, This might not be the cheeriest thing to watch in the middle of the night. I think deep down I wanted to take the plunge into my despair over my breakup and really feel the pain. And I did. I woke up with what Humbert Humbert called *pavor nocturnus*—complete and total, all-enveloping Night Panic. You know, heart pounding for no reason, cold sweats, racing brain, thoughts of spinsterhood.

There were two things that calmed me down: infomercials and Vanessa. And her sage advice and friendship, unlike Facersise® (get your face skinnier with a VHS tape and creams!), was free and enhanced my life, since we met loaded with textbooks our first day of freshman year in college. Vanessa is a tall blonde who is modelesque in looks and even smarter than she is drop-dead gorge. From midnight Chinese food Hoover-vac feasts to psycho-long walks to endless phonefests into the wee hours, she was like the sister/shrink I never had. I once saw a needlepoint pillow that said TRUE FRIENDS ARE THE ONES YOU CAN CALL AT 3:00 A.M., and headache came on, and he said he had to go. I never heard from him again.

About a year later, after a couple of failed mini-relationships, I really hit the nadir. For some reason, all my best friends had boyfriends. I bitterly lamented the fact that I was utterly and completely alone. Except I wasn't. I had roommates. Small, furry gray roommates.

The shrieks began when a *pavor nocturnus* fit woke me. I had that inner battle of "do I deal with getting out of bed to pee or not?" I tried go back to sleep, but once I recognized my bladder, I eventually had to go. I was heading to the bathroom when I first saw a mouse/rat (they're both so gross, they're indistinguishable to me, but I believe the city has only rats, and the country has mice). It darted across your two-by-two kitchenette, which was not unlike the proportions of an airplane bathroom, and I thought I was going to pass out. I tripped and fell, scraping my knee on the Pottery Barn sisal, and didn't seem to care about the blood gushing out of my knee as much as the fact that I was living among rodentia.

I called your owner and freaked. Her cold response? "Welcome to New York, kid." I informed her I was from New York and never had four-legged squatters. She dispatched her exterminating company, Roachbusters, whose logo naturally was a Ghostbusters sign with a cockroach instead of Casper. Nice. Two weeks later, I could still hear them scampering. I called your owner again, saying perhaps if she had sent a company called Mousebusters, we wouldn't have this problem. Eventually, thanks to mousetraps, which I had the pleasure of hearing snap in the night, the problem was solved.

But more than anything, the mice forced me to make plans every single night. Gone were the dates with Orville Redenbacher and Time Warner cable; I had to leave to avoid other sightings. I made a voiced-out-loud pact with the mice that they could hang as long as I never saw or heard them and they shat under the sink.

So I started leaving you and going out. All the time. Vanessa and I were so inseparable on the junior benefit circuit, people thought we were lesbians. Or if I didn't have plans, I'd put on my earphones and walk for miles and miles, à la Forrest Gump, minus the beard and retardation. I started going to plays again, even by myself. One theatrical plunge was so therapeutic, it began to take over my life. You must have wanted to shoot me for blaring *Hedwig and the Angry Inch* every second for a year. My friend Trip and I went to see the amazing musical in the West Village, and when we came out, I was singing the songs at the top of my lungs down Jane Street. He stopped and looked in my eyes. "You're back," he said. "We lost you there for a little while, but now you're back." I burst into happy tears because deep down, I knew he was right. That was the reason Vanessa had spoken of: I hadn't been fully myself in my previous relationship, and I was at last returning to my kooky uncensored side.

As winter thawed, I left you more and more; those long walks I was taking became longer walks—to Wall Street and back to Seventy-sixth, even round-trips to Brooklyn. So I thought I'd walk the New York Marathon, why the hell not. Seeing as how I am the worst athlete ever to roam this earth (think JV volleyball, benchwarmer), it was a true miracle that I finished it. I think it was some crazy challenge for myself that I knew I'd never do again, but I had to do it once just to prove after nights and nights of lonely walks that I could actually leave you and go into the world. All five boroughs, to be exact.

My cute parents were freezing at the finish line, waiting for me, complete with GO, JILL, GO! signage, not realizing I'd finished way earlier than planned. I staggered home alone in my silver cape-thingy and, of course, my medal. I remember walking in and looking around your space. I was exhausted and could barely haul my ass to the shower, but I felt so proud: Despite the fact that my body was near collapse, my head was strong.

A few months later, I went on a blind date with a guy named Harry whom my grandma Ruth fixed me up with—the grandson of her friend Betty. My first thought was one word: Oy. Just what I needed, a dweeb who is such a power-nerd, he needs his nana for a fix-up with an NJG. But my life was so shtetl, because sure enough, it was practically love at first sight for me. He was a beyond adorable, scruffy nugget in his Harvard Ski Team pants (double-whammy hotness factor of brains and balls), and after dinner, we walked and talked and venue-hopped for hours. At four A.M., he put me in a cab and gave me a kiss on the cheek, asking if we could have dinner again two nights later. Natch, I said yes, beaming and giddy.

Unlike many nights coming home to you, tonight had elated me. There had been so many evenings of dashed hopes after a supposedly fun party where I was in the back of the cab, hanging it up for the night, my only fun to be with *Saturday Night Live* upon my return.

But this time, as I put my key in your door, I heard the phone ringing. Huh? I ran up the stairs. The clock read 4:17 as I picked up. "I just wanted to make sure you got home safe," Harry said.

The next morning, at my *Sex and the City*–style recon brunch with Vanessa, I told her I had met my husband. It turned out I was right. Twenty months later, we were married, and it was your threshold he carried me over when we returned from our honeymoon. Being in love made your ceiling's peeling paint less of an eyesore, the cacophony of the neighbors more muted, and the gray critters less scary. Suddenly, you were a palace—well, maybe not quite a palace, but my rose-tinted glasses transformed you from lonely bachelorette pad to love nest, filled with smells of cooking for two instead of microwave-popcorn-as-dinner in sweatpants.

Apartment No. 5, sometimes I think that if only I'd had a crystal ball, I would have enjoyed our time together much more. If I had known I'd fall in love and be settled with work and be happy, I could have relished those years and not stressed so much. But knowing the future would have ruined it, because it was my hard times with you that got me to where I needed to be. It was in the four walls of your living room where I pep-talked myself back from the downer days. It was in your bedroom where I chatted with my best friends. Sure, I was lonely, but that time alone helped solidify what I wanted and who I really was. In the end, the fairy-tale ending was not because of Harry—he didn't save me—it was because of you. You helped me get independent, you returned me to my old self, and you delivered me to Harry when I was ready. And that is why, despite my nightmare neighbors and cheesy pheasant hallway wallpaper and mice and Moby and assoholic landlords, I am so happy we met. I don't miss you, but I will always love you.

Girls Can Do Anything!

By Leanne Shear and Tracey Toomey

Starting when we were about five years old, both of our mothers posted similar signs that exclaimed GIRLS CAN DO ANYTHING! We each took the sign quite literally, and at any given point in our young lives, whenever anyone asked us what we wanted to be when we grew up, we'd answer decisively, "A doctor," "A teacher," or "An astronaut!" Funny, the one occupation neither of us ever blurted out was "A bartender!"

Seventeen years later, we both stood proudly at attention, dressed in cap and gown, on the stages of our prestigious universities. Tracey was set to shoot her big scene in *A Beautiful Mind,* which went on to win an Academy Award. Leanne was about to begin a high-powered consulting career at Sterling Group in New York City. We'd each put down security deposits on a sixth-floor walk-up apartment in the East Village, hit IKEA, and started making payments on our student loans. Our mothers were right—we girls *could* "do anything." Neither of us could wait to dive into the future.

Little did we know that under a year later, we'd be drowning together in a sea of soiled bar rags, discarded beer bottles, and abusive customers. Our seemingly ideal post-college occupations quickly dissolved in reality. It turned out that getting lead roles in Ron Howard films and moonlighting in Tony Award–winning

Broadway shows was challenging, indeed. Pounding the pavement en route to auditions every day was exhausting, and the rejection could get unbearable. Statistically, the average *working* actor in New York books only one job out of every fifty auditions. Tracey's plan of getting signed by a high-powered agent immediately after graduation, touring the film festival circuit with her latest brilliant film, and being on *Letterman* before her twenty-third birthday seemed a little improbable. For that matter, becoming the first twenty-three-year-old executive vice president of a leading consulting firm wasn't a piece of cake; not that this was even what Leanne had dreamed of. The job at Sterling was, for her, a one-way ticket to New York City, where she could get settled, make a few bucks, and one day break into Pulitzer Prize–winning journalism for *The New Yorker*. However, she found it all too easy to get mired in office politics in her "cushy" job.

Tracey's character on *All My Children* got written off the show, and without "Nurse Linda's" salary, she couldn't make ends meet. Meanwhile, Leanne made the switch from corporate America to a "career" in freelance gossip-magazine writing. We both needed fast cash, not to mention a little bit less stress (even a little fun), in our professional lives.

Onieal's Grand Street, a former speakeasy in SoHo with a dark mahogany carved ceiling and long, burnished bar top, provided the perfect backdrop for our introduction. Leanne had gotten the bartending job at Onieal's through a friend at Penn, and Tracey scored the same gig a couple of months later, after meeting the owner at another bar. Our first night together behind the bar, while we were sweating through the demands of two hundred Red Bull–amped Wall Street execs, we happened to look up from the sour-apple martinis we were churning out, to notice that we had the exact same hip-shaking move to Bryan Adams's "Summer of '69." A best friendship and bartending partnership was born.

One night (actually, one early morning), after we'd dragged

four enormous fly-covered trash bags to the curb, we settled onto stools at the deserted bar and opened up a bottle of Rex Hill pinot noir as part of our post-work, wind-down ritual. We started re-hashing the night's war stories.

"Can you believe that girl who fell down the stairs?"

We'd both laughed when the perfectly coiffed, petite blonde who'd apparently had one too many Jolly Rancher shots pulled herself off the sticky floor and slurred threateningly, "I'll sue you!" before stumbling out the door.

"What about the country-line-dance guy? That was hysterical."

In a sea of white and blue button-down shirts, a lone redhead in a loud plaid flannel had tried to corral the entire crowd to line-dance to hip-hop. "Come on, y'all," he'd twanged, "I got ninety-nine problems, but a bitch ain't one!"

Before we knew it, the seeds of a book were taking hold.

Our schedule involved bartending together five nights a week until five A.M., then meeting bleary-eyed at Starbucks a few hours later to work on our manuscript. We went from shots of whiskey to shots of espresso without missing a beat.

While researching our novel, we came across an interesting piece of information: The first-ever female bartenders were actually prostitutes in German beer houses. They served not only pints to patrons, but a hell of a lot more if the price was right. During the time we worked on the first draft of the manuscript, we found ourselves dealing with customers who made remarks like "Nice rack" or "I love it when you bend over to get my Corona, sweetheart." More often than not, these customers assumed we didn't have an ounce of intelligence or drive in our "pretty little heads"; they asked us condescending questions like "Did you finish high school, honey?" As bartenders, we were viewed as objects, programmed to smile blankly and robotically turn out cocktails. We needed the money to pay the bills, but at times we felt like we were compromising our character. Girls could still "do anything," including supporting themselves by bartending, but they had to be prepared for how they would feel after some guy casually inquired, "So, what kind of a tip do I have to give you to get you to come home with me tonight?"

Too many nights ended with laments as we wiped down the bar. "I hate when that guy John comes in here," Tracey would say. "He always makes me feel so uncomfortable."

"I know," Leanne would agree. "Every time he comes in, I put on my sweatshirt because he's always staring at my chest."

"I'm so tired of getting hit on by old, gross men who think they're allowed to say whatever they want to us because they think we're just idiot bartenders."

We weren't the only ones who were uncomfortable with our new roles. When we first announced to our mothers that we'd abandoned a traditional career path in favor of slinging drinks, their distress was palpable. Of course they worried about our safety and lack of health insurance. But as it turned out, their concern was motivated by something even deeper. They felt that their generation of women had made so much progress toward sexual equality, paving the way for us to be the first group of women to have every career opportunity imaginable available. Neither of our mothers was a bra burner, but they had both taken part in the movement. If they'd made sacrifices to stand up for feminist ideals, why were their daughters choosing to bartend and willingly put themselves in a position where they were objectified? The irony was impossible to ignore. We were told girls could "do anything" by mothers who had lobbied for equality of opportunity. Little did we know that there were limitations on "anything." It certainly didn't include bartending.

Friends and acquaintances were also surprised by our decision. Whenever people we knew from college happened to come into the bar, we were plagued by shame and struggled to keep the awkwardness in check. Our investment-banker friends came into Onieal's dressed in starched shirts and conservative suits, while we wore beer-soaked, skimpy halter tops and perilously short miniskirts. An acquaintance from Leanne's alma mater booked her birthday party at Onieal's and filled the bar with her usual coterie of perfectly pressed, flawlessly manicured acolytes. When she arrived, she simpered up to the bar and ordered a glass of Veuve Clicquot. She did a double take when she recognized Leanne, exclaiming with a tinge of surprise and derision, "What are *you* doing back there?"

When a fellow actress from Tracey's conservatory (who at that moment happened to be starring in a major Broadway show and a popular ABC sitcom) popped into Onieal's for a cocktail, she remarked pityingly, "Don't worry, Tracey. Your time will come, honey. You won't be bartending forever."

Our college-friends-turned-Manhattan-roommates generally left for work as we were coming home from work. There's nothing like meeting your roommate—fresh from a post-gym shower—in the elevator when you're stinking like stale Jose Cuervo and have mascara oozing down your cheeks. "Rough night?" she'd ask, her tone modulating between sympathy and disgust. People who once knew us as excelling in literature classes, at cross-country meets, or in the theater now found us scrubbing glasses, frantically serving hordes of demanding customers, and fielding lewd pickup lines like "Is that a mirror in your pocket? Because I can definitely see myself in your pants."

So why *did* we choose to bartend? Aside from the obvious benefits—fast cash, a built-in social life, endless networking opportunities—being a bartender is one of the only professions without an arduous corporate ladder to climb. There are plenty of politics involved in securing plum shifts at a lucrative spot, but once you get the job, you make the same amount of money as the guy standing next to you who's been doing it for thirty years. Bartending is the ultimate in immediate gratification. And as products of the ADD generation—results-oriented versus process-oriented—we wondered why we would wait ten years to make money when we could do it instantly. Plus, bartending freed up our days so we could progress in our respective artistic endeavors.

On top of working together on our novel, Leanne was getting published in *New York* magazine, and Tracey was landing roles in successful independent films. In contrast, one friend of ours took the hierarchical route at one of the biggest talent agencies in Los Angeles and worked hundred-hour weeks answering phones and making photocopies for a high-powered agent who couldn't be bothered to so much as glance at the screenplay our friend was toiling away on. The assistant-level job didn't pay enough for gas to get back and forth from work; she wouldn't be promoted to junior agent for another five years; and to top it all off, her screenplay seemed doomed to forever collect dust in her desk drawer.

Meanwhile, we were spending our free time auditioning and submitting freelance articles, working on our book, and spending our surplus cash on new computers and new head shots. Bartending became infinitely more bearable once we had the novel to work on. The idea of writing a book based on our experiences behind the bar justified the job itself. Instead of just being a place where we'd exploit ourselves to make a quick buck, the bar was also where we conducted all our research.

However, we learned that bartending is a double-edged sword, and we often wondered if we'd made the right decision. There's no such thing as a promotion in the bar world, and the money quickly levels off. When we first started working together, we developed a following of loyal, big-tipping customers who came to the bar to see us in action. On any given night, we could walk away with upward of three hundred dollars, sometimes much more. But as we got deeper into our twenties, friends started ascending the rungs of the corporate and financial ladder, while our income remained constant. One close friend became the youngest vice president at Morgan Stanley and was a millionaire by age twenty-eight. In sharp juxtaposition, our idea of career advancement had become working at the hottest club in the Hamptons.

To compound it all, we found ourselves constantly battling against the stereotype of the female bartender. At low moments, we felt like those German prostitutes in filthy, crowded beer halls. We couldn't help but notice that our tips had a funny way of increasing exponentially as our necklines plunged (the bar world's only form of a "raise"). We were toeing a fine line between propriety and the need to make a decent living in a work environment where sexual harassment was practically in the job description. In the corporate world, while sexual dynamics certainly play a role, a woman is usually protected by anti–sexual harassment statutes. Can you imagine an arbitrator responding to a scantily clad bartender's gripes about a customer commenting on her body after she'd been doing shots and flirting with him all night? The bottom line is, if we didn't entertain a man's advances, we wouldn't get tipped. In our hand-to-mouth existence, every dollar counted, even the ones we felt shitty about working for. We incessantly grappled with the question "How much is this money worth?"

Harassment wasn't always as overt as inappropriate comments or touching. One regular customer purported to be a Hollywood producer who worked with the likes of Steven Spielberg and Tom Hanks. Feeding on our vulnerability (and ambition), he enticed us both at different times with promises of movie roles and screenwriting credits. To an aspiring actress or writer laboring behind a bar, such promises are manna from heaven and cause for fierce hope. We found out later that he was a fraud. It was nearly a rite of passage at Onieal's to think you were going to be discovered through his next film.

Furthermore, going home with a patron from the bar created a loaded situation. After we'd been serving a guy all night long (an exchange of goods and services for cash), we couldn't help but feel that energy carry over into the intimacy—the beer-hall bartender/prostitute rearing her ugly head once more. The roles had been clearly delineated as server and client, and it was impossible to ignore the dynamic. We always felt we were pigeonholed as "the bartender," and all the stereotypes of the label haunted us. In the end, the paradigm precluded an authentic connection.

If a bartender does decide to hook up with a customer, and it doesn't work out, one of two things can happen. Either the guy stops coming to the bar altogether, which can result in a major loss of business for both the bartender and the establishment; or he could become a veritable stalker. He knows when and where he can find you, and there's nothing to stop him from coming in to see you. A fellow bartender at Onieal's met a seemingly great guy while on the job and started dating him. She ended things with him after a couple of months, but he refused to accept the breakup. He came in every shift she worked and beseeched her to take him back. When that didn't work, he sat at the bar all night glowering. His visits became increasingly threatening, and eventually, she had to quit Onieal's. This wouldn't have been a problem if she'd worked at a PR firm; he never would have made it past the security desk. Girls could still "do anything," but there may be a price involved.

It was undeniable: Scandal and debauchery really did lurk behind every dark mahogany corner, and sex, power, and alcohol weren't the only ingredients in our toxic cocktail. Fellow bartenders were stealing fistfuls of cash nightly—instead of ringing drinks into the register, they'd simply pocket the money. One of the clubs we worked at in the Hamptons felt like the Enron of the bar world. Embezzlement was so rampant that the place filed for bankruptcy. We weren't immune to the seduction of more and more cash. At times the bar world's vices coalesced in a way that made us feel as dirty and stained as the dollar bills we peeled off the bar.

We never could have survived our tenure behind the bar without each other. Since we met—whether bartending, writing, or just grabbing a margarita—we've spent nearly every waking moment together. It was almost painful whenever one of us had to bartend without the other; we didn't make nearly as much money without our dual chemistry, didn't have anywhere close to as much fun, and didn't have anyone to get our backs. When the psycho girl in the Hamptons reached across the packed bar and grabbed Tracey's hair to get her attention, Leanne was at the ready to have her thrown out. When Leanne had "beer tears" after a customer called her a bitch, Tracey overcharged his credit card and sent him on his way. Let's be honest, it's never fun to jump up on the bar and dance to "Sweet Child o' Mine" by yourself, and drinking red wine after a long shift without your partner is downright depressing. The bar became an emblem of our friendship and business partnership; we entered the nightlife netherworld and escaped it as a team.

When we first started shaking martinis, neither of us had any idea where it would take us. We thought it would be a way to pay the bills while we pursued acting and writing. Throughout every long, liquor-soaked night, we were waiting for our professional lives to begin, when in fact we were living them the whole time—accumulating research for a career neither of us had ever imagined. After our moms acclimated themselves to the idea that we wouldn't follow a safe career path (and once we had an actual book deal for *The Perfect Manhattan*), we all redefined our ideas of what success connotes. As five-year-olds gazing at our GIRLS CAN DO ANYTHING! signs, we had a narrow, definitive view of success. Now we're not so sure. In bartending, success was easy to measure—at the end of the night, the register spit out a summary of the night's sales, and the tip bucket was an easy gauge. Ironically, as published authors, we're still judged by how much we sell.

Still, no matter what our rank is on Amazon.com, there's no denying that our partnership and friendship made us twice the women we would be on our own. We've learned that girls really can do anything, especially if they have each other.

An (Un)Literary Tour of My Twentysomething Mind: Journals 1995–1999

By Megan McCafferty

September 12, 1995 I was watching *Melrose Place* last night. For a moment I thought, *Wow. Life after college sure is sexy and exciting.* And then I remembered that I *was* living life after college. And that it sucks.

I probably shouldn't say this, but I was always skeptical of books like this one, in which an assortment of celebrated writers draw upon their personal trials and tribulations to prove that you, dear reader, are not alone in your angst. I could never buy into the takeaway wisdom proffered in these types of essays, the sunny "I did it, so can you!" spin put on any life crisis suffered by those who have come out triumphantly on the other side.

Don't get me wrong, I'm not discrediting my fellow authors. Back then my fractured state of mind was in no condition to judge the soundness of anyone's advice. I was too mired in the mess of my life to accept that these successful women had once been stuck in their own existential muck. I'd skim through the pages, roll my eyes, and think, Easy for you to say, Ms. Best Seller. Life sucked and now it doesn't. Woo-hoo for you.

So what makes this essay any different? I have proof.

I started keeping a diary in fifth grade and continued to do so for the next fifteen years. My most prolific period was between the ages of twenty-two and twenty-six, immediately following my college graduation in 1995 until the sale of my first novel in 1999. If you were to read the diaries kept by any one of the other contributors to this anthology, they might reflect an epochal time of great creative development. Perhaps *their* journals capture the burgeoning brilliance of an artist in bloom, with poignant prose that bursts with energy and stuns you, dear reader, with heart-breaking insights into the state of our world at the dawn of the twenty-first century.

It's a pity, then, that you won't get to read those journals. Because mine are shamelessly all about ME! ME! ME! And oh, what a disaster I was.

September 26, 1996 I'm twenty-three and I conduct search-and-destroy missions for gray hair. I'm twenty-three and I scrutinize my face, trying to separate the temporary lack-of-sleep undereye bags from permanent wrinkles. I'm twenty-three and I'm obsessed with how my ass is falling so far and so fast that it will soon be indistinguishable from the backs of my knees. I'm twenty-three and last night I tried calculating the optimum percentage of my pay to take out for my 401(k) plan. I'm twenty-three and I feel . . . so . . . fucking . . . *old*.

I wrote in the pre-blog era, for my eyes only, so my journals are both self-absorbed and unself-conscious. I never imagined anyone else would read them, so I was wholly uncensored. Especially when I was drunk.

February 17, 1997 I am alone in my apartment. And I am also drunk. I finished off a bottle of white zinfandel, using a glass that has no mate because I dropped it on the kitchen linoleum months ago. It's MY glass and I drink from it when I AM ALONE. Any gifted alcoholic worth her Pulitzer would be drinking something smoky and dark and sad, like bourbon. But no, when I get wasted, it's with something sweet and pink and just so goddamn cheerful. This seems to be adequate proof that I'll never amount to much as a writer.

My twentysomething self would be mortified to find out that I'm making these private thoughts public. Why betray my poor misguided self? (And when I say "poor," I mean literally, as in living unsubsidized and without a trust fund in New York City on $21,000 a year before taxes.) Why remind everyone how I guzzled white zin with ice cubes? (Klassy!) Or how I got a ridiculous Rachel haircut and wore my impossibly high-waisted, tapered jeans with disposable hoochie tops from Strawberry? How I mangled the pronunciation of "zeitgeist" and "fois gras"? And couldn't remember the difference between *The New Yorker* and *New York* magazines? I did a pretty bang-up job at embarrassing myself the first time around. Why call for a reprise?

June 2, 1997 I bought a lottery ticket today. I want to win the $70 million jackpot so I can escape this crowded, unfulfilling existence. You will know if I've won if I never write in this notebook again.

I'm fine with exposing my youthful foibles for one reason: I'm over them. Not only am I over them, but I'm happier now, in my early thirties, than that pessimistic twentysomething ever could have imagined. My current contentment has everything to do with what I wrote in my journals, which is why it would be hasty to dismiss them as vapid testimonials to the type of anguished pseudo-philosophizing that is the luxury of those who don't have more pressing concerns. All my well-documented sources of fear, frustration, and self-flagellation have worked themselves out in one way or another, and that painstaking process helped make me the person I am today and will be tomorrow.

August 2, 1995 This is how low I am on the masthead: I don't even have a cubicle. I have to get promoted to move on up to a cubicle. Dare to dream, Meg. Dare to dream . . .

Yes, I'm veering into chipper "Take it from me, sista, everything happens for a reason" territory. Stick with me. Because what these journal entries lack in literary merit, I hope, is made up in their therapeutic benefits. Okay, smarty, perhaps *you* already know better than to drink pink wine from a box. But you picked up this book for a reason, so I'll bet that my post-college preoccupations aren't totally dissimilar to your own as you navigate this strange, semi-autonomous period, when you're technically on your own but in no way feel like you qualify as an adult; when you discover that what you thought would make you happy doesn't, and what you thought you wanted isn't what you want at all. When you're afraid that every wrong decision you make now is setting you up for decades of regret. When you not only don't know who you are anymore but wonder if you ever did.

March 17, 1997 My mother tries to tell me that coming home from work cranky and exhausted is something that you just have to put up with as an uncontrollable fact of life. I refuse to believe her, but I have to wonder . . .

I've chosen entries that focus on My Career Angst and Quest for Deeper Meaning in Life. I've selected this subject over other popular topics (such as My Rapidly Descending Ass and Other Insults of Aging) because I know from too many conversations with similarly disillusioned friends that this is a nearly universal aspect of the twentysomething experience. While the specifics are surely different, I hope that you can take comfort from my doubts about ever being able to live up to my own expectations. And if you can't relate to my worries, perhaps you'll get a schadenfreudian lift from knowing that you're less clueless than I was at your age.

(Note: These entries have been edited for clarity. And occasionally for stupidity.)

May 13, 1995 It's my last weekend of college and I'm the only one at this damn school who hasn't landed a job. I've been told that I shouldn't worry about my future because I've got a gift with words. Yet somehow I didn't manage to impress the powers that be at the prestigious publication known as the J. Crew catalog.

"Are you a FASHION MAVEN???"
Apparently, the Khaki Queen couldn't draw her own conclusion about my fashion mavenness by taking one look at the electric-blue power suit and patent-leather pumps my mom bought for me on clearance at the *other* JC, as in Penney. When KQ asked me for my thoughts on ribbed versus unribbed T-shirts, I knew I was doomed. I would never be a copywriter for J. Crew, which is appropriate because I am *not* a fashion maven and don't give a shit about denim and all its myriad fits, rinses, and washes. And this is why I'll have to move in with my parents and work as the token exchange technician at Lucky Leo's Arcade for the rest of my life.

For the record, I also lost out on a similar position with The Princeton Review, who asked me to mock up an ad for their latest testing materials; I was so bored by the assignment that I drank Rolling Rock and watched *Melrose Place* instead. And I wasn't even granted an interview with a granny magazine that regularly features butter cookies and quilts on its covers.

At the time, one rejection after another, I couldn't see that these so-called failures were crises averted. Losing out on these jobs did not mean I was destined for a career on the boardwalk in Seaside Heights, New Jersey. It simply meant I was the wrong person for them. Period.

But even jobs I *was* right for weren't right for me.

July 7, 1995 I've been a working woman for one week and I've already gotten to the point where I shrug my shoulders and mouth "Whatever" when my roommate asks how my day went. How can this be? I'm working at a teen magazine. Isn't this the job I've wanted ever since I first laid eyes on *Sassy* magazine in ninth grade? I'm the only person I know who got the exact job I wanted after graduation. But there's something missing. Maybe I'm just not used to the nine-to-five grind, which is really more of the eight-to-seven grind, but my overtime pay is the only thing keeping me over the poverty line, so I'm not going to complain. Um. Too much.

August 2, 1995 My job means no more back-to-school shopping. I used to love trying on my fall clothes and watching myself enact a September scenario in the mirror, always an extremely animated play in which I was fascinating and funny and secretly lusted after by one cute boy or another. If I wasn't so traumatized by standardized tests, a back-to-school wardrobe might have been a salient reason to apply to graduate school. In what, I have absolutely no idea. I just wish I had a syllabus to follow for my life.

Despite my insecurities, I thrived in the magazine industry. I was blessed with a benevolent first boss who noticed and nurtured my talents, thereby helping me advance quickly in what can be a very cutthroat field. And yet no success assuaged my fear that

I was settling into a life in which bland discontent was the best I could hope for.

March 7, 1996 Yesterday at my first PR breakfast, I found myself in a hotel ballroom full of young, thin, tall(ish) women, all in variations of the women's magazine editor uniform: twinset, short skirt, knee-high boots. It scared the shit out of me. Am I one of them? Do I want to be? *They* seemed happy to be there.

September 19, 1996 I got promoted today. I'm now making $10,000 more than I was less than a year ago. Unreal . . . Supposedly, my boss was telling attendees of the sales meeting that I am the next superstar. I'm not sure if this is limited to the magazine or is open to the whole company or the publishing industry at large. Why not broaden it to *all* media in *all* its forms, even those that have yet to be invented? I envy others when they succeed, and yet I can't ever take my own accomplishments seriously.

September 28, 1996 Scary but true: My alarm clock went off at seven-fifteen A.M. and I jumped out of bed, ready to go to work. Then I realized that it was Saturday, and I had set my alarm simply because THAT'S WHAT I DO. So I fell back asleep and had a dream in which I started editing, line by line, a story about pedicures that doesn't exist in the real, waking world, even going so far as to write an intro that went something like "Feet. Without them, you'd fall over. So why not be nice to them for a change?"

AHHHHHHHHHHHHHHHHHHHHHHHHHHHHHHHHHHHH.

I always knew that my venting, though cathartic, wasn't enough. Wanting to write a novel was one thing. Actually writing one was an altogether different proposition, which is why many wannabe novelists get so stuck on the former that they never get around to the latter. Of course, this phenomenon is by no means limited to aspiring authors. It's so much easier for aspiring *anythings* to complain about one's fate instead of doing something to change it.

May 7, 1997 Last night I read my journals from the end of high school through my sophomore year of college. I couldn't help but notice a recurring, narcissistic theme: I AM DESTINED FOR GREATNESS. I bring this up because I keep waiting for the moment that everything will come together—when I'll finally make use of my sense of humor and way with words and know what I'm doing with my life is right. Right now lack of time is my favorite excuse. That if I had more time, more free weekends, I'd spend them being brilliant ... Do homeless derelicts still believe— despite all the evidence to the contrary—that they are still destined for greatness? Homeless derelicts probably spend more time on their would-be novels than I do.

June 10, 1997 My writing instructor at the New School urges us to write, write, write ... Other writers sacrifice all—sleep, food, sanity—for their art. But I won't even sacrifice a sitcom—a rerun, at that.

Like many of my friends, I felt firmly entrenched in the life I had chosen by the time I hit my mid-twenties. After all, I had been working for *almost three years*. To do something as drastic as quitting would mean starting all over again from zero. Instead of seeing freedom in a fresh start, I rejected it as an unacceptable acknowledgment of defeat. I felt trapped and totally out of control.

August 13, 1997 I just left an ATM vestibule patrolled by a security guard. I didn't say anything to him. He didn't say anything to me. A pack of rowdy guys came in. They didn't say anything to him. He didn't say anything to them. I don't know how he can show up for a job during which no one ever says anything to him and he never says anything to anyone else. I wonder if *he* ever has sleepless nights about fulfillment and finding a sense of purpose.

October 20, 1997 I just had a frightening experience. I was on the subway to work, and at Wall Street I started to feel a little thirsty and slightly nauseated, like I do if I work out too hard and don't drink enough water. I breathed deeply, which is usually enough to get through any nausea. But it wasn't working. Between Brooklyn Bridge and Fourteenth Street, I started seeing stars and heard everything through a filter inside my head. I was hot and felt beads of sweat boiling on my upper lip and brow. I took off my jacket, shut my eyes, leaned across the door, and thought, This must be what it feels like to die. Someone got off and I grabbed his seat. No one sat next to me, which confirmed what I already knew, that I looked really fucking scary. I glanced up at one point and saw an older woman looking at me with concern but saying nothing. This whole time I was able to tell myself to keep calm, that I was almost at Grand Central, where I could (ironically) get some air. We pulled in to the station, and my sight and hearing returned to normal. But I still feel woozy and sweaty and not right.

I think I had my first panic attack.

January 1, 1998 I should be ecstatic about my new job at the biggest-selling women's magazine in the world. But I'm not. When I hung up the phone after hearing the news, I sobbed and not with joy. This has nothing to do with the new job and everything to do with me. I'm so beyond making resolutions.

March 11, 1998 I see my name on the masthead of the most widely circulated magazine on the planet and I wonder who that person is. I feel like a fraud.

September 4, 1998 I can't come up with any scenarios for this month's quiz. In the past, I could whip up quiz questions replete with references to threesomes, bondage, and masturbation with phallic produce. But now . . . nothing. I wonder if I'm failing intentionally, so I can be liberated through unemployment.

And then, when I was twenty-five, under three months after I got married, my back exploded. Specifically, my L5 disk blew out, spewing its contents into my spinal canal, causing excruciating pain and partial paralysis from the waist down. I endured emergency surgery, three months of bed rest, a year of intense physical therapy, and countless hours of introspection.

It was the best worst thing that ever happened to me. Obviously, I don't recommend self-actualization through spinal surgery. But this unexpected, unwanted disturbance required me to make major changes in my life. Without it, I often wonder how much longer I would have succumbed to soul-sucking inertia.

October 22, 1998 Friends and family have joked about how this is the perfect time to start my Great American Novel. I'd settle for the Not Bad American Novel. Deep down, I still hope to be a novelist someday. I think of all I've accomplished by twenty-five—and even though I tend not to want something as soon as I achieve it, I think it's all been part of a growth process. So I *do* see myself writing a book someday. But not like this, under the influence of painkillers, from my bed as I recover from back surgery. I think my book will come from a more organic origin.

Oh fuck. When did I start using terms like "growth process" and "organic origin"?

December 2, 1998 I'm taking a break before physical therapy. "Break" is a loose term, since I haven't done anything today besides watch back-to-back episodes of *90210* on the FX channel.

I've spent the last two and a half months recovering from surgery and obsessively thinking about my past. I've reread all my old short stories, pored over my journals, I even read every letter I wrote to my husband before we got married. I should come out of this whole horrendous experience with something lasting to show for it, something besides the two-inch scar on my spine. I think my biggest no-brainer pseudo-revelation is that my *job* isn't the problem, *I'm* the problem. And my life won't change unless I make a change. Yes, I am now officially resorting to the most hackneyed platitudes, the likes of which are written in brightly colored paperbacks published independently out of many amateur authors' basement self-help headquarters.

December 29, 1998 I already have many things that under-thirty women aim for. A happy marriage, a high-profile, well-paying job, interesting friends. I guess what I want most is the *confirmation* that I'm living my life the way it was intended. By whom, I don't know. It would be so much easier if I could just find God. But there's no chance of that. Though I must admit that I was sucked in by those commercials for the Church of Jesus Christ of Latter-day Saints in which seemingly well-adjusted people are miserable about their lives. In one, an impeccably groomed woman is out to lunch with a friend and she plasters a smile on her face and gushes about how happy she is about her promotion, but she doesn't have anything else to say and she breaks down and starts to cry and the worried voice-over announcer suggests that anyone who can relate to this woman should call for the free no-obligation book, *The Way of Life* or some such quasi-Bible babble. And I thought, Is there anyone who doesn't relate to this woman?

January 25, 1999 I was watching a bad teen flick the other night, a poor rip-off of *Sixteen Candles*, starring Jennifer Love Hewitt. It made me wish that . . . well . . . I certainly don't want to relive those insecure teenage years, and yet something about that movie didn't make me want to be twenty-five and counting, either. My birthday is in two weeks. Twenty-six bothers me more than twenty-five because it's closer to thirty than it is to twenty. And to be almost closer to thirty than twenty and have no idea what I want to do with my life for the first time since I was fifteen and discovered *Sassy* magazine and swore that my destiny was to be a magazine writer/editor, well, it's no wonder I was feeling nostalgic for high school.

February 5, 1999 Lately, I've been very open about my malaise, which is tantamount to career suicide in this cat-eat-catty industry. It's clear to me that I'm intentionally undermining myself because I *want* to be fired. I actually fantasized about having another herniated disk, just so I could just drop out for good.

April 9, 1999 I wrote "WORK ON BOOK" in my notebook and circled it for emphasis. Just thinking about this novel I'm *not* writing makes me more excited than anything I *am* writing for work.

I told friends and family that I was working on a novel. Naturally, they asked about its progress. I felt ill at ease when I recognized that the thing about me that was most interesting to other people was, in fact, completely hypothetical. I felt not unlike Jack Nicholson's writer-turned-nutcase character in *The Shining,* only I wasn't even putting in enough time at my keyboard to pound out page after page of "All work and no play makes Meg a dull girl." To put an end to this shameful charade, I finally started writing almost as much as I was bitching about not having time to write. Soon I was writing as much as I was bitching. Then writing more than bitching. Eventually, the most miraculous thing happened.

The bitching stopped.

October 6, 1999 I've been unhappy for a long time. And my only reason for sticking with this chosen career was fear. Of failure, yes. But mostly of the unknown. My position is not the problem. There are many people in this industry who love what they do, who wake up excited every morning to go to work, who get a genuine sense of satisfaction from a job well done. It doesn't matter what magazine I work for or how many promotions I get or how much money I make: I won't ever be one of those happy magazine people, because editing is not "it" for me. Of course, I'm petrified of finding out that writing this novel won't be "it" for me, either. I have to take that risk. I can always get another job. But not another life.

October 15, 1999 I quit. I don't have a job or a book deal. But I've got freelance assignments lined up, thirty manuscript pages, and a meeting with a literary agent. For the first time in ages, I'm not worried about the uncertainty of my future.

I feel . . . free.

This is going to sound unrealistic and corny and just too, too, perfect. In fact, it's precisely the sort of thing I used to mock about books like this. But it's the absolute truth: Those were the last words written on the last page of my last journal.

And you know what, dear reader? I still feel free.

Woo-hoo for me.

Hired, Fired, and What I Wore

By Alison Pace

Dress for the job you want. This is what they say to you when you are trying to figure out what to wear for your first job out of college, or your second, or your third. My question to "them" is this: What if you are one of those people who always has nothing to wear?

No matter how much time I spend shopping, no matter how much of my salary I devote to my wardrobe, no matter how many hours I spend angsting about it—and those hours, believe me, are numerous, second only to thinking about the fact that oftentimes I feel fat—I don't have anything to wear. I am one of those women who stares forlornly at her closet, hating its contents. I am convinced that no matter what may be in it, it isn't right, isn't what I really, truly need. A combination of being decisionally challenged and possessing both a great capacity for buyer's remorse and rather short legs has left me on the other side of fashion.

The other side of fashion, in case you are lucky enough not to know, is where fashion is not a friend, not a source of entertainment and pride, but rather, a great font of intimidation and fear. Though I am not one of them, I am very aware of the fact that there are many women for whom fashion is a friend. My friends Cynthia and Kimberly are among them; they always look nice, so pulled together every time I see them, and I have reason to believe that fashion for them might be fun. The way it is for me with beauty products. With beauty products, I'm fine. I know exactly what I want and am not at all hindered by uncertainty, indecision, or even remorse. I can say with the utmost assurance and confidence that I like Stila eye shadow in Grace and Wheat, Trish McEvoy bronzer and blush, and Laura Mercier cover-up. I love Sue Devitt Triple C-Weed whipped foundation like few other things in this world, and I would run through oncoming traffic for Chanel Glossimer lip gloss in Blizzard. But with fashion, I'm a wreck. It was always this way, as far back as I can remember. My mother will tell you, maybe even if you don't ask, that the low point of her parenting career was trying to find me a sweet-sixteen dress.

My first job out of college was as a receptionist/assistant at a contemporary art gallery in SoHo, back when SoHo was all art galleries, before it was a mall. Let's call the gallery Editions, and my boss there, let's call her Anna. Anna was a fabulous-*looking* (the emphasis here is all on the looking) blond woman who had a great affinity for Armani suits and Marlboro Reds and whose idea of lunch was a TheraFlu tablet. Anna often delighted in having me order her a coffee every morning and disappearing upon its delivery so she'd never have to pay.

It was not until the first snow arrived that year that the mood began to strike her for an afternoon cappuccino from Dean & Deluca. It was a fifteen-block round trip I embarked on frequently, whenever the skies clouded over and opened up. The Gap rain boots I took to wearing, in order to always be at the ready, did not look good lined up under the desk next to Anna's Manolo Blahniks, and did not accomplish a tremendous amount toward increasing my clothing confidence.

It was then that I first remembered someone saying how you're supposed dress for the job you want. Well, I wanted Anna's job and not at all because my first few months working in the art

world had endeared me to it; mostly because I think that somewhere in my logic process, I figured that if I had Anna's job, she
wouldn't be there anymore. On my next trip home, one in which
I had previously promised my father that I wouldn't cry about how
much I hated my job, since it upset my mother, I negotiated the
long-term loan of four of my mother's suits. In retrospect, I probably should have clued in to this a bit faster, but the high-end
suits did not, in the end, endear me to Anna.

"Is zis Armani?" she inquired one day, fingering the fine material of my suit jacket's sleeve.

"No," I said, tapping my Marlboro Lights on my desk with a
flourish, packing them, just as I'd seen her do with her Reds. She
narrowed her already squinty eyes and asked me, "Barneys Private
Label?"

"Yes," I said, when what I really should have said was "Express."

Anna had a greater capacity for meanness than anyone I have
met since. And she was meanest to me when I wore my mother's
suits. Something about the navy blue gabardine of my Barneys
Private Label pantsuit always filled her heart with the desire to
embark me on fun projects that involved power drills, mopping,
or, if it was raining, a great need for a summer roll from the luxe
noodle shop Kelly & Ping (she loved them so, when she was off
the TheraFlu). Kelly & Ping, not unlike Dean & Deluca, was perhaps the farthest point from our gallery that you could get and
still be in SoHo.

After almost a year spent working for Anna, doing not much
more than running through SoHo in inclement weather and repeating "Editions" over and over again into the phone, I was left
with no greater understanding of the art world, the world itself,
for that matter, nor any idea of what I wanted to do in it. At the
end of that year, I found myself with a burgeoning persecution
complex, quite a lot of regret over a misguided shopping excur-

sion at Betsey Johnson, and the thought that it might be time for a rethinking of the career.

I'd started out in college as an English major. All throughout grade school, junior high, and high school, I'd been steadfastly convinced that one day I'd be a writer. But somewhere along the way in college—American University, land of big socks and big hair and big sweatshirts adorned with Greek letters—I both developed an aversion to letting anyone see my writing and got bitten by the art history bug. I switched my major to art history. While my other just-out-of-college friends worked at banks and PR firms and ad agencies and went to graduate school and made friends with their coworkers and classmates, I sat alone day after day in a poorly heated loft space where I was yelled at by a German woman with a propensity for throwing summer rolls at me.

Convinced that all of art history had been a terrible mistake, that really, *truly*, what I was supposed to be was a writer and clearly not an art gallery employee, I applied for my MFA in creative writing. When the image of myself as an MFA student filled my mind, that image of me didn't seem worried at all about what to wear, and I think she was wearing a pair of really cool jeans.

Having established a fine tradition of thinking things through and leaving myself lots of options, I applied only to Columbia. While I waited for what I somewhat inexplicably believed to be my surefire acceptance, I felt that in the interim, I should seek employment somewhere other than the art gallery, as the very thought of staying, now that I was going to be a writer, was, frankly, unbearable. I cast around for ideas for something temporary.

A friend from high school had recently started dating a woman who worked as a salesperson at Ralph Lauren; it was how they'd met. He'd been buying a shirt and special-ordered another so that he'd get to see her again. When I first met this woman, I instantly liked her. She was pretty and funny and elegant, beautifully attired in blackwatch plaid and cashmere. Not only did I want her to be my new very best friend, I became enthralled by her tales of a 50 percent employee discount on clothes, 70 percent if it was something you'd wear to work, and bus trips to a magical place in New Jersey called the Employee Store, where everything was wholesale. Upon further investigation, I learned that while there was not a sales position at the Ralph Lauren flagship store on Seventy-second and Madison, there was one available at Polo Sport, right across the street. The interview went so well, I hardly thought twice when they asked me if I was comfortable wearing body-conscious clothes.

"Sure," I said, and they gave me the job. The job that would enable me to leave the gallery, to trade in the well-heeled glamour that was kicking my ass for the sporty chic that hopefully would not. I thought it all seemed great. I thought it would be the perfect way to tide myself over until graduate school began. I thought I'd be fashionable and free from my smoke-filled enslavement at the art gallery, and I thought it would be fun. I tendered my resignation happily, even though for some reason, I cried when I did it. Anna bid me farewell and asked if she could use my employee discount. It was the last time I ever saw her. I left Editions and SoHo and the art world behind and headed uptown to Polo Sport.

It turned out that I was not all that comfortable in body-conscious clothes. Or at least not in the ones chosen for me. On my first day of work, the head of HR took me through the store and selected an array of outfits for me. Equestrian jodhpurs and ascots and knee-high riding boots; a pair of white ski pants and a plaid mohair sweater; and a velvet mini skating dress, complete with beret, were the least distressing of the outfits selected and then Polaroided, lest I forget how to accessorize them. Once during a break, I was standing outside by the employee entrance, decked out in a skintight white unitard (I have never been, just so you know, slim of thigh) and a bright orange vest adorned for some reason with a giant '3.' I noticed an old boyfriend from college fast approaching along Seventy-second Street. Our eyes met, and he waved. I froze, mortified, my faux-fur après-ski boots glued to the cement.

"Alison?" he said, not sure if it was really me. And this is what I said:

"No."

I was so out of my element, so far away at that moment from any version of myself I'd known, that the thought of dealing with someone who hadn't liked me that much when I *had* been myself was incomprehensible.

In the employee lunchroom at Polo Sport, a commonly heard phrase was "If you really want to, you can be a size two." A co-worker turned me on to diet pills, and I lost fifteen pounds and got a bit irrational, which is the only way I can explain the fact that I cut off all my hair in the manner of an early-nineties-era Linda Evangelista. Being around all the beautiful clothes all the time, and all the people who talked about clothes all the time, pretty much all I wanted was the clothes. I spent far too large a percentage of my salary and commissions on clothes, and Ralph Lauren, even at 50 percent off, is quite expensive. Seventy percent off wasn't happening for me, since all the clothes they selected for me to wear in the store were at best not clothes I wished to purchase and at worst completely upsetting.

I spent a tremendous amount of time riding a shuttle bus to the Employee Store in New Jersey with many of my fashion-obsessed coworkers, feeling somewhere in the back of my mind like a bit of a groupie. I spent an even greater amount of time thinking about cashmere. And when my rejection letter arrived from Columbia, even though they wished me luck in all my future creative endeavors, I thought a lot about failure, about being washed up, and about making far too many mistakes. I was twenty-three.

I decided I should work in magazines. As I continued to toil away at Polo Sport, working on my folding skills and fashion sense, I began to send my résumé to magazines. And then came the phone call I'd never expected, the one from *The New Yorker*. I would put those words in italics even if magazine titles weren't supposed to be italicized, because in my mind, *The New Yorker* just can't be uttered without a great deal of emphasis.

"This isn't an editorial position," the human resources man told me on the phone. "Are you interested at all in the business side of things?" Truth be told, I was not much interested in the business side of things, but it was, after all, *The New Yorker*.

"Absolutely," I said, and, clearly impressed with my zeal for the business side of things, the human resources man from *The New Yorker* told me when to come to the magazine to interview for the position of an assistant in advertising sales. *Sales*. Among the things I had learned at Ralph Lauren: I was most certainly not a latent fashionista; diet pills are bad for you and make you a little bit crazy; I never should have cut off all my hair, as it was looking much less French gamine and much more terrier who had jumped into a pool; I was terrible at anything that had to do with sales.

"Sounds great," I said.

My interview the following week with Jarrod D., advertising sales executive, went very well. He wore tweed and spoke glowingly about how much he loved *The New Yorker*, how he loved being a part of the magnificent history. He talked passionately about how we would be a team, about how any task we did together, no matter how mundane, would in actuality be important. Engaging. Because we would be doing it on behalf of the continuing tradition that was *The New Yorker*! He was so alive, had so much conviction, yet amazingly was very solid, very calm, very cool, and very collected. Standing there in his little office, I wanted to one day call him pet names.

Having a crush on my boss, for a while at least, made it easier to stomach the fact that my job was exceedingly secretarial, that my only activity of any interest was when I'd get to go to the cartoon library to find the perfect cartoon for a campaign. Because I had not a lot else to my name other than a hell of a lot of Ralph Lauren clothing, I arrived in the advertising sales department of *The New Yorker* each day resplendent in overpriced cashmere. Not only did this not turn my boss's eye, did not make him forget all about his stylish and beautiful and successful girlfriend (who shopped at Bergdorf Goodman and whose Isaac Mizrahi suits were sometimes delivered to our office) in favor of jumping headfirst into the murky waters of a possible sexual harassment suit, it also did not endear me to Bronwyn, the other advertising sales executive whom I assisted. Despite the rather country-club connotations of her name, Bronwyn liked to tell me that *The New Yorker* wasn't a country club. She also liked to inquire several times a day whether I—or any other random passerby, for that matter—thought she'd ever get married.

After two years of being an advertising sales assistant by day and a writer of overwrought short stories that I wasn't altogether sure I ever wanted to show to anyone by night, I had a talk with Jarrod about my future career at *The New Yorker*.

"I'd love to be in editorial," I told him. "I want to be a writer," I explained.

"That's probably not going to happen," he said. "The guys down in editorial, they all went to Ivy League colleges; they were all editing their Ivy League college newspapers." I hadn't worked on my non–Ivy League school paper, had never even contributed an article after taking European Art History 101: Cave to Cathedral. If I haven't already made this clear, I worshipped Jarrod. On top of being erudite and dreamy and Ivy League–educated, he had a far better handle on his career than I did mine. If he didn't think I could be a writer, then the matter surely was solved: I couldn't.

Immediately after that conversation, I began to wonder if I'd been wrong to abandon all the time I'd spent in school learning about art history. I was soon utterly convinced that I had been. The only thing that seemed to make sense was to spend some more time in school learning about art history. So I applied to graduate school for—yes—art history, and when I was rather quickly accepted, I said goodbye to *The New Yorker*, to Jarrod, and to being a writer. I saw the version of myself, the one who wore really cool jeans and sat all day, deep in writerly concentration at her laptop, walking slowly away. I didn't try to stop her.

During the summer months before school started, I worked at a special-events-planning firm. I don't remember much about what I wore that summer to the special-events-planning firm, but I remember my boss there, Yvette, wore a muumuu every day. I have always been deeply mistrustful of someone who wears a muumuu without irony. I learned that, for me, event planning is neither interesting nor fun. A tremendous amount of time is spent at parties where you are not invited to partake in any of the festivity but only in the setup.

Fashionably speaking, graduate school was a snap. I wore jeans and Banana Republic sweaters every day, and afterward, I went to work at Sotheby's. I learned so much there, about paintings and research and auctions. I learned a lot about fashion there, too. Exceedingly preppy fashion. Going to Sotheby's each day was like being in a time warp, and right back at my fairly preppy high school. I think some mornings I may have rooted around my apartment in a desperate attempt to unearth my field hockey stick before I remembered what decade I was in. Everyone at Sotheby's wore headbands; everyone wore ballet flats and loafers. Fashion conformist that I'd turned out to be, I wore headbands and ballet flats and loafers, too.

I learned that big sunglasses should be worn on top of one's head at all times, even if you were inside, even if your hair was already secured in a ponytail, even if it was nighttime or smack-dab in the middle of a thunderstorm. I learned that apparently, one could never go wrong with an Hermès scarf tied in the manner of a tourniquet around one's neck. And, of course, I busted out my spoils from my tenure at Ralph Lauren. I will admit for the sake of this essay that I did wear the riding boots, though never the jodhpurs. I went on dates dressed like this. It sometimes does not seem a complex mystery that I am now in my thirties and still single.

After three years at Sotheby's, I moved on to do research at a gallery. Like a girlfriend who returns to her cheating boyfriend, I'd conveniently forgotten all the reasons why I had run, kicking and screaming in my mother's Barneys Private Label suit, from my first gallery job. I remembered quickly enough.

I remember the three years I spent at my second gallery job— during an art market crash, no less—as the Patagonia Years. I was so professionally unhappy at this gallery job, felt like such a career failure in every definitive sense of the word, that I believed the only way through was to get in touch with my inner nature girl. During the Patagonia Years, I again spent too much of my salary on clothing, this time mostly on microfiber and fleece. I spent almost all of my vacation time camping and hiking and, once, on a particularly trying excursion, white-water rafting.

Over the years I spent at what turned out to be my last full-time job, I learned that what my inner nature girl wanted was to stay in. I learned also, I imagine a few years too late, that no job is worth being as unhappy as I was there. And I learned that if you put your mind to it, you really can change things. I started working on my novel while at the gallery. I'd spent close to a decade doing things I wasn't really sure about. It was time to stop writing things I didn't want to show to anyone, and to start writing something I would want to show to people, maybe even a lot of people. It was time at last to put on a proverbial bathing suit and jump into the deep end of the theoretical pool.

I was wearing a bright blue Izod dress the day my boss explained to me that I was being "downsized," and that sometimes things like being "downsized"—something that felt to me so much like being fired—were the best things that could happen to a person. Though it took me a while to realize it, I don't think truer words have ever been spoken. And I don't think I'll ever forget that dress.

I'm convinced that I've been granted a fair share of good luck, and that maybe this good luck was granted from sticking it out at the gallery until they didn't want me to stick it out there anymore. I truly believe that I am getting to give this whole lifelong dream of being a writer a shot because of some good karma I picked up somewhere along the way.

Along with my slight persecution complex and my ever-so-wee issues with commitment, I might be what people call a later bloomer, if you will. I needed to try on slightly more than a few hats in order to find the one that fit. And the one I'm wearing now, the writer one, I didn't even hold in my hand, let alone put on my head, until I was thirty. I've learned that that's okay. All the missteps along the way, if nothing else, have given me something to write about.

These days for work, which takes place in a corner of my apartment, I wear yoga pants, which I feel are a bit more fashionable than traditional sweatpants. I have a few "going out" outfits, and this new thing going on with the universality of jeans as an item of clothing to be worn everywhere is a godsend. I have a few pairs of really nice shoes. Shoes never make you feel fat. Of course, no matter what my work dress code has happily evolved to, there are still pitfalls in my fashion life. The current trend of tight-fitting T-shirts is not one that flatters me, since I'm not slim of arm. Lunch meetings freak me out; yes, I always, without fail, feel like I have nothing to wear. But it is a feeling that ties me to my past in an almost nice, familiar way.

I have a sense that no matter how much money I may one day make—you know, when I'm the next J. K. Rowling and all—if

Banana Republic is one day replaced in my world by Henri Bendel, if the second floor at Bloomingdale's one day becomes the sixth floor at Bergdorf Goodman, that I still won't have anything to wear. But I have learned that though I am seldom happy with what I am wearing, I am, several careers, a few broken hearts, and two novels later, quite pleased with the person wearing it.

And I've learned something else, too. No matter how good it looks, no matter how nice you are to it, Ralph Lauren cashmere just isn't going to hold up for ten years.

Trade-offs: Why I Sold My Soul for Apartments

By Donna Freitas

You're never going to believe this," I said to my then-boyfriend, Jonathan, and his roommate, Jason, who were helping on move-in day, waiting for me by their truck. I'd just descended the long staircase that led up to the residence hall I'd be running in less than three weeks. I'd just keyed in to my apartment for the first time.

"Is it that bad?" Jonathan sounded worried—partly, I think, for my sake, but in part for his own. He'd be spending a lot of time there, since he was dating me.

"You are going to die when you see it," I began slowly, trying to overcome the shock I had felt just moments before when I opened the door and peered inside my new home for the first time. "It's the most gorgeous apartment you've ever seen."

"It is?" Surprise and relief registered in Jonathan's voice.

"It is," I said, reaching over the side of the truck to start pulling out my belongings. Now I couldn't wait to set everything up. I wanted to start living there immediately. "And it's all mine," I added, sighing. I'd never had a place to myself. And now this! It was too good to be true.

All thoughts of the job that came with the apartment (or was it an apartment that came with a job? I couldn't remember now) were gone as we began the long treks up and down that staircase, carrying my clothes, books, everything I'd accumulated during college and since into the place I would live for the next four years. Upon seeing it, I was convinced it had to be worth at least *at least* $2,000 a month if I'd been renting. I was in Washington, D.C., after all, and rents were not exactly cheap, especially if you lived by yourself.

The second time I keyed in to the front door, and the first that Jonathan and Jason laid eyes on my new digs, my jaw fell to the floor alongside theirs as we took in the insane luck that had found me somehow, through a decision to take care of first-year college students, of all things. The three of us spilled into the spacious office, my residence hall office, with its brand-new desk and walls lined with bookshelves, the first room everyone met when entering my apartment. Best of all were the huge windows on the back wall that looked out onto beautiful trees and endless colorful sky, the sun just starting to set and barely hanging under the top window frame. My apartment was almost high enough to see the Potomac River and near enough to go jogging there every morning.

When I opened the second door, though, the one that led beyond my work space to the place I'd live, I found the best part of all.

My apartment was gigantic, the living-dining area an enormous L-shape, the long side of the L lined with those same gorgeous windows, eight in all, that, when opened, made you feel as if you were sitting outside on a porch in summer. Light streamed in everywhere. Around the corner from the dining area was a separate kitchen with spacious countertops and more cabinets than you can imagine. Down the hallway off the living room (it actually had a hallway) was a bathroom with a linen closet (my first closet!). Last but not least, at the end of the hall, was my bedroom—my beautiful bedroom! With four more windows, that same spectacular view, and most shocking of all, a walk-in closet big enough to change in—with space enough for all my clothes and shoes, not only hanging space for everything I owned but shelves galore as well. I could see it now: each sweater in its neat place, my shirts and pants spaced out on the clothing rack so I could view each and every one individually and never forget what I owned, my shoes lined up neatly on the extra shelves—kitten heels on one, flats on another, and boots lining one wall on the floor.

I was in heaven.

Who knew dorm living could be like this?

I decided then and there that my new job in residence life was the best thing that had ever happened to me.

I was going to be living it up free of charge! I couldn't believe my luck.

The first time I did it—took a job in residence life—it was for the job, not for the gratis living arrangements.

When I got the call offering me the position, I was thrilled. The fact that my new job as a community director in residence life at a nearby university came with an apartment—a free one—was low on my radar. Barely an afterthought. I won't lie and say I wasn't excited about the idea of living without paying rent every month, or phone bills, or cable, or electric, or Internet. When you are twenty-four and in graduate school, free cheese samples at the local Dean & Deluca can be exciting, never mind a space to lay your head without any monthly bills to pay. It all sounded wonderful, this particular side benefit of the job I was agreeing to take over the phone, explaining that yes, I could move by August 1. I shook my head happily and smiled when my new boss said that the hours were flexible and wouldn't interfere with my classes. Accommodating my course schedule was paramount.

I took the job knowing exactly what I was getting into—or so I thought initially. I took the apartment, sight unseen, by default.

I clicked the off button on my phone, cradling the receiver in place, and looked around the tiny, dark room where I was living at the time, a room that barely fit a bed and dresser, a room that looked remarkably like the even tinier, darker room I had rented two years earlier, both of which came with a bevy of housemates living outside my thin walls, some of whom I got along with well, others whom, let's just say, I disliked with a deep abiding passion. With only one window—one barred window looking out onto a small walled-in brick patio—even in the brightest sun, my room still felt like a dungeon.

Wherever I was about to live couldn't be worse than this place, I told myself. Nothing could be smaller or darker or more awkward than the houses I'd lived in since graduating from college three years before—houses that were filled to the brim with too-tiny rooms and too many occupants. I would be happy with whatever was given me, I thought, and reminded myself that no matter how small it turned out to be, I wouldn't complain because at least it was free.

Most important, I was fully aware that my future free-of-rent living arrangements came with their own, rather unique price tag: My new job required me to live in a first-year residence hall, otherwise known as a dorm, a college dorm, on campus at the university where I'd soon be working.

"I am going to live in a dorm," I repeated over and over, to get used to the idea.

Not just any dorm, either. I mentally prepared myself to move back into the same residence halls where I'd lived as an undergrad. When you work in residence life, which I was about to do, you live with the students; "living in" is what it's called. I was about to live in and manage a staff of resident assistants (RAs) where four hundred first-year students would be my most immediate neighbors. I focused on my excitement about the position and pushed aside thoughts of my dank college rooms.

I convinced myself not to expect much.

As August 1 approached, I began taking down my dresses and shirts from the steel wardrobe bar I had squeezed across from the bed (I didn't have a closet). I gave away the nightstand and the old blue wooden dresser with the drawers that didn't close (the dorm was furnished, apparently). The only things that would be cumbersome to move, that were always cumbersome to move, were the mountains of clothes, the too many pairs of shoes, and the millions of books I trekked wherever I went and inevitably would have no space for when I arrived.

I had no idea what was about to befall me.

I had no idea I was moving into a palace.

That I was to be spoiled, ruined for life, when it came to living space.

That I would become addicted to jobs in residence life for the pure and simple fact that people who work in residence life have the best apartments in the universe. In exchange for zero dollars.

They don't accept cash in res life. They take your soul instead.

But in those naive and blissful first moments, when I took in the reality of my new living situation on move-in day, any anxiety I had about what "living in" might entail melted away into a single peaceful concept that warmed the soul. I had yet to give up on an idea that could be summed up in a single word: home. Well, two single words: *my* home. Mine!

When I was in college, some friends dreamed of the day they'd walk down Wall Street in a well-tailored suit, carrying the requisite Coach bag, on their way to long hours with high salaries and bonuses to match. Others would go straight on to law school, med school, or MBA programs to spend several years investing in a career that would later land them jobs that paid back these initial outlays tenfold (literally). I, on the other hand, went a different route. A philosophy major as an undergraduate, I harbored visions of someday donning the fancy robes of the academic, a newly minted Ph.D. marching to the strains of "Pomp and Circumstance" on graduation day to take my hard-earned place among the faculty.

A noble path, I thought. I was going to become an intellectual!

Of course, getting your Ph.D. does not exactly put you on the fast track to accumulating a wardrobe worthy of Carrie Bradshaw; nor does it support the *Sex and the City*–style habit of dining out with friends at fancy city restaurants and downing Cosmos at fifteen dollars apiece, all habits from which I suffered. Though I was secure in my choice of career—one that would earn me a nice lifestyle in terms of time and job satisfaction (I loved to write and teach)— becoming a Ph.D. in religion was not likely to accommodate my affinity for everything obscenely expensive in the categories of vacation, food, clothes, and shoes. Each year that passed following college, as I watched my friends' salaries grow to four and five times what I was earning as a teacher, their end-of-year bonuses often matching my entire yearly salary in one fell swoop, I became more frustrated and insecure about my choices, my lifestyle, and the state of my purse. I felt good about what I was pursuing, but feeling noble about one's life choices just doesn't pay the rent.

Or buy you Prada.

Or afford you sushi on a nightly basis.

And I wanted what all my friends suddenly had: I wanted to be able to go my own way, get my Ph.D., *and* eat out at expensive restaurants with my investment-banker friends, drop ten dollars a drink, plunk two hundred down for those adorable kitten heels I saw at Neiman's—all without batting an eye or hyperventilating over the depletion of my bank account down to nothing because I just ate two orders of salmon sashimi instead of getting the cheaper cucumber roll.

So with my sudden, unexpected discovery of the perks of working in residence life—the free palace apartments, the free everything—it was as if fate had turned to me and said: "You *can* have it all! You can pursue your dreams and spring for hundred-dollar dinners! Voilà!" It was as if I'd found the magic answer to catching up to all my financially successful friends. I'd no longer lag behind in fashion and lifestyle. Soon I'd be living the life without a bank-statement care in the world!

No more nights in for this chick, because her days of monthly bills were over.

Within a week of when I moved, my apartment was set up and I was beaming, joyfully inviting friends over for dinner or lunch or coffee at my new apartment that looked like a model set for *Trading Spaces*. Blue accents in the bedroom. Reds and oranges in the living room. Fresh flowers adorning the dining table and towers of colorful books lining the walls. I'd arranged not one but two sitting areas, the first away from the windows with a small table, easily removed to accommodate the pullout bed and therefore overnight guests; the other a huge space blanketed with outdoor light, with three comfy chairs and a sofa all surrounding a long coffee table that practically had "I'm perfect for socializing" written all over it.

And socializing in my new home I did. Just about every day.

For two weeks.

For two weeks I lived the life I'd always wanted. I shopped. I updated my wardrobe and bought new pairs of shoes to fill the extra space in the walk-in closet that was just begging for attention. I ate all the sushi I wanted without a care in the world.

For *two* weeks.

Then came my first day of work. And move-in day for students. And being on call for nighttime crisis duty. And the screaming all night outside my gorgeous windows. And the fire alarms at two A.M., four A.M., sometimes raining, sometimes snowing, and sometimes twice in a row. And the constant knocking, knocking, knocking on my office door, which was, of course, attached to my apartment, and the students whose voices I could hear through the inside door saying, "I know she's in there. She *lives* in there. Keep knocking until she comes out." And the getting yanked out of bed in the wee hours of the morning for every possible scenario you could imagine, from roommate conflicts that erupted into screaming matches to utter destruction on the sixth-floor post-Friday-night drunken debauchery to nighttime trips to the hospital after someone's attempted suicide.

Oh, and then there was the time when one student showed up with her RA at six A.M. because her bathroom sink fell off the wall and shattered on the tile floor.

"Isn't this a job for facilities?" I asked innocently, stupid me, thinking I was the wrong person for the job.

The girl looked at me angrily, and the RA stared nervously.

"Well, the thing is, it's kind of a roommate conflict," said the RA.

"Did the roommate yank the sink from the wall because she was mad at you or something?" I asked, still confused about why I was in my bathrobe at my desk at six o'clock in the morning.

Before my RA could respond, the angry girl blurted out: "The sink fell off the wall because my roommate was having sex on it with some guy! With me in the other room!"

Oh. Of course she was, I thought, now accustomed to the fact that anything was possible on my watch.

And soon I knew *exactly* why they gave people in my position palaces for homes. That was how they kept us working: They offered us apartments no one in their twenties could ever in their dreams afford, especially not in a city, in exchange for sucking the life out of us on the job, making us endure twenty-four-hour total insanity without discrimination for things like sleep and eating in peace. Or even having sex in peace (we had pagers). And they knew, the bosses in residence life *knew,* that once they got us into the apartments, once we saw what we could have, it would take a lot, I mean *a lot,* for us to actually decide to leave.

Well, leave I finally did.

After all the chaos, the sleepless nights, the swearing I'd never sign on for this madness another academic year, the times when I went knocking on Jonathan's door over the river in Arlington, crying, begging for a home away from home just for one evening, the crazy, the *always* crazy, situations students conjured up for me at the worst possible moments, I put in my notice for that job, which meant giving up my Washington, D.C., castle and those shocking freebies—free cable, free phone, free Internet, free electricity—of which all my friends were jealous.

And I didn't think it could be done!

I left that palace of an apartment in exchange for another, even more spectacular palace in one of the best neighborhoods in my favorite city of all: New York. My new place was going to be smack-dab in the middle of Manhattan, overlooking Union Square Park, on the penthouse floor. The penthouse! Who needed a free D.C. apartment when you could be living it up in New York City?

You see, this was the only way I could have given up my gorgeous home of four years in Washington. The only way I could have moved out of my beloved apartment was if I found another, better living situation somewhere else.

I couldn't believe my luck when I first saw it. It was even more amazing than the amazing I already knew, and it was in Manhattan. Manhattan, of all places! My new apartment was awe-inspiring, absolutely jaw-dropping. It was going to be fabulous living there. People would die when they came over, I thought, not believing that luck had found me twice.

Oh yeah, and it might have come with a teeny, tiny bit of employment. In residence life. And twenty-four-hour on-call crisis duty without any days off. Ever. And responsibility for almost a thousand students. And a staff of more than thirty people. And inflexible working hours (I was doing my dissertation by then, so who needed flexibility? Not me). It's also possible that my brand-new, gorgeous Manhattan flat with a view of Union Square Park right next door to Blue Water Grill (which I highly recommend, if you are ever in the city—great sushi) may possibly have been located in a residence hall—albeit one with a fantastic location.

Before I knew it, I'd sold my soul. *Again*.

So the second time it was for the living arrangements, not for the job.

I thought I knew what I was doing. I even thought I was clever! I'd found the perfect way of landing myself a place in the Big Apple, a city famous for its impossible rents and almost as impossible to find apartments. I'd heard horror stories from my Wall Street–walking, Coach bag–toting friends about living arrangements with no windows at all, or, if they were lucky, a window facing a brick wall. In Manhattan everything was small, small, small and cramped, and as dark as dark can be. But for once I had job skills my friends lacked, so residence life was my ticket into the city, *the city*, bypassing the faraway boroughs of Brooklyn and Queens and situating myself straight into one of the most coveted neighborhoods in the city.

All for free! I mean, who gets free apartments in Manhattan?

Just like last time, the satisfaction was immediate. When friends came by to see my new Union Square home, they took bids on how much I'd have to pay if I were renting. At least

$4,000 a month, most would say, and some even ventured as high as $5,000. I'd smile knowingly as I ushered friends in the door, eager to hear their reactions, which were always gratifying and immediate.

"Oh. My. God." Those were popular words when people saw it for the first time.

"I hate you," said with a part mocking, part serious tone, was another common response.

"This is insane. And you have a dishwasher!" Everyone was always stunned that I had a dishwasher.

Through it all, I chose to ignore that little promise I'd made to myself to never, ever, *ever* again in my life sign up for one of those godforsaken, crazy, all-consuming jobs like they have in residence life.

And just like last time, the satisfaction was shockingly short-lived and the pain of the job unbearably long. There were days when I worked twenty-four hours without a break and without eating. There were times when I worked two months in a row without any days off, responding to crisis after crisis, rich parents threatening to sue over their son or daughter's insufficient air-conditioning or my attempt to adjudicate them for running a drug ring in the hall (do parents have no morals anymore?), and one student who went so far as to try and hit me when she got caught breaking university rules. I'd imagined many nights of dining out at Blue Water just next door but instead found myself half asleep and pajama-clad at eleven P.M., ordering expensive sushi to go at the bar while all the chichi patrons stood staring at my shockingly un-chichi attire. Who had time to eat out? I had students with needs. Crises to respond to. Disgruntled staff. Exploding toilets. You name it.

I'd eat my fancy sushi at my desk.

I lasted two years in that apartment (I mean job). It took getting married, finishing my Ph.D., and an attractive offer of a coveted tenure-track faculty position for me to at last give up my gorgeous rent-free apartments in fantastic locations—and the residence life jobs that came with them.

I rejoiced when I put in my notice.

But I cried long and hard when I parted with My Apartment. My Union Square Apartment.

Last night I was at a party talking to the woman who has it now (My Apartment).

"Is this your last year, or will you stay on another?" My tone was friendly, but somewhere in the dark depths beneath this simple question lay an envy greener than the arugula I am continually staring down on my salad plate, force-feeding myself this leafy substance that makes me feel at once healthy and starved.

"To be honest, I can't imagine doing this another year. I mean, my training is for something totally different. High school students," she answered casually. Her eyes fluttered at me as she spoke, long blond hair falling in perfect waves around her face, as if it were perfectly normal to talk offhand about what she had of mine, as if it had never changed hands, as if this history didn't exist between us, fool that she was. The color in my soul shifted from the bright, edible green of arugula to dark forest, just over the border from the blackness of hate.

"Really," I said, making my tone carefully even, so as not to betray the emotions welling up inside. "So you're leaving, then? That makes sense. It's been what, three years now?"

"Three years this August," the blonde confirmed. But suddenly, she lowered her voice to a whisper and said as if we were coconspirators, which in a way we were, "If it weren't for that apartment, I'd already be gone."

"Isn't it amazing?" I whisper quickly back, my envy beginning to dissipate.

"The job is crap. But I'd have to move out of the city if I quit.

I couldn't bear to live in what I could actually afford in New York after this."

"I know. The view is unreal."

"I died the first day I saw it."

"I did, too! I had to stifle my thrill out of fear the interviewer would mistake my interest in the job for what I really wanted: the apartment I got in exchange for employment."

"And the closet space. Five floor-to-ceiling fully shelved storage spaces! In Manhattan!"

"One and a half baths!"

"Entire walls of windows!"

"All that sunlight!"

"Penthouse level!"

"And two balconies! One over the street and the other the courtyard!"

"You couldn't get a better location if you were a millionaire."

We sighed together, bonded over a mutually experienced living space and the horrid dilemma of giving it up. My envy turned to a feeling of warmth. I had already broken the vicious cycle: I had gotten out. Granted, she still had what I would always long to have back and never would. But looming ahead of her was the black, inevitable day of moving out. And that blackest of moments was fading ever farther into my past.

I'd gotten back my soul.

I knew how hard it would be for this woman to regain hers.

In this moment I knew I was beginning the long, hard process of letting go of the palaces where I had spent my twenties, accepting the thirtysomething reality of living in a slowly gentrifying area of Brooklyn, the only place where my husband and I could afford to buy. I am sad to admit we are almost always broke and eat a lot of pasta, but happy to say I no longer am on call twenty-four hours a day, nor do I have students banging on my door at three A.M. in a drunken stupor.

The price of my independence—our independence, now that I am married—was steep. I occasionally entertain the thought of going back, and I know my husband occasionally longs for me to, but I refrain; I know, we both know, that my sanity is not worth a free apartment. No matter how great the location. No matter how many balconies it has. No matter how much shopping is just a stone's throw from the front door.

Though sometimes I do think it might be worth a new outfit and shoes at Barneys.

Sigh.

Lie #2

"I'll have everything I need to live the life I've always wanted"

Breaking Up (with MasterCard) Is Hard to Do

By Cara Lockwood

It was the hardest thing I've ever done—breaking up with my credit cards. We were sitting at the kitchen table, just Master-Card, Visa, and me.

Me: I'm sorry, but we can't see each other anymore.

MasterCard: Was it something I did? (tears starting to brim on the holographic bank insignia)

Me: It's not you. It's me. I'm the one with the spending problem.

Visa: But didn't I offer you an 8.5 percent APR? Free balance transfers? Wasn't I there when you needed to fly to Dallas to watch your ex marry that empty-headed Melissa? And what about all those trips to Crate & Barrel for wedding shower gifts that you know very well your (cheap) college friends are never going to repay? That means nothing to you?

Me: I know. I'm sorry. I'm going to have to cut you up now.

MasterCard: You'll be sorry when you want to get those Franco Sarto boots. Or that Banana Republic sweater. But don't come crawling back to me, because I'll be in pieces.

Me: I know.

Visa: How about one more charge before we call it quits? For
old times' sake? I think the Gap is having a sale.
Me: Don't make this harder than it has to be.

It was a difficult time. MasterCard and I had had a relationship
since college. When we met, it was a sunny fall day in my sophomore year, and I needed a new pair of jeans.

I knew we were destined to be together because the guy sup-
plying MasterCard applications was also giving away a free water
bottle, and I didn't have any dishes for my dorm. It was fate.

At the time I didn't know why Citibank was giving out free
water bottles. Now I realize they were doing it because I was about
to embark on a lifetime marathon of shopping so exhausting I
would need frequent water breaks. I realize now how thoughtful
MasterCard was. They didn't want me to have any muscle cramps
during the semi-annual sale at Nordstrom.

The funny thing about credit-card applications in college
is that they don't seem like a serious financial venture. I mean,
when you get student loans, they don't hand you a free T-shirt or
a coupon for subs at the local student hangout. When you get a
home loan, they don't hand out frequent-flier miles. That would
cheapen the heavy responsibility of being in debt up to your eyeballs.

No, credit-card companies don't want to scare you away. Look
at the cards themselves, which come in a bright array of different colors. Some of them with cartoon characters. This isn't *real*
money. It's play money. Monopoly money.

So you can see why I didn't take credit cards seriously. Anything
that comes with a water bottle can't require too much responsibility, right?

My first heady purchase with my own (not my parents') Master-
Card was at the Gap. I bought three new pairs of jeans to replace

the ones I'd lost to a terrible accident involving a stray tube of lipstick in the dryer.

It was the start of a beautiful courtship. MasterCard wooed me with gifts from Bloomingdale's, Old Navy, and DSW. He wined and dined me in the best restaurants, bought me popcorn at the movies, and whisked me away on exotic weekend trips to Mexico. He bought me flowers and groceries and ordered takeout. We rented movies, and when I forgot to return them, MasterCard paid all my late fees. MasterCard picked up my dry cleaning. He paid for my gas. He bought birthday gifts and wedding gifts and baby gifts for my friends. When I got my first apartment, Master-Card was there to furnish it. When I got into my first car accident, MasterCard was there to replace my fender.

I worried that my whirlwind romance with MasterCard was leading straight to heartbreak. In my more sober moments, away from the shopping mall, I knew that racking up hundreds and then thousands of dollars of debt was not a good idea.

It was bothersome, like when I (briefly) dated an Israeli paratrooper in college. He had anger management issues and once got into a fight with a homeless man outside a movie theater. I knew he wasn't marriage material, but I dated him thinking it would be okay until Mr. Right came along.

MasterCard was the same kind of relationship. It was destructive, but it was a temporary fix. Something I would rely on until my career took off, until I could handle things on my own. I knew that one day I'd be making enough money to pay off my debts and buy things with cash. I'd either get a promotion or I'd win the lottery. Either way, I wouldn't have to stay with MasterCard forever.

MasterCard never failed me, and all he asked in return was a monthly minimum payment.

There are no two words in the English language more seductive and more dangerous than "minimum payment."

"I don't have two hundred and fifty dollars for that Coach bag," I'd tell MasterCard.

"But it's on sale! Buy it right now and you'll save a hundred dollars instantly," MasterCard would say. "It would be fiscally irresponsible *not* to buy it. By not buying it, you're throwing away a hundred dollars."

"You speak good sense, MasterCard, but I still don't have two-fifty for the regularly three-fifty bag."

"Go ahead and get it now, and through the magic of minimum payment, you'll owe me only two dollars," MasterCard would tell me. "And you have to do it, because that bag will Change Your Life. That bag will become your Trademark. That bag will help land you the promotion you'll be coveting. Some guy at the grocery store will notice that bag, and you'll fall in love and get married. You have to do it. I'm just allowing you to buy it now and pay me back later."

Of course, I knew two dollars for a Coach bag didn't make sense. I knew they were piling on the interest charges, but I wasn't alarmed. I was an English major, and math wasn't my strong suit. If I successfully calculated a tip, I felt number-savvy. Interest was beyond me.

Now, I'm sure the founders of Visa and MasterCard probably sat in a boardroom somewhere saying, "This sounds like a crazy idea, but hear me out. There are thousands of English majors out there who can't do math. Really. *And* they never read the fine print. We'll bill them for millions before they ever catch on."

So I didn't realize then that the $250 Coach bag would turn into a $2,500 lifetime investment to Citibank. That the running tally of revolving credit showed up in gray on my bill. It's as if MasterCard didn't want to upset me by showing me my total balance in bold. It was a faded gray, easy to overlook unless you went looking for it. And I never did.

Studying your credit-card statement too closely would be like staring too long at your cellulite in the changing room mirror. No one needs that kind of reality check. Who could withstand such a blow to the self-esteem?

I know this is what psychologists call denial, but let's face it. Denial feels good. Denial is a warm, snuggly blanket you can wrap yourself up in (just like that Ralph Lauren cashmere throw I found on sale at the outlet shop).

I had my balances spread out over three cards, so I didn't have to face the fact that I'd gone into the five-digit debt range. I could look at my cards and think that I would pay them down, just as soon as I a) got that promotion or b) won the lottery.

Every year I'd vow to get out from under my debt. Every year, as with a New Year's resolution I didn't intend to keep, I'd pay down one of my credit cards. That credit card would stay at zero for about two months, and then the balance would pop up on another one, just like Pop-a-Mole. It was spring cleaning. Every year I'd clean out the dust bunnies under my entertainment center. And every year they'd grow back, just as large and scary as they were before. It was like having my vacuum on the wrong setting—I spread dirt from one part of my apartment to the other without really cleaning anything up.

It got to the point that the stress of looking at a credit-card bill required me to have a glass of wine when I opened it.

I started having dreams where my teeth would fall out, or where I'd be drowning under thirty-foot ocean waves filled with floating luggage. I was drowning in debt, and while I could stay in the happy place of denial most of the time, sometimes the debt would not be ignored.

I didn't tell my friends or family about it, because I didn't want them to know how out of control I'd let things get. In my family, I'm the responsible child. I didn't want to disappoint my parents. My dad, after all, had given me stern lectures about the value of a dollar. My mom bragged to her friends about my financial independence.

My friends knew I spent a lot, but so did they. Like any good addict, I surrounded myself with people who did what I did.

And I have what every big spender needs: a Spends More Than I Do Friend. You know her. We all have one. As long as you have a Spends More Than You Do Friend, then you feel practical. I had a friend who used to pay full price at the Gap. I was twenty-four and thought this was crazy. Full price at the Gap! All you have to do is wait two weeks, and whatever you want typically goes on sale. Full price! It's like walking into a street market in Mexico and taking the first price that's offered. You're likely to insult the Gap employees.

My Spends More Than I Do Friend also made more than I did, but that's not the point. The point is: She had a bigger credit-card debt than I did, by at least double. If I had a love affair with MasterCard, she had a codependency relationship. Mine was healthy. Hers, pathological. As long as she was in more debt than me, I was fine.

I told myself it was no big deal. I'd take care of it one day, just like one day I'd start that 401(k).

But the very fact that I kept it a secret meant that I was ashamed I'd let things get so bad.

I tried cutting back my spending, but I seemed to cut back the wrong things. I started taking my lunch to work ($8 per day savings), but after work, I'd go out for dinner and drinks with my friends and plop down $70. I canceled my subscription to *InStyle* ($24 savings) only to spend $25 on mascara. I'd cancel cable ($50 a month savings) only to rent movies from Blockbuster and wind up with $60 in monthly late fees. And no matter how hard I tried, I couldn't get rid of the $100 Target tax (whenever I go into a Target, they ought to charge me $100, because I can't leave without spending at least that much).

I just kept sinking deeper and deeper.

Life in your twenties does not lend itself to practical spending. For one thing, there are the gifts: weddings, babies, birthdays. There are the for-your-friends necessities: the bridesmaid dresses, the plane tickets (to go to those weddings), the trip to Vegas when your best friend of all time gets dumped by her asshole of a boyfriend.

There are the endless (and I mean endless) rounds of drinks you buy at happy hour, because without happy hour, work is just, well, *work*.

There are the thousands of dollars you spend in search of a boyfriend (hopefully fiancé). Your mom had it easy. She ran into your dad in Psych 101. These days most of us spend a fortune looking for our soul mate. I'm talking about spa treatments (including waxing, hair highlighting, hairstyling), new outfits, bar tabs, online dating membership fees, gym fees, makeup, skin-care products, dating advice books, dieting advice books, and all the first dates where you offer to go Dutch and he *takes you up on it*.

Then there are the things you buy to convince yourself that just because you're twenty-five and you wear panty hose every day to work doesn't mean you've lost your college "cool quotient." These include concert tickets, extreme sports merchandise like Rollerblades, gadgets of any kind, CDs by bands you pretend you know but don't, new mobile phones, cable (so you can watch *TRL* and *Cribs*) and anything you see (and I saw) in *InStyle* magazine.

I bought all these things and more.

Still, I told myself I was fine. Oh, sure, I'd get a promotion, and then instead of decreasing, my debt would increase, but that's normal, right?

Everyone had debt. If everyone had it, then I didn't really have a problem.

I was fine. That is, until I got married.

I'd been living with my husband for years before we got married, so you wouldn't think there'd be any surprises. But we'd kept our finances separate all that time. We split everything—the rent, utility bills, and groceries. And we never argued. It was a nice arrangement.

My husband knew that I liked to shop. Quite a lot. He teased me about it.

But he didn't hold this against me. After all, if it wasn't for me, he'd still be renting his pastel-sprinkled patchwork couch from Rent-A-Center and using the *Star Trek* drinking glasses he once got free at Burger King.

My husband knew I had some debt. The key word there is "some." By "some" I mean I told him about one of my credit cards.

He had a strong position on debt: He didn't like it. He had this insane notion that you should actually save money. But what he didn't know didn't hurt him.

Things would have gone on like that if we'd kept our finances separate, but my husband had another crazy idea that being married meant that all of our property—assets and debts—would be shared.

So we opened a joint banking account. Suddenly, I had another person looking at my bank account and credit-card statements. And not just any someone. A frugal someone. My husband is practical. My husband doesn't like to shop. My husband has a savings account that has been steadily growing since he was ten. My husband, unlike me, has a Ph.D. in chemistry and can do math. Real math, not the Jedi mind tricks I was using to balance my budget ("emergency" purchases, such as a dress to wear to my ex-boyfriend's wedding, do not count as actual spending).

"You realize you have twenty thousand and ninety dollars on your credit cards, right?" my husband said to me one day while he was poring over my statements and looking at all that near-invisible gray print.

"That can't be right!" I exclaimed, even though I had a sinking suspicion he was right. I looked at the statements: $8,000 on one, $5,000 on another, $3,000 on another, and $2,000 on two more. As far as I was concerned, having them on different cards meant I didn't have to add them all up. That was why I had them on *different* cards.

"Have you ever done a budget?" he asked me.

"Of course I have," I said. And I had. But I never *stuck* to a budget. Budgets were like science fiction. Maybe a Cara Lockwood in an alternate dimension managed to spend only $20 on dry cleaning last month, but the Cara in this dimension spent $67.

My husband asked me to accurately record all my spending, as if I were on a Weight Watchers diet. It was then that I realized I had a spending problem. Specifically, I discovered two things: 1) I really like shoes and 2) I buy a lot of gifts. It's true. Nearly a third of my MasterCard spending went to my friends and relatives. Birthday gifts, wedding gifts, baby shower gifts, bachelorette party gifts, sorry-you-lost-your-job gifts, you-bought-me-a-gift-so-I-have-to-buy-you-one gifts.

What can I say? MasterCard is so thoughtful that way. It's why we are soul mates.

"You realize," my husband said. "That we can't buy a house until we pay this down."

And then it hit me: I would be living in bad apartments forever. Forget the two-car garage. Forget the cars, even. My future would be me as a bag lady wearing all those sweaters I'd bought on sale at www.jcrew.com.

I went to one of those websites that calculates how much house you can afford. I punched in my debt load and my salary and the down payment (none!), and the online calculator told me that I could afford a house that cost $35,000. Unless I wanted to raise my family in a Honda Accord, I decided that MasterCard had to go.

But it was so difficult to break up with MasterCard. We'd had so many years of good times. So many years of living beyond our means. I couldn't just dump him like that. Not after all those trips to Target and IKEA. Actually following through on the breakup was a lot harder than I ever thought it would be.

My husband, I'll admit, shamed me into it. It was a lot harder to justify (another) pair of black shoes from Nordstrom when I had someone asking me why I needed them. I decided to do it because I wanted to get out of debt, and because I was tired of my husband having the high ground.

So I sat at the kitchen table and cut up my credit cards, one by one.

Without MasterCard, I had to pay cash for everything, which meant that nine times out of ten, by the end of the month, I didn't have money for food. For the first time in my adult life, I had to make choices. Hard choices. Buying shoes at the beginning of the month meant that I might be eating peanut butter sandwiches for ten days straight until I got paid. Without MasterCard, I had to say no to trips with the girls, no to dinners out, no to lunches out at work, no to movies, no to everything.

Overnight, I transformed from the Fun Friend to the Lame Cheap Friend. Instead of being the first one to offer to buy a round of drinks, I had come down with an affliction of Alligator Arm—my arm's too short to reach the bill. While all my friends browsed the Origins counter, I became the Generic Walgreens Products girl. I had to say no to concert tickets at $85 apiece. No to a girls' trip to Las Vegas. No to yoga classes. No to my gym membership. No to highlights. No to pedicures. No to brow waxes. No to brand-name anything.

My wardrobe became tattered and out of date, my hair was a mess, my complexion like a week-old pepperoni pizza. Even showering with the sharp metallic scent of generic shower gel depressed me.

I realized that for years, MasterCard had shielded me from the ugly reality of life: Being poor sucks.

Instant gratification is so much easier to live with, but the fact is, the only way to get out of debt is to spend less. For a long time. Forever, possibly. Making more money and then spending more money will not be the solution. There's simply no other way out.

It's like dieting. There's no silver bullet to losing weight. There's no magic pill. You have to eat less. Period.

Debt is the same way. You have to spend less. Period.

But it's hard. Because MasterCard wouldn't leave me. He kept showing up in the mail and in my e-mail box. Begging me to take him back. He'd drunk-dial me at two A.M., reminding me of all the fabulous shoes that could be mine at the Nordstrom's semi-annual sale. He'd call me and offer me free magazine subscriptions or ten thousand frequent-flier miles that could be used for that trip to Italy I always wanted. He'd give it to me for 0 percent APR the first eight months.

He would show up in the hands of my friends, taunting me with how easily he'd moved on, and how much fun he was having with them at Bloomingdale's.

After I had paid him down to zero, near my twenty-eighth birthday, I let him back into my life on the condition that we would only be friends. But the romance was over. I could never again let him wine and dine me, never again let him take me away on romantic trips. That first blush of credit-card love would never be recaptured. I was a responsible adult now, with a mortgage and a husband who opened my mail.

I had to pay my balance in full every month.

"I heard there's a sale at Pottery Barn," MasterCard says. "You know you could sneak me out. For old times' sake. Your husband would never know. You deserve four-hundred-and-fifty-thread-count sheets!"

"I'm putting you away now, MasterCard. Be good or I'll have to break up with you again."

"Remember that time I took you to IKEA?" MasterCard says wistfully. "I bought you a lot of nice things that day."

"You sure did, MasterCard. You sure did."

But the fact of the matter is, MasterCard could never buy me peace of mind. And that is truly priceless.

Money Doesn't Buy Happiness, but It Comes Damn Close When It Buys a White-Tableclothed Meal and a Few Bottles of Wine

By Laura Caldwell

After two months in law school—two months during which my head was swirling with arcane phrases such as "caveat emptor" and "res ipsa loquitor" and "voir dire," none of which I understood in the slightest—a friend called with what he promised would be a beacon of light.

"This is going to be great for you," said George. "I know law school is a bitch, but this is just what you need."

"Tell me," I said, glugging from a can of day-old Mountain Dew and eyeing a stack of textbooks about my height.

"We're starting a supper club."

"What do you mean?"

"You know, friends getting together once a week to eat and drink."

"Sounds good." I perked up. I imagined free meals at the homes of our college friends, the ones now working at banks and family-owned companies and who rented cool, urban apartments decked out with Ralph Lauren furnishings. It would be such a break from the airless airplane-hangar feel of the law school's library, not to mention my own mildewed basement apartment.

"We're starting next week at Charlie Trotter's," said George, naming one of Chicago's most well known and god-awfully expensive restaurants.

"Maybe I'll skip a week," I said. "On second thought, I'll skip it altogether."

I was incredibly lucky: I had a benevolent family who paid my tuition, but that rarely left one cent toward electricity or oatmeal, not to mention taxicabs, cute clothes, or dinners out. And my law school had made students sign a contract promising not to work the first year—not that there was time.

"You've got to do it," George said. "It wouldn't be the same without you."

"I can't afford it."

"I'll pay for it."

I admit this was a tempting offer. I was poor in a way I hadn't known before, and I wasn't above hitting up guys for drinks. But George was a friend. A good, solid, wonderful friend whom I sensed I wanted around when I was fifty years old.

"I can't let you do that," I said.

"Just for the first week."

"Where are you going next?"

He named a stylish Michigan Avenue eatery that would set me back at least a hundred bucks. I knew that hundred dollars could also buy about forty-seven packages of ramen noodles and ten six-packs of Bud Light.

I passed on the supper club. Instead, my poor friends—other students, public school teachers, and ad agency interns—and I fed ourselves on bar popcorn and bakeries that offered free, if minuscule, slices of bread.

Every week George called with critiques and raves of the restaurants the supper club had visited. Every week there was another fantastic story. Once they met a celeb who was in town filming a movie, and they partied with him until the wee hours. Another night, a bar owner sent over a platter of oysters flown in from Brazil, along with a case of Dom Perignon. Yet another night, the dinner somehow led to backstage passes at the House of Blues.

I grew bitter. It wasn't that I felt entitled to fabulous nights out and long dinners with friends, but why did law school have to be so damned spartan? Would the work ever, *ever* pay off? And even if it did, was I missing some of the greatest moments my friends would have?

Meanwhile, I was making plenty of memories in law school; I just didn't realize it at the time. My friend Melinda and I threw a tiny yellow ball back and forth across a library table as we quizzed ourselves on the tenets of civil procedure, peppering our discussions with anecdotes about boys and families and the cheapest places to buy beer. During those times, I was usually wondering why I wasn't wearing high-heeled pumps and dining with the supper club at Gibsons.

Later, when I was wearing pumps every day to work and preparing endless motions for summary judgment, I would wonder why I wasn't in a pair of jeans, slumped in a library chair across from my girlfriend.

While I feared working for a living, I couldn't wait for a real paycheck. I would not only join the supper club, I would be its president. I daydreamed about how it would feel, waltzing into a nice restaurant, breezily announcing my arrival to the maître d', consulting with the sommelier about pinot noir versus cabernet, debating with my fellow diners over a chocolate mousse for dessert or just a glass of port wine. I knew little about the detailed process of dining out, but I knew I wanted it. I wanted that world.

Ultimately, law school passed quicker than I ever would have thought possible. Legal employment, which for me had seemed as likely as a future in Chinese foot binding, came blissfully quickly as well. I had exactly one second interview and exactly one job offer.

I stepped behind the desk at my new law firm, knowing I understood little about the law and even less about how to "practice" it. I prayed no one would notice me or the nice chunk of change that was now seeping annually from the firm's bank account into mine. It wasn't the highest-paying job around, at least not for a law school grad in the early nineties. Many of my friends were making tens of thousands more. And yet now I could buy as many packs of ramen as I liked. I could even afford a loaf of that bakery bread I used to get for free.

I called my friend George and proudly announced my self-nomination into the supper club. Wouldn't they be lucky, I thought, to have a new fresh face, someone eager and reasonably smart and not too bad to look at. But I learned that our friends had moved on to new and more exciting endeavors. They were buying houses and making dinners at home. They were traveling, George said. Some were pregnant. It was just too hard to get a big group together for dinner every week.

My disappointment was palpable. I had missed out on the supper-club era. I had missed what were surely golden memories made during a golden time. For a while I tried to cajole the old members of the supper club back together. I scheduled one large dinner after another only to have them disintegrate—*too busy, too crazy, we've already been to that restaurant four times*. I resigned myself. The supper club was gone. It was one of the things I'd simply missed out on, and the fact that I had gotten a law school education wasn't too bad an exchange.

Yet it didn't seem so great an exchange at first. Practicing law was *tough*, or at least much more mentally challenging than law school, something I hadn't anticipated. Law school was made out to be such a burden that I'd assumed the light at the end of the tunnel would be a bright, pleasant, and easy practice, along with lots of respect and more than a little money to go to dinner.

I decided not to wait for the members of the supper club. I decided the money that wasn't going toward my student loans would be funneled right into a fund called Nights on the Town. I was the sole manager of this fund, and the city was mine for the taking. I started going out to dinner, and not just at the local pub that offered day-old popcorn. When the guys at work asked me to join them, I jumped at the chance. We tried Indian and Thai restaurants. We went to upscale Italian trattorias. When another associate wanted to introduce me to sushi, I batted down the initial throat closing that accompanied the thought of raw fish and went for it. Sometimes I went out with dates (a girl like me never says no to the joy of free food), but I also went with friends and with girlfriends and sometimes just with my lonesome, which I was surprised to find wasn't lonely at all.

One of my most vivid memories of those initial days dining out was a dinner with my now-husband. Like me, he had been lucky enough to grow up with a fantastic family and (in retrospect) fortunate enough that his family had made him work for at least some of his supper. For one of the first big dinners of our dating life, my husband suggested a restaurant called Ambria, which I'd heard was the Shaq Daddy of restaurants in my neighborhood of Lincoln Park. I was sure the supper club had dined there repeatedly, and now I was finally going to experience it.

For Ambria, I chose an outfit that was dressy (and therefore fitting the venue) but also sexy (and therefore fitting the fact that I wanted to end up in bed with this guy very, very shortly after dinner). I felt fantastic as I checked my hair one last time and straightened the black miniskirt and sheer blouse I'd chosen.

But when we got to the restaurant, time screeched to a halt. My tiny and adorable skirt was nothing short of inappropriate.

Everyone else was in suits or classic, elegant-looking attire. My hair, which I'd fluffed to an extreme, just felt fluffy. The other diners shot looks from my skirt up to my blouse. Quickly, I went from feeling super-fabulous to super-slutty, from fashionable to utterly unsuitable. And it wasn't just the looks of the other, more elegant diners that made me feel this way. It was the whole white-tablecloth experience. I wasn't used to such formality, such presentation, such *silverware*. I was used to eating out of a package with my hands or utilizing a plastic fork to chomp food from Styrofoam containers.

I practically crawled to the table.

Yet once we'd gotten into our dinner, I left behind the embarrassment and marveled at the forks that appeared over and over, replacing one another. I went to the restroom, enchanted when I returned to find my napkin refolded in a precise triangle and standing at the ready on my plate. I loved how all the glasses—for water, for wine, for champagne—sparkled at me. I delighted in my boyfriend, in the delectable cuisine, in the sheer scrumptiousness of it all. I forgot that, compared to the other diners, I was dressed like a backup dancer for Ricky Martin.

After that night, I continued to eat out whenever I could. In fact, as I began working harder and harder as a lawyer, I found it was simply easier to hit a café for dinner at the end of the day, rather than deal with grocery shopping or preparing food. And with the dining frequency, I grew accustomed to that world. I lost the butterflies of my first night at Ambria. I lost my dining innocence.

But even after all these years of spending more time in Chicago restaurants than in my own kitchen, and paying more for dining each year than I did for my law school tuition, I still love dining out. I love the white tablecloths and the cheery, deferential waiters. I love picking up a spoon for soup and knowing there'll be a different one when I want to stir sugar in my coffee, a spoon I won't have to wash. I love the candles on the tables and the wineglasses that don't hold a smear of pink gloss from the last time I used them. I love watching the other patrons, guessing whether they're on their first date or their last, striking up conversations with women in the restrooms for impromptu dining reviews.

I still feel special when I sit down to a white tablecloth and a place setting, and I still feel like a superstar when a waiter puts a plate of fish or a Cobb salad in front of me. But when I think about it, I realize the only thing that brings me such happiness, such pangs of pleasure, is money.

We're told when we're in our early twenties—and certainly any time we have to pinch pennies—that money can't buy happiness. This axiom is accurate, certainly. Anyone who has seen a friend or acquaintance marry someone primarily for money knows this to be true.

Yet we can't ignore the fact that money does grease the wheels of life. It makes day-to-day living a hell of a lot easier. Don't want to walk to the subway because your heels are too high? Take a cab. Feel like going to see your sister in Phoenix, even though the plane tickets just went up a hundred dollars? Who cares, it's worth it. Spilled red wine on that favorite white sweater? Wipe your tears and head to BCBG for a new one.

For me, money brought the luxury of dining out, something made so special because of the years I couldn't even entertain the idea. I'm not wealthy, and I still have to give up certain things in order to visit all these restaurants. I don't splurge on boots unless I can envision wearing them for at least five years, and I try to stay clear of expensive makeup, heading instead for the Walgreens cosmetics aisle where I've been buying mascara forever.

I still dine out whenever I can, wherever I can, and I enjoy the hell out of it. But I miss the wide-eyed innocence of that first night at Ambria. I actually miss my naïveté and wish I'd cultivated it more. I wish I hadn't struggled so hard to be the smooth customer who could order wine with ease. Naïveté and innocence, it seems to me, are something to be recognized and reveled in for the short time they are yours. If you don't enjoy these traits, if you try too hard to be unaffected and oh-so-cool, then all you are is a young girl in an inappropriate blouse, waiting for some food. Relishing your innocence, though, makes everything glint and gleam. I'm glad I did, because although my dining innocence is gone, memories allow me to keep a wide-eyed fascination about the process.

As a poor law student, I was irked that I couldn't be one of the members of the fabulous supper club, but I swear I'm grateful now. I'm grateful for every bite.

The Real World

By Erica Kennedy

For some strange reason, I believed my first apartment out of college would be a small one-bedroom that I would inventively decorate on a shoestring budget. I'd probably live in Brooklyn, where I'd be able to afford more square footage, as opposed to a tiny, suffocating box in Manhattan with a shower in the kitchen. Every morning, after waking in my charmingly spruced-up apartment, I would quickly throw on a cute but professional ensemble, then brave the subway rush hour and maybe grab a muffin on the way to my entry-level job, which I'd bitch about after work with my equally cash-strapped, recently graduated pals. The saving grace? It would be a job in a cool industry—media or fashion—and after working long, thankless hours for a few years (three at the most), I would be rewarded with a higher-paying and more emotionally fulfilling position with many, many perks. And then I would move, perhaps to a loft, very possibly in SoHo.

What the fuck was I thinking?

A possible answer to that question is that I had a chaotic, wildly dysfunctional childhood, raised by a mother who was pathologically hysterical. It felt like I was acting the role of the normal, high-achieving suburban girl, and when I got behind the curtain, it was chaos. As a result, my grasp on what was normal was tenuous. The life I imagined was closer to an episode of *The Mary Tyler Moore Show* than to anything within the realm of possibility.

My first apartment turned out to be not an apartment but a room. My ex-boyfriend from college was living in an old house with rickety stairs in Boerum Hill, Brooklyn, with two other guys from school. When one moved out, lucky me moved into a room so narrow and dusty that it felt like a broom closet. Thank God I was completely over my ex, because every weekend I could hear him having sex with random women in the next room. Other than that, living with the boys was a joy. The kitchen was always filthy, as was the bathroom, and when we had a mouse, I amused them with my screaming and frantic pleas that they "do something!" They never caught the mouse, and whenever it would scurry through the living room while they were getting stoned, they'd point and say, "Hey, there's Ben."

When a former classmate from Sarah Lawrence asked me to house-sit his airy Manhattan duplex, I jumped at the chance to escape the Brooklyn slum I called home. Late one night, as I luxuriated on his cool sheets, I found myself watching *Baby Boom*, which I had already seen. "Your well's run dry," the bumbling handyman tells Diane Keaton, a New York career woman who has fled to picturesque Vermont with the adorable baby she's inherited from a long-lost cousin. Her dreams of an idyllic life in the country are going down the tubes as repairs on the old house eat through her savings, and this is the final straw. She flips out and, before passing out in the snow, shrieks, "I'm not prepared for a well to run dry! I just want to turn on the faucet and have water! I don't want to know where it's coming from!"

I burst into tears and sobbed for an hour, staring up at my friend's fifteen-foot ceilings, thinking, I know, girl, I know! That was how I felt every day for the first few years of my post-college life. Like flipping out. Like it was all too much. Nothing was as I had imagined it would be, and every day brought a tidal wave of problems for which I was not prepared. The only reason I didn't have a breakdown sooner was because I was so perpetually shell-shocked, struggling to keep my head above water, too numb to feel much of anything.

I never mapped out how much it would cost to sustain this fantasy life that I thought was an attainable reality. I just assumed that this was how life would be—the same way you assume, when you book a hotel room, that there will be a bed in that room. But when I opened the door to the real world, I found out the bed was extra. And so was everything else.

Many of my friends, either middle-class like me or completely-out-of-touch-with-reality rich, were equally ill equipped to deal with the daily struggles presented by living on their own. I think someone could make a killing with a company that offered real-world tutoring. Just as you prep for the SATs, RWT would prep you for the practicalities of life, addressing things like balancing your checkbook, deciphering your credit report, maximizing cubicle space, and managing to get to the cleaners before they close. I had one Beverly Hills–reared friend who once said in a sociology class that her family was middle-class. That comment was met with outraged objections, as everyone knew she was the daughter of a legendary actor. She defended her statement by saying, "Compared to most people we know, we are. We don't have a plane." She would leave all the lights on in her first apartment because it scared her to come home to the dark. Then one day before walking out, she made sure to turn off all the lights. "I actually looked at the Con Edison bill," she explained. See, now in RWT, they would teach you that.

Those first few years, I felt like a bucket of ice-cold water was being thrown in my face on a daily basis. I'd known I would have to struggle, but I'd thought those lean years would still be fun, that one day I'd look back and laugh. They weren't and I don't. And it wasn't a few years, it was more like a decade. I'm still recovering.

The Mouse House was an example of how far and how quickly I'd had to scale back my expectations once I started poking around in the real world. A month after graduation, I told a real estate broker I was looking for a one-bedroom with lots of light, ample closet space in an elevator building; a doorman would be a plus. It was as implausible as my walking into Sotheby's tomorrow for an auction, paddle at the ready.

I thought it was my lucky day when I saw a huge rent-controlled one-bedroom in a prewar doorman building in Brooklyn Heights. But it was the worst possible thing that could have happened, because it only perpetuated the fantasy that I would be the black Mary Tyler Moore. My application was denied, of course, because there were probably a hundred applicants vying for such a plum deal, and I'm quite sure all of them made more than the whopping $20,000 a year I was pulling in.

Then there was the little problem of my credit. I'd signed up for a Visa freshman year, and then when I couldn't pay, I gave the annoying man who kept calling both the home and work numbers for my mother, who had no idea I had a credit card. He took it up with her, and though she was pissed, she paid up. Lesson unlearned, I got a Barneys card senior year. When I could not pay that one off, I just pretended the bill didn't exist. I never paid off the nine hundred or so dollars (it seemed like a lot then), and that mistake—what the good folks at TransUnion call a "charge off"—remained on my credit report for seven years. It probably brought my score down hundreds of points.

I now live in a lovely apartment in the Heights that's a stone's throw away from that first apartment, which I fantasized about for years. It took me ten years (and a book deal) to afford the apartment and neighborhood I imagined I would move into straight out of college.

But one thing did work out as I'd expected. I got a low-paying job in a cool industry. I was hired to do college promotions at an upstart hip-hop label called Rowdy Records. I had no desire to work in the music industry, but then again, I hadn't a clue as to what I wanted to do. Sarah Lawrence, a liberal arts school that doles out "evaluations" instead of grades and doesn't require students to pick a major, didn't exactly help me focus. Working at a record label sounded like a cool job, especially since the label owner, a super-producer named Dallas Austin, who'd produced most of TLC's hits, was the same age I was, twenty-two. When the general manager, a friend of a friend, offered me the job, he apologetically told me the salary. I didn't think about taxes or all the expenses I would incur living on my own, without help from parents, like a lot of my friends had. I was just happy to have a job. And a cool one at that.

Since Rowdy was a company of young people (no one except the general manager was over thirty) and the office was supposed to look hip—and "rowdy," I suppose—we were all allowed to paint our offices any color we liked. I was out of the office the day the painting was done, and my colleagues picked my color. When I came in the next day, my office was hot pink. It was like spending eight hours a day trapped in Barbie's dream house.

All in all, though, life at Rowdy was pretty fun. I remember mentioning at a party that I was going on a business trip to a music convention in San Francisco. Another recent college grad asked incredulously, "You go on business trips?" They were dumbfounded to discover I also had my own office with a door, an expense account, and the ability to order Town Cars at will. (Still clinging to fantasy of what my life would be, I found none of this odd.) The permissive company policies were in line with the attitude of our boy-genius boss, who took a laissez-faire approach to running the company. He lived in Atlanta and spent most of his time there making music, while Rocky, the label's general manager, ran the show in New York. On one visit to New York, Dallas came into my office in the afternoon and said, "I wanna go to the movies. You wanna to go to the movies?" I told him I couldn't. "Why?" he asked. "Because I'm working," I told him. "Okay," he said. "What time do you get off?"

My job as college promotions director was to call all the college radio stations and get our label's songs added to the playlists. The first song I worked with was by a group called 95 South, named after a highway in Atlanta. I didn't particularly care for the song, and I didn't know how to "rap" to the college DJs about it. So I just badgered them with calls, discussed whatever they wanted to discuss—school, their girlfriends, you name it—and then asked them to please add the song to their rotation. There was some kind of chart released every week (like Billboard, but for college airplay) that rated the top twenty-five songs, so Rocky knew exactly how I was doing. After four years of college with no grades, now I was being graded every week at my job! My song inched slowly up the chart until, a month later, 95 South had the number one most added song on the college playlist. Rocky was so proud.

But what good did that do me when I had to go home to my dusty broom closet and eat spaghetti . . . again? It wasn't even Ronzoni, it was generic. Brand-name food was a luxury I could not afford. So were cabs, new clothes, snacks at the movies, that muffin I'd imagined I'd grab on the way to work. After putting my twenty-thousand-dollar salary into context, I felt duped. So I went to Rocky to complain. "When am I due for a raise?" I demanded, the lax atmosphere leading me to believe it was perfectly okay to speak to one's boss this way. "Another ten months, maybe," he told me with a shrug. I told him I could not live on what he was paying me. He answered with another shrug.

Desperate, I began plotting ways to make more money. I considered getting a second job. Added bonus: A night job would keep me out of my broom closet. That's what I did, got a second job—sort of. When Rocky decided he needed an assistant, I went to him with a proposal. What if I continued doing college promotions and took on assistant duties as well? Then, instead of paying someone else a full twenty-thousand-dollar salary, he could just pay me ten thousand dollars more. And he went for it! Being his assistant didn't take much time or energy (I'd known it wouldn't), and in just two months, I had gotten a ten-thousand-dollar raise. That was a small victory—until Dallas moved the company to Atlanta, and I found myself unemployed.

My situation was made more appalling by the fact that a lot of the people I knew were either rich of their own efforts, had rich parents, or were dating/about to marry into extreme wealth. Don't ask me why that was, but I would have preferred some poor friends. While those around me were shopping and running off to the Hamptons, I was collecting coins to put in the Coin-O-Matic so I could afford my weekly supply of generic pasta.

Having friends with big apartments did come in handy during extended periods of homelessness. One month when I was between apartments, I lived in the penthouse of hip-hop mogul Russell Simmons, whom I had known since high school. It was not as glam as it sounds. He'd abruptly fired his live-in homeboy manservant, and he allowed me to stay in one of his guest rooms until he could find a replacement. That was all well and good for the first three weeks, when he was in L.A. Then he came back and duty called. On top of my full-time job at Rowdy, I had to shop for Russell's groceries, pick up his dry cleaning and movies at Blockbuster, call the cable company to fix the television in his bedroom, which wouldn't pick up BET ("It's the only channel I watch!"), and so on. One night he buzzed me on the intercom and demanded I go to the store and get him a bottle of cranberry juice ("And make sure it's Ocean Spray! I don't know what that other shit is that you got in the refrigerator!"). It was almost midnight. I refused.

I went to Stuyvesant, arguably the best high school in New York. I was a college graduate who'd spent my junior year at Oxford. How had my life amounted to this? I didn't want a fabulous spread like Russell's, which he'd bought from Cher along with all her weird furnishings. I just wanted a place to call my own.

Russell was so mad, he ran down from the upper floors of the apartment, where he stayed ensconced, communicating through the intercom like God, and gave me a dose of reality face-to-face. "The payments on this place are fourteen thousand dollars a month. If you want to pay seven, then you don't have to go to the store and get me anything!" I got the cranberry juice, and the next day he threw me out.

I lived such a nomadic existence that I cannot remember the sequence of all the addresses and couches where I laid my head. There was the beautiful Park Slope house where I lived with two roommates, one of whom stayed up all night bouncing a basketball in his room, which was directly over mine. Then there was a teeny-weeny "two-bedroom apartment" that would have been a small studio if you'd knocked down all the walls. It was on a great block in SoHo that at night was overrun by giant, bold rats. All the vermin dancing in the streets made it difficult for my roommate and me to get people to come over. "What the fuck," said one guy I dated, who would never walk me to my door after dark. "It's like they're putting on a production of *101 Dalmatians* out there!" He'd drop me off on the corner, and I would sprint down the block with my keys out, hoping I could get inside before one charged me.

By then I was working in PR for a fashion company after years of freelance jobs that barely paid my rent. As when I'd worked at the record label, I had no interest in being a publicist. It was just another job that came along by happenstance, and I took it because I was directionless and in need of a steady paycheck. It wasn't until I was twenty-six and in therapy that I asked myself,

"What is it that you really want to do?" As Oprah would say, it was an "aha moment." Not the answer, just the question. I had always been an honor student, I had gone to great schools, and I had been out of school for five years before I asked myself that simple question. What would I do even if someone weren't paying me to do it? What was my dream job?

The answer was: writing for magazines. It was that simple. I had been reading every magazine under the sun since I was a teenager, everything from *Vogue* to *Sports Illustrated*. I'd always been told I was a good writer, and when I'd interned at a women's magazine in my senior year, they'd allowed me to write a few short pieces. I'd never thought I could make a living doing that. But was I making a real living doing anything else?

So I quit my PR job. Just like that. I took a few classes at the New School on how to break into magazines and, feeling that I had to make up for lost time, pursued my goal with a vengeance. Six months later, I was getting yelled at by a superstar musician while interviewing him for an *InStyle* profile. "Are you a fluff writer? Is that all you're ever going to be?" he bizarrely berated me in the wee hours at a downtown lounge while his two bodyguards stood in front of the banquette. "It felt like a boxing match," I told my editor later. "He kept punching me and punching me. I just wanted it to end. But the bell kept ringing. Ding, ding. Next round."

I wanted to go down and stay down, but I couldn't. Not when I'd scored my first magazine feature in a magazine people actually read; when there was a $3,000 paycheck on the line; when I'd slept on people's couches and dragged myself out of bed to go to jobs I abhorred; when I'd finally gotten my own apartment and that month's rent was due.

I was twenty-seven when I was finally free of roommates. I found the apartment in *The Village Voice*. I couldn't even tell what it looked like because I saw it at night, and the electricity wasn't turned on. I had to be out of my other place ASAP, so I bombarded the rental office with calls until they said it was mine. It was a dingy studio that partially faced a brick wall, but it did have three walk-in closets, a large separate kitchen, an elevator, and a part-time doorman.

I spruced it up little by little over the five years that I stayed there, hustling for freelance assignments to make the rent. Then I upgraded to a charming one-bedroom down the block, where I started working on my first novel. My tumultuous post-college years, which I'd thought of as a total waste, provided much of the material for that novel, which was published in 2004. Now I spend my days in my Brooklyn Heights home office, working on my next book, and every Sunday I hit all the open houses in my neighborhood, because the time has come for me to buy a home to call my own.

Plan B

By Megan Crane

When I graduated from college, I was vastly unprepared to deal with the Real World.

I don't mean that in a vague, metaphoric way. I mean that I was *totally clueless.* Not only did I not know how to balance a checkbook, I wasn't entirely sure how to go about writing a check. I don't think I *had* checks, or even a bank account, come to think of it. I spent four years in college without once doing laundry on campus, preferring to wait until I could drag mountains of dirty clothes home to my unamused mother. (Those were the grunge years, luckily for me. It was fashionable to wear the same flannel shirt for months. Or so I kept telling myself.) The only job I'd ever held was as a decidedly bad camp counselor, the sort who let the kids do the kinds of things for which parents these days go to court. All I knew about the Real World was that everyone talked about it the way they'd talked about menstruation back when they separated the girls and boys in elementary school and forced us to look at "sanitary napkins": something unpleasant as well as unavoidable, that for some reason made people already experiencing it lofty and smug.

I wasn't overly concerned about my cluelessness at first, because I'd drunk deep of the Kool-Aid at my fancy college. I had been "taught how to think," the commencement speaker, herself a graduate, thundered as I sat in the sun with my mortar board clamped to my head, wondering whether I was supposed to feel different.

I had a lot of time to think about differences in my first months of Employment in the Real World. Mostly, I thought about the difference between working hard in school, which had always seemed to involve a lot of time for sleeping, and working hard out of school, which seemed to involve work and very early mornings. There wasn't enough coffee in the world to make waking up before dawn okay.

The Real World, I thought almost daily on my pre-dawn commute, just wasn't much fun.

Back in college, I'd been vocal about the things I felt weren't fun. Like final exams or several papers due in the same week. Or any courses involving math or foreign-language skills, neither of which I possessed. Or sharing a bathroom with hundreds of other students, many of whom had questionable hygienic practices.

I quickly discovered that senior-level seminars entirely devoted to one stanza of an obscure poem were *way* more fun than days spent crouched on the floor of an improperly heated file room, sorting through the expense reports of sales representatives at a large corporation in the wilds of Mahwah, New Jersey.

Who knew?

The fact that I knew how to think did not, it turned out, hold much weight with the regular inhabitants of the accounts payable department. Amazingly enough, they, too, knew how to think, even without the benefit of an elite education. And what they thought was that I was a spoiled, overly entitled drama queen with few to no marketable skills.

It was hard to argue with this assessment, particularly when my parents were weighing in with their own version. They were focused more on the unpleasantness of living in close proximity to my collegiate habits (leaving all lights on all the time, avoiding laundry until there was not one item of clean clothing left, etc.) and corresponding collegiate attitude (snotty). Neither of which would be any of their concern, of course, were I to move out on my own.

In theory, I was ready to move out right that second.

In practice, I was afraid.

I had only recently suffered the indignity of my first paycheck, complete with my first exposure to taxes. Surely I couldn't be expected to pay bills or leisure expenses with a paycheck that did not compare favorably with the allowance I'd received at sixteen. Someone had to be kidding.

As that first fall wore on and turned into an equally listless winter, I came to realize that this wasn't a joke. It was my life, and while it was less gleaming and fabulous than I'd expected, I was making it significantly worse than it had to be with the temp positions and the squatting-in-my-childhood-home nonsense.

I took the first temp-to-perm position I could find. At the time I felt empowered and, yes, excited to be making a commitment to the workforce. In retrospect, I have no idea what I was thinking. I could not have been more ill suited for the job as a customer-service representative at a medical laser company if I'd tried. For one thing, my attitude and entitlement issues did not exactly make for excellent—or even competent—customer service. For another, I had less than no interest in medical lasers and wasn't afraid to say so. Other things I didn't much care for included: arriving at work at eight-thirty A.M. every single morning, returning from lunch in a timely fashion, and my boss's obsessive (in my opinion, pathological) attention to details he felt I should be on top of, like the filing system.

My foray into customer service for medical lasers would last only a year, but the important thing was, it got me out of my parents' house. It took a real, steady job to help me get over my fear of paying rent. Not that I stopped being afraid of it, really. I just stopped making excuses for not doing it. After about eight months of wearing out my welcome at my parents' house, I bit the bullet and moved into my first apartment in Hoboken, New Jersey.

Finally, I thought.

Finally, I could live the way I wanted to live, without interference from my parents and their near-criminal lack of understanding. More important, I wouldn't have to conduct my vastly superior version of living in my childhood bedroom, complete with narrow twin beds and stuffed animals I couldn't quite bring myself to throw out.

Bring on my *real* twenties, I thought, filled to the brim with smug anticipation, for surely my greatness was about to swell up and carry me off into the limelight. I'm ready to leave this teenage stuff behind!

A year later, I was rethinking my zeal.

It had been a tough year. Some things I learned in my first year out on my own in my real twenties:

- Dorm rooms are easier to clean than apartments, especially when you don't know how to use a vacuum cleaner, a duster, or, let's be honest here, a cleaning implement of any kind.
- Shopping for groceries, it turns out, is like cleaning: unpleasant, tedious, and has to be repeated almost immediately. Also very expensive.
- It's still easier to load up three months' worth of laundry in the trunk and do it at Mom's, where there is also a stocked fridge.
- Rent is really annoying, especially when you have suspicions about your landlord with the faint Italian accent and the suspicious henchmen.
- Real life kind of sucks.

I didn't let any of these things get in my way, no matter how much zeal ebbed away. I got a Very Important Real Job in a Very Important Real Big-City Law Firm, because my parents often told me I was argumentative, and who knew? Maybe that meant I should become a lawyer. Also, the customer-service thing had been doomed from the start. So I moved myself and my eighty zillion possessions into a tiny studio in what was then the far reaches of Spanish Harlem, and I told myself that I was *filled* to the *brim* with the *energy* of the city!

In truth, what I was filled with was nostalgia. I hung out only with college friends, all of whom also lived either in studio apartments or with their parents, and we talked about college. Now that we'd had time away from the place, we were less consumed with how claustrophobic and jaded we'd felt socially, and way more obsessed with how little work we'd done when we'd had a four-year paid vacation at our disposal.

Why, I wondered, had I found it necessary to moon about for four years, carrying on about sad dead Victorian women and their sad poems—often about death, as it happened, or love, which usually amounted to the same thing in thematic terms—when I had an entire college at my disposal and conceivably could have learned something useful? Like, say, a marketable skill? Because the other thing I'd discovered since graduation was that "learned how to think" was not a bullet point interviewers were interested in reading on a résumé. Computer skills and words per minute, that's what made interviewers smile, or so I'd heard. A mention of an independent study on Anglo-Saxon elegies? Not so much.

I felt misled. Cheated. Some of the people I'd gone to college with had taken advantage of different information. These people had learned how to type, or had taken business classes in between frat parties, and were now raking in serious salaries. These people had obviously received instruction about how to function as adults, while I had learned how to drink seventeen White Russians in a row without toppling over. Oh yes, and how to think.

What I thought then was: This is unfair. After which, to make myself feel better, I would buy something. Shoes. Chocolate. The *Pride and Prejudice* miniseries starring Colin Firth. Elizabeth Bennet hadn't had to worry about boring jobs, marketable skills, and credit-card debt. Elizabeth Bennet had simply had *fine eyes*, and presto! She was rewarded with Mr. Darcy.

Right about the same time, I discovered that I harbored an abiding hatred for the minutiae of the law. If lawyering involved thundering about justice in courtrooms like the assistant district attorneys on *Law & Order*, then I was in. Who didn't want to expose injustice in the middle of a tense courtroom scene? If, however, lawyering was about extremely boring details—which it sure seemed to be—then I wanted nothing to do with it.

"You should always put on your résumé that you're detail-oriented," my extremely detail-oriented friend had told me when I was interviewing for my paralegal job.

"What does that even mean?" I asked. "What details am I supposed to be oriented toward? Who gets to choose the details? Or do you mean any details at all?"

"You asked for my help," she snapped. "So just put it on your résumé, okay?"

"I don't know what makes you think I have a résumé in the first place. I've had exactly one job, and they're one phone call to the eight-hundred number away from firing my ass as it is—"

"Listen to me," she commanded. She was, of all my college friends, the one who had the best job. She knew where to buy suits and how to wear neck scarves. I didn't even own a neck scarf. I was too busy wearing flannel and pretending I lived in grunge-era Seattle to think about business accessories. I was a little bit in awe of her, actually.

"I'm listening," I said.

"When you put down that you're detail-oriented, it tells your employer that they can depend on you to do what they want without having to run around checking up on you," she explained. "It's a shorthand."

I considered.

The truth was, the only details that interested me were the details of my histrionic social life, those of my friends' equally histrionic social lives, and those of the (okay, I'll admit it) histrionic television shows I watched obsessively. Details about my job? Snore. In case I had any doubts about this, there was my tenure as the Worst Customer Service Representative Ever to remind me that while I probably had some work-related strengths somewhere (and I was just taking that on faith), details weren't part of them.

"Here's the thing," I told my friend. "I don't think I care about details. I think I'm goal-oriented. Especially if the goal in question is me being rich one day and not having to work anymore, or write résumés in which I wax rhapsodic about temp jobs I hated, or anything like that."

"That's fantastic, and I look forward to sipping mai tais aboard your yacht," my friend retorted. "But if you want this job, pretend you're anal. Detail-oriented. *Just do it.*"

Which was no doubt how my law-firm supervisors got the impression that I actually *wanted* to spend whole weeks of my life page-checking tedious documents and digging about in file rooms.

Once again, I was miserable. I needed to do something new. I just didn't know what to do. So I decided, after a trip to sweet, temperate Atlanta in early March, when it was snowy and hideous in New York City, that maybe the problem wasn't me or my inability to focus or my lack of responsibility or my constantly changing mind (no matter what my parents thought). Maybe it was the fact that I'd lived in and around New York City since I was three years old. It didn't take much in the way of rationalization: I sucked down the Geographic Cure like it was candy.

Everyone says the Geographic Cure doesn't work, and that's probably true in the long term. But who cares about the long term in your early twenties? I didn't. I hightailed it out of Manhattan and, for the next ten months or so, was completely consumed with building a new life in the New South. That's why the Geographic Cure works in the short term: You're too consumed with the creation of a new life and identity to worry about your old ones, and once you have time to let the past creep up on you, you can just move again. You could keep it up indefinitely.

I returned to customer service, because that was the area where I had the most job experience, ironically enough. It was also the area where I had the most attitude, but somehow, my new employers failed to notice that at first. I didn't have time to concentrate on the fact that I'd returned to the kind of job I already knew I hated, because I was adapting. I was introduced to Real Live Southern Belles, bless their hearts. I learned how to drawl. I discovered I was a Shockingly Rude Yankee—well, that wasn't really a new discovery. Life was pleasant enough, y'all, if not exactly exciting.

Then one night I took it into my head to calculate my future salary, allowing for small cost-of-living annual raises, to see when I might start making real money at my pleasant enough, but not exactly interesting job. It was something like $45,000 by 2078. Which meant I wasn't likely to be sipping cocktails aboard my personal yacht anytime in the foreseeable future. At that rate, I wouldn't be able to afford a cruise on someone else's yacht.

When I recovered from my swoon, I fanned myself with my vast selection of credit-card bills. The Geographic Cure had clearly worn off and was no longer distracting me from the mess I'd made of Plan A. I needed a Plan B.

Plan A, the plan wherein I found meaning in some yet-to-be-determined career, thrived in an office environment, and wore separates dictated to me by the "work attire" pages of fashion magazines, wasn't working. A quick survey of my "career" thus far made that more than clear. At best I was an indifferent employee, and I was so rarely at my best.

I generally worked about one day in five. The rest of my work hours I spent talking to my friends across the United States courtesy of the office 800 number, napping beneath my desk, writing longish short stories on my hard drive, and endlessly scrolling around the Internet. I was habitually tardy, argumentative—especially when faced with authority figures—surly without provocation, bored, and often reading novels when I was supposed to be doing something work-related.

Plan B, I figured, would have to be the kind of plan that took the very things making me such an awful employee and turned them into strengths. After all, I'd exhibited the same behavior in every job I'd held down. There had to be a place for me, a place that celebrated the very things my current employers used against me in performance reviews.

How about a place where I wasn't expected to turn up every day, and not until late in the day? How about being encouraged to engage in spirited debate, especially with authority figures? Even surliness could be looked upon as intellectualism in certain circles. I was sure I wouldn't be bored if I wasn't trapped in a cubicle, and if I could just find something that celebrated reading instead of punishing it.

It came to me in a flash of light one day, when I was loitering in my local bookstore, fingering stacks of books in the new-paperback-fiction section: graduate school.

Well, not really a flash. Graduate school had been lurking in the back of my mind ever since senior year of college, when my savvier classmates were already applying to further years of study, the better to avoid the job market altogether. But it was in that bookstore that I thought: Graduate school is the place for me.

The more I thought about it, the clearer it seemed to me that graduate school was my Plan B. Graduate school in literature, particularly, would solve all my problems. I could spend my days the way I already spent them: reading, writing, and shooting my mouth off, except in graduate school, that sort of behavior would be called "studying" instead of "slacking." Moreover, with vague aspirations of "being a professor or something," there was my "career" sorted out in the space of a single application. I knew right then and there that graduate school was the Cure for My Indecisive Twenties.

Bring on Plan B, I thought. It's about time.

I couldn't know then what would happen in graduate school, or how different Plan B would turn out to be from my great expectations. But that's a different story.

Lie #3

*"I'll know myself—
and what I want"*

Pride and Prejudice

By Anna Maxted

I graduated from Cambridge with an average degree and a big head. So confident was I of my own worth that, with no journalistic experience besides a review for the university rag of *The Rescuers*—a super-cute animated film about rodents—I applied to *The Guardian*, a serious national newspaper, for the position of news editor. I received a most cordial rejection letter. I grudgingly curtailed my ego, followed my mother's advice, and got myself a job as a cub reporter on the *Jewish Chronicle*.

The JC is a fine publication with high standards. However, it isn't cool and never was. To the general public (the Jewish community in particular), its cachet ranks alongside *Dogs Today*. With the brittle conceit of a twenty-one-year-old, I remained convinced that I deserved to proceed straight to greatness, and two-timed my kind employers with a couple of illicit weeks on the *Sunday Times*. After ten days of photocopying, I slunk back to the JC, where at least they tolerated my Gypsy Rose dress sense and allowed me to write.

This was an interesting decision on their part.

I was a fan of my religion, but I wasn't *learned*. In fact (and I don't use this expression lightly), I was pig-ignorant. I conducted a telephone interview with an Ethiopian who had stowed away to Israel. I handed in my copy to the news editor, who was puzzled by my repeated references to the "Swiss Canal." *Were* there canals in Switzerland? Wasn't Switzerland a bit of an unnecessary detour? Eventually, a colleague with some basic knowledge of the globe suggested that perhaps it was a spelling error, and what I meant was the *Suez* Canal.

As I recall, I was embarrassed but defiant. (The Ethiopian's English was barely decipherable.) I hated to admit I was at fault in any way, whatsoever. I needed to be seen as cute *and* clever. For the majority of my teens, I'd been the fat, square kid at school. At university, I'd dieted myself skinny (too skinny), reinvented myself, acquired a smarter accent. Cambridge University was a useful shield to wield, because if you'd studied at Cambridge, you *must* be clever. (If only they knew.)

Everyone believed in the new me except me. To be honest, I didn't know *what* I was, what I wanted to be. My actual self, I felt, was pretty dull and unimpressive, so I was forever trying out different identities. I was like a magpie. If I saw something that I thought was appealing, I'd take it. Even today my personality is littered with remnants of stolen affectations. I cross my sevens, continental-style. I say, "Hello there!" as a greeting. I dance a bit like Elaine on *Seinfeld*, but it wasn't meant to be that way—it seemed cool when Julia Louis-Dreyfus did it. I have embarrassing jewelry in my bedside drawer; for my twenty-first birthday, I asked my parents for a string of pearls. I was a Jewish girl from North West London, what the hell did I want with a string of pearls? I know. I wanted to fit in with the posh, horsey girls, all honey-blond hair and plums in their mouths, fresh from boarding school. I had nothing in common with them, and they knew it. I must have worn the pearls once.

So in my early twenties, whatever I looked like, I appeared to be something I didn't, at heart, feel I was.

In retrospect, my colleagues' faith in me was astounding. Maybe they believed the hype, or perhaps they thought that despite the silly accent, the touchiness, and the odd dress sense, I had potential. I was sent to interview the chief rabbi about something not very important. I met his second in command (that might not be the official term) and breezily stuck out my hand. He took three steps away from me, his back against the door, and my smile froze on my face. I remembered, too late, that an orthodox Jewish man is forbidden any physical contact with a woman who is not his wife.

"Oh, Chr— Sorry!"

"No, no!" he replied with a grin. "I'm just holding the door open for you."

Looking back, I see that few people took me as seriously as I took myself. When you're that age, you *have* to take yourself seriously—you're fighting against the world, most of which assumes you to be foolish and trivial (as if). I was allowed to review Blooms restaurant in Golders Green, a bastion of good old artery-hardening Jewish cooking, the sweet carrot tsimmes, the lokshen pudding, the salt beef, the whole caboodle. I took a male friend who worked in the city (I'd harbored a crush on him throughout college and, sternly resistant to the fact that he had no romantic interest in me whatever, hoped to seduce him with my glamorous reinvention as a streetwise hack). Sadly, that particular avenue of credibility was closed to me when the waiter pinched my cheek and addressed me as "Choochy Face."

I was battling the tide, I suppose, because the community thought of the JC as their property. Their attitude was slightly abusive—I can only compare it to a Jackie Collins heroine and her relationship with the Mexican maid. Once a housewife rang me up and bullied me into attending her twelve-year-old son's school play. She expected a big write-up in the theater pages. I sat through a long amateur production of *Oliver Twist* in a cold hall, as she surveyed me through narrowed eyes. I pretended to scribble notes, all the while whining inside like an orphaned puppy.

As in every community, there were plenty of people looking for love, some of whom were already married. To certain men I met through work—in their defense, they didn't really know me—I seemed like good wife material. I repelled the advances of a guy from the Jewish Sailing Club. (Boat people, ugh.) A member of the Board of Deputies took me out for lunch and informed me that there were nine calories in an olive. But I was safe in the office, or so I thought. Valentine's Day and I rarely troubled each other, but in my second year of employment, on February 14, I received a pink card.

It had a cartoon of Shakespeare on the front, penning a sonnet. Inside was a rhyme (sub-Shakespeare) written on a manual typewriter. It was singing someone's praises, but the grammar was so convoluted, I couldn't quite understand—was it the wonder of me, or the wonder of . . . him? I showed it to a girlfriend. "Anna," she said. "I'm very much afraid he's talking about himself."

I shoved the card in a drawer. If it didn't relate to me, I was bored. My world was small. My ego needed constant tending because, while it was puffed up, it was also delicate as eggshell. Not even a hardy duck egg—I'm thinking one of those tiny pale blue shells that you sometimes see broken and empty on the pavement. A week later, a freelance journalist who worked occasionally for the JC rang and asked if we might do lunch. As we weren't particularly friendly—she was middle-aged, with the sense and mannerisms of a twelve-year-old—I couldn't imagine why. Did she know of a job I might want? Imagine my surprise when I took one bite of my tuna sandwich and she burst out, "Crusty the Clown is madly in love with you!"

Crusty was one of the high-ranking editors (though, behind his back, an object of ridicule). He was married with children, fifty if a day, and—if I might paraphrase Jane Austen, to emphasize the acidity of my disdain—he had neither looks nor personality to recommend him. My mouth fell open like a parrot's beak.

Middle-Aged Girl continued, "He's ready to leave his wife and kids! He's set up a flat in town! The chemistry is so strong, he knows it must be reciprocated!"

Those were her exact words—I remember them precisely because the breathtaking insult of their delusion was seared into the spongy surface of my oversize ego. Fine (I guess) if he wanted to indulge in disgusting, inappropriate fantasies about a girl who was young though not quite ugly enough to be his daughter—and perhaps we should overlook the moral footnote of a wife and kids—but how dared he implicate *me* in his foul imaginings? My rage was unparalleled. The conceit of studenthood was still a crisp protective shell around me, but Crusty's assumptions cracked it open and left me gasping in the cold wind of reality.

To quote Ms. Austen again, "we all have our level," and mine—now that I was forced to consider it—ranked as several stratospheres above his. His was in a prehistoric bog, with mudskippers.

"I have a boyfriend!" I spluttered, a weak and inadequate defense against two people who were, in fact, mad.

"But when you finish with him . . ." she said (not a question).

"I'm not going to finish with him!" I cried. "I am *not* in love with Crusty! Not now, not ever! I respect him as a person"—a great lie—"but I am not in love with him." She didn't believe me but conveyed the message to Romeo nonetheless, then rang me later that afternoon to say coldly, "Crusty the Clown is very upset. He said you were giving him signs."

I could think of one sign I'd given him.

I couldn't laugh it off because the offense was so serious. The early twenties are all about image. They have to be, because behind the labels that establish you as identical to, and therefore acceptable, to your peers, there is frantic uncertainty, self-doubt, misery, and angst, which is a good deal less appealing. It felt to me as if Crusty the Clown had seen through everything I hoped to be, to what, in my darkest moments, I thought I really was: an ugly, stupid creature who deserved to marry an old toad.

What saved me was another asset common to twentysome-things: brattishness. No way was I going to be crushed by such an oaf. There were no kids, no spouse, no mortgage, no worries to sap my energy. I had all the bounce in the world to rebuff the assault on my self-esteem (and none of the sophistication to effect it with subtlety). Nothing was more important than resurrecting my pride. I had the luxury of time, and no perspective. I brooded for hours, thinking of devious, ingenious ways to make myself feel better and to punish Crusty for his transgression.

Naturally, in the end, I appeased my sense of mortification by telling the story to the entire office, including the editor in chief, who laughed himself purple in the face. He was giving me a lift home at the time (we lived in the same smart suburb, as I was still residing with my parents, yes indeed), and he nearly crashed his company car, he was laughing so hard. Every time he glanced at the stunned, bleak expression on my twenty-two-year-old face, he laughed harder.

"Kiddo," he said (he was an American, in case you wondered), "welcome to the real world."

The One Who Got Away

By Melissa Senate

My shrink at the time diagnosed me with the Groucho Marx joke of not wanting to belong to any club that would have me for a member. (The club, in this case, was a guy named Greg.) I laughed it off.

"Nothing funny about it," the shrink said. "It means you don't think you're good enough."

The first time I met Greg, he liked me fine but was sort of, maybe, I don't know, possibly/potentially getting back together/having a moment with his long-term ex-girlfriend, who had the same name as my sister, which extra-bugged me. The second time I met Greg, a year and a half later, he fell madly in love with me.

Suddenly, I was his dream girl. Me. Which meant there had to be something wrong with him. I believed this without remotely being aware that something must have been wrong with me for thinking such a thing. *I don't want to join any club that would have me as a member* . . . I was much more comfortable the first time around; after all, I had something to do, which was to win him over. I had to work for membership.

I was twenty-six when we met. I placed a personal ad in the *New York Press,* an alternative weekly newspaper; he responded. We had a "me, too" conversation on the phone for over an hour.

Me: "I'd better confess up-front that I smoke two packs of ciga-
    rettes a day."
Him: "Me, too—and menthols!"
Me: "I'm an editor."
Him: "Me, too!"
Me: "I work at Harlequin, on romance novels."
Him: "I work at *Popular Mechanics*, on science and technology
    articles. Hey, our readers are married!"

We both loved Indian food. Woody Allen movies. Red wine.
Smoking while eating Indian food and drinking red wine. He
lived downtown and I lived uptown, but he didn't make fun of the
Upper East Side, like everyone else who lived below Fourteenth
Street. Another "me, too" was cats. He had two—Mitchell and
Spike. He also had a newt and a tankful of crazy fish.

On our first date, he picked me up in a car (a first for me, as I
lived in New York City, where no one *I* knew or dated had a car);
he'd been on a business trip to check out giant squid for an article
he was writing. The giant squid sold me. Greg was not going to be
your average guy, which meant I was likely to fall for him.

I fell. He turned up wearing a dark, spylike trench coat. He reminded me of Humphrey Bogart. Six foot one. Lanky. Smart, sexy
dark brown eyes. Good brown guy hair, curlyish but very short.
He was masculine and the most polite guy I'd ever met. And he
was even more liberal than I was. We ate chicken tikka. He introduced me to mysterious green sauces. We drank red wine. He impressed me with stories about interviewing an astronaut who had
walked on the moon; I charmed him by naming all the Harlequin
romance euphemisms for "penis" and "vagina."

I thought he was out of my league. Greg was six years older,
from Washington, D.C., the graduate of a famous prep school, an
Ivy League college, and a prestigious master's program. His by-
line was on countless articles about science and technology (two

things I knew nothing about). He'd even published a children's book on how trains worked. I thought he was too smart for me, too "been there/done that" for me, too everything for me. But I could tell he was attracted to me, and he did ask me out again. Sure we'd have nothing to talk about on a second date, I dressed hot. A Miracle bra. Sexy heels. We did very little talking on date number two.

This went on for a month or so, until the sort of, maybe, I don't know ex-girlfriend and a weekend in Montauk presented themselves. Greg was the sort who couldn't even entertain the thought of another woman while dating someone, so that was the end of me. I was hurt, in both heart and ego, but a few months later, I fell madly in love with a guy named Doug, another magazine editor.

I was twenty-seven. Doug was my first big love. Except that I was the only one in love. He merely liked a lot, liked having a girlfriend. Still, our romance was exclusive, seemingly serious, and included family functions and vacations abroad. Six months into the relationship, Greg called to say hello, to see if I wanted to get together. He explained about the weirdness with his ex. I told him I was madly in love. He wished me well, and that was that. Ha, I remembered thinking. So there! Take that!

Six months after that call, my one-year relationship with Doug was over, and I was a brokenhearted mess. I needed . . . something. And so I called Greg in order to have an immediate date with a guy. We made plans to see *Four Weddings and a Funeral*, and as we exited the theater, I spotted Winona Ryder and Dave Pirner of Soul Asylum arm in arm, in their weird long wool hats and striped mittens. The sight of them—young, gorgeous, in love—made me feel so wistful, so wanting. When Greg asked if I wanted to go back to his apartment for a nightcap, I said yes.

As our taxi headed down Second Avenue and passed the East Village, the neighborhood where Doug lived, the wistfulness dissipated. Now I just felt sick. Lonely. Miserable. I was in a cab with another guy who hadn't loved me. But Greg wasn't the one I wanted to love me.

In Greg's apartment, the moment his hands touched me, the moments his lips were on mine, all I could think about was Doug. How in love with him I still was. I could see his face, his body. Until I opened my eyes, and there was Greg's good-looking face, Greg's rock-hard body. It was the first time I experienced a silent scream.

But I wanted to be wanted. And so I closed my eyes. Afterward, as he left the bed for a few moments, I lay there and cried, confused, sad, wanting something else, *wanting*.

The next morning Greg taught me how to do the *New York Times* Sunday cryptic crossword puzzle. He made me cups of tea, eggs, English muffins. He practically fell over himself to make sure I was happy, had everything I needed and wanted. He stared at me googly-eyed, something you notice when the guy doing the googly-eyed staring has such intense, intelligent eyes. Oh, and did I want to stay the afternoon and . . . evening, perhaps? We could see a movie, grab some Thai, and then snuggle for the night. My reaction to all this I-am-crazy-about-you-ness was a deep sigh.

So maybe that's what it took: I'm into you, you're not into me. You're into me, I'm not into you. I didn't think I had the energy for it. But I was wrong; it was what sustained me.

A few months of affection and googly eyes and planned dates and homemade romantic dinners and every-night phone calls, and I was ready to spontaneously combust. Greg was everything I wanted in a guy, but he wasn't the guy I wanted. Worse: If Doug was the guy I wanted and he didn't feel that way about me, why did Greg? Something must be seriously wrong with him. I broke up with Greg.

"But I love you!" Greg said. "Everything's great between us!"

And it was. Sort of. Except for how I felt. I shook my head. I cried. He thought I was crying over my confusion about us, and it was enough for him to let me go for a couple of days. To think. But I was crying because the wrong guy was saying the right things, which made me mad at him.

It's not easy to work as a romance-novel editor and be broken-hearted. At Harlequin Enterprises, it's all romance, all the time. I wanted what I was reading day in, day out. Which was fantasy. But there was some serious reality involved in my relationship with Greg, in the dynamic between us. Our chemistry was romance-novel hot. We had everything in common. I adored him. I loved the way he made me feel about myself. I could spend an entire weekend in his company, feeling as though I'd never need anything else in the world but him. There was no reason in the world why I shouldn't love him. I wanted to love him. All I had to do was *feel* it.

At times I did. For a few days. A week, a couple of months. And then poof, I would be at work or riding the Second Avenue bus or buying paper towels, and the feeling wouldn't only be gone, it would be replaced by revulsion. I would have to end things, extricate myself from him.

I'd wake up in the middle of the night wondering what was wrong with me, why I couldn't love the guy I clearly loved.

"Because you don't!" friends insisted.

"Because you're scared," Greg said.

"Because you don't want to belong to any club that would have you for a member," the therapist reminded me again and again.

The more I retreated, the more in love Greg fell. The more he fell, the more I retreated. Every few weeks, or every couple of months, I would break up with him in high drama, running away tearfully to catch a cab. Once I came back for only a week.

"My friends tell me I'm the biggest loser for taking you back," he'd say, those intense eyes soft on me. "But how can I not? I'll always take you back, no matter what. I love you so much, Melissa."

It feels good to be loved like that, by someone you admire. But when the need for the fix wears off, the feeling is cut off. Stopped. It's like suffocation. And the only way to breathe is to break up. Break up. Mope. Feel lonely. Feel stupid for giving up a great guy. Whine to friends who are sick of hearing about it.

"If you loved him, you'd be with him," they said over and over during the course of two years. "You're not in love. Move on."

The problem was that a very quiet piece of me, very far down, knew that I did love him. I do love him. I don't. I do. I don't. Do I? Or don't I? Why can't I love him? Why, why, why? My girl-friends weren't the only ones rolling their eyes at the same old story. During our off periods, I would ask this on dates with other guys, launch into my history with Greg, completely clueless that I was boring, selfish, and a really bad date. One guy (whom I actually liked) snapped, "It sounds like you *do* love him. You talk about him enough. On dates with other *guys*."

I talked about him everywhere, until the answer from friends was to press their hands over their ears. So I got more serious about therapy. After telling me I had the Groucho Marx dilemma, my therapist went on to say that my questions, my issues, my problems, my very life, had nothing to do with Greg at all. According to the therapist, most gigantic guy problems can be linked back to a woman's relationship with her father. "And you have a textbook case," he told me. "Your father walked out on you and your family when you were nine, and you never saw or heard from him again. If your own father doesn't love you, why would you expect any guy to love you? How could you possibly take seriously any guy who does? We deal with that, we deal with your problem. And maybe this guy Greg will still be available when and if you do."

It seemed like such a cliché. And it wasn't like I hadn't thought of it myself. Anyone could have connected the dots if I'd ever talked about my biological father, which I hadn't. Except in therapy, when it was pulled out of me. In elementary school, the year my father left, my teacher wrote in my report card, "Getting Melissa to respond to questions is like pulling teeth." I remember being unable to talk then, unable to express or explain why I couldn't form a thought. But the shutting up and the not dealing started early and continued for way too long. By the time it became necessary to start talking, to start dealing because this perfect-for-me guy was making me break my own heart, I couldn't, wouldn't, see it. It had nothing to do with my father, I insisted. And my friends backed me up. "You just don't love him," they said. "You want to, because he's in love with you. Because you're twenty-eight . . . twenty-nine. Because he seems perfect for you and you want to love him. But love doesn't work that way." And on and on about how the heart knows what it wants.

In the course of two years, I broke up with Greg at least twelve times. Once, toward the end, I decided to ignore myself and just say yes. I forced myself back to him, to accept being loved. And when he spontaneously proposed marriage at three in the morning in an Irish pub, I said yes. Our engagement lasted until we hit open air—four minutes later. Once again, I went home alone in a cab.

And so did he. The worst part about being so self-absorbed, self-centered, self-everything, is that at the time, you have no idea how much damage you're inflicting. But you can't care about breaking someone's heart if you can't believe yourself capable of breaking a heart in the first place.

The accepted and unaccepted proposal was the last straw for Greg. He wrote me a long letter telling me he was going to accept that I didn't love him, that he was, as the song said, going to bow out gracefully. *But remember, I'll always be here*, he wrote. *I can't not take you back.* I dropped the letter as though it were on fire. I was scared. He was letting me go this time.

But there was already another guy, of course. Another all-consuming, night-and-day romance. The new guy and I both charged full speed ahead *and* held back, which made it work for a few months. I'd had a few of these ridiculous relationships interspersed in my relationship with Greg. Instead of being with Greg, for example, I chose a guy who told me no woman could ever compete with his fantasy of Sheryl Crow. Another guy informed me on the first date that he was obsessed with his stepsister and wasn't sure if he ever loved his last girlfriend, whom he'd dated for six years. These were the guys with whom I was sharing my time on earth instead of Greg. The therapist assured me that one day I would "get it." I'd wise up.

I'll always take you back. How can I not? I love you so much, Melissa . . .

Greg's words and the conviction behind them sustained me during the times I wasn't with him, when I was with idiots. When I was doing what I thought I needed to do without realizing that I needed something entirely different.

Six months after Greg bowed out gracefully, the new guy and I were having dinner in our favorite restaurant, and he said, "My mother is uncomfortable with our relationship because your brother is married to a Chinese woman. She's worried what she'll have to say to your sister-in-law across the Thanksgiving table if we get married. She's not even sure if the Chinese celebrate Thanksgiving. Do they?"

We didn't finish dinner. I told my boyfriend that his mother (with whom he lived at age thirty-one) was a racist. He was furious. I was furious. We argued the few blocks to my apartment.

Him: "She's not a racist! She's just ignorant!"
Me: "That's what racists *are!*"

As we headed inside, we continued arguing. To shut us both up, I pressed play on my answering machine.

I remember very little of the message. A woman's voice. "Hello,

Melissa, this is Greg's mother." And then there were the words: "Ruptured brain aneurysm. Come." And then: "I'm afraid it's irreversible."

Irreversible. Irreversible. Irreversible. I stood there, in shock, unhearing, unseeing. Echoes of the word "irreversible" over and over.

You can't be prepared for some things. Childbirth is one. Another is seeing someone you love—someone who loved you—dead. When I visited Greg in the hospital the next morning to say goodbye, he was gone, for all intents and purposes. There was a life-support machine that would do its job for one more day.

When someone you love and love deeply in a way that you can't understand is gone, just gone, so suddenly, no goodbyes, no nothing, irreversibly, irrevocably gone, you, too, disappear. Slowly and not abruptly, as he did. I disappeared from my own life in little ways at first. To everyone's shock, I left my beloved job of several years, with its security, its built-in long-term friendships, its familiarity. I moved out of the studio apartment I'd lived in for seven years, despite it being $710 a month, rent-controlled, on a beautiful block. I began climbing the huge stone steps to the Catholic church on my corner to light candles for Greg (even though I'm Jewish and he was Protestant) because it gave me something to do. And when I stopped knowing what to do, I started dating again: my drug of choice. I moved in with my new boyfriend (not the one with racist mother)—who all my friends thought was a jerk—after three months. And I cried a lot. At home, at work, on the bus, on the streets. I developed a weird and rare swallowing disorder that my therapist pounced on: "You literally can't swallow what's going on in your life!"

In the hopes of avoiding major stomach surgery, I underwent a procedure involving anesthesia. My boyfriend picked me up afterward, and as we exited the hospital, with me slightly dazed from the anesthesia wearing off, he said, "You know what I don't get? *You* like your hair when you blow-dry it straight, and *I* like it straight, so why did you leave it curly today?"

I stared at him. "I just had a balloon blown up in my lower esophageal sphincter," I screamed. "And because it didn't do what it was supposed to do, I have to have major surgery! Why are we talking about my hair?"

"I'm just saying" was his response.

Even dazed and disoriented, I felt the lightbulb finally turn on over my curly head. This was whom I'd left Greg to meet one day? This was whom I was waiting for? This was my future? I broke up with the boyfriend and moved out three weeks after moving in.

There was a new apartment. A new job. A struggle to figure myself out.

Two weeks before Greg died, to celebrate my thirtieth birthday, my mother took me on a trip to New Orleans. A wild-haired, wild-eyed fortune-teller read my palm on the streets of the French Quarter for five dollars.

"Whatever you're doing," he said, looking at me pointedly, "you're on the wrong side. Like, if you're a film director, you should be an actress."

"I'm a book editor," I told him. "But I can't write a novel, so forget that."

He shrugged and went on to the next palm.

Greg smiled when I told him this. "Of course you could write a novel. You could do anything. But the palm reader is also telling you that you should be with me. Like, whoever you're dating, you should be dating Greg instead." He smiled again and squeezed my hand.

I didn't know what to say, so I said nothing. That was the last time I saw Greg alive and well.

*   *   *

Many people said to me, "Wow, if you'd married him, you would have been a widow at thirty." But I would rather have been a widow at thirty than not have married him. I might have known what to do with my grief, might have been able to accept my grief, which I didn't feel quite entitled to in a strange way. The mysterious illness I'd developed forced me to focus on my health. So I gave up dating and stopped smoking. I became a vegetarian. I started running. But no matter how much I tried to change myself for the better, make the old me disappear, there I was. Full of grief, guilt. Full of me.

A few years after Greg died, an editor with whom I used to work told me that her publishing house was starting an imprint devoted to chick-lit books, and since I was a serial dater who lived in Manhattan and worked as an editor in book publishing (in other words, a living, breathing chick-lit cliché), if I ever wanted to try my hand at writing a novel, now was the time. I had nothing but time. And so I stole some of my life for a plot and wrote a novel called *See Jane Date*, seemingly about a serial dater but really—and possibly perceptible only to me—about Greg. About us. About me. About insecurity. About love and loss. Writing that book saved my life. So did the CD I listened to over and over while I wrote (*Fumbling Towards Ecstasy* by Sarah McLachlan), pressing repeat for one song in particular, "Hold On": "Hold on to yourself/For this is gonna hurt like hell . . ."

And so it turned out that the wild-eyed fortune-teller on the streets of New Orleans had been right. Whatever I was doing, I was on the wrong side, but it wasn't as simple as going from book editor to author, from guy of the moment to Greg.

I'd been on the wrong side of *myself*. That's the truth about life in my twenties.

Twenty-eight Is the New Eighteen

By Shannon O'Keefe

One Sunday morning in the not so distant past, I woke up with a distinctive purple bruise on my left hip that darkened with the day, an arm sore to the touch, and a certainty that there is nothing worse than feeling legitimately disappointed in yourself. After greeting one day with a hazy memory of the last—which doesn't include the fall that led to the bruises, but does involve having gone to a party with my ex, after which I tried to pick the lock to my front door, MacGyver-style, with a bobby pin—I realized my purse was missing.

All this at a quarter to twelve, just after I'd woken up with the lights on, on top of my comforter instead of beneath it, wearing my ex's much-too-big-for-me-T-shirt over a tank top. I had one, two, perhaps three peaceful if disoriented moments before ratcheting my body up and looking from clock to watch and back again. I had a brunch date (worse, a blind date) at noon, and no purse, no phone, no keys, no money. My roommate gave me twenty dollars as I ran out the door, my hair barely brushed, my teeth slightly more so. Brunch was frenetic. I couldn't stop talking and was more taken with the mysterious bruises than I was with him, his conversation, the mimosa that grew flat, or the quiche I barely ate. We had been exchanging e-mails following a set-up, and I had written at length about how much I liked food—cooking and especially eating. Yet there I sat, a naturally thin woman at a great French bistro, pushing around the food instead of devouring it. He probably thought I was anorexic, manic, and a liar. In addition to being our first date, it was also our last.

The episode reminded me of another ill-conceived brunch during my freshman year of college, when those types of mornings were supposed to have begun and ended. My aunt and uncle were passing through town and offered to take me to breakfast. I saw these relatives once, maybe twice a year, and if I'm thin now, you can only imagine what I looked like at eighteen (Bones was my high school nickname). I had woken up just in time to meet them, with the memory of shots, lots of them, rolling around as clearly and urgently as the corresponding memory of countless trips from bunk bed to toilet. Still, I felt terrible about canceling, so I went, and it was even more miserable than I had imagined. I ordered the lightest thing on the menu, despite their insistence that I "eat up." I tried to convince them that I wasn't big on breakfast; worse, I had to excuse myself several times over the course of our meal to dry-heave in the diner restroom. But I made it through. I kissed them and said my goodbyes before going straight to bed. It wasn't until later that evening, when my mother called to say that my relatives had asked her about the eating disorder I didn't have, that I realized I hadn't made it through at all.

The worst thing about reliving a morning like that ten years later, without exception, is first having believed that I never would. That I'd left all such unfortunate moments behind in an earlier era—part of the school of hard knocks, of lessons learned—part of my past, as opposed to my present. It's the realization that however mature I think I've become, I'm still acting like a kid; that at twenty-eight, I'm behaving in exactly the same way that I did at eighteen. And while my mother wouldn't be proud of my behavior, it's more important to me at this point that *I'm* not proud of my behavior; that I'm still waking up and feeling like I haven't aged at all, like I haven't learned a thing.

Following brunch with the blind date, my frenzy faded, and I became rather morose as I walked to the party locale to pick up my purse. When I rang the bell, there was no answer. So I went home, but again there was no answer, leaving me locked out for the second time in twelve hours. A friend was working at a bar down the street, so I walked there and forced him and a fellow waiter to listen as I gushed over how irresponsible and stupid I'd been. I spared no detail—no detail I could remember, anyway. How steep the fire escape had been on the way down and how I couldn't imagine having gone back up. How I had drunkenly kissed a friend of my ex's following a game of flip cup, which I hadn't played (with good reason) since college, and during which I'd actually thought dancing on a table dripping with booze might be a good idea. How when I'd called my ex that morning for information on the whereabouts of my purse, he'd suggested I call my new boyfriend for the details. My friend's reply? A very deadpan acknowledgment that he, at twenty-six, had recently passed out on a street corner from drunkenness. My street corner, in fact. And it had taken six policemen to wake him. So by comparison, he assured me, I had nothing to worry about. "War wounds of the urban young," my bartender friend said, before passing me his bottle of water and patting me on the head as he left to take another order.

Like every respectable child of the psychoanalytic age, I want to take this opportunity to blame my parents. You see, as the only girl of four children in a house where my mom got it all done—the cooking, the cleaning, the ironing (the O'Keefes were nothing if not neatly pressed)—I was the one who was supposed to be just like her. Responsible, hardworking, unwavering, and, you know, female. I expected to be married by twenty-one, just like she was. I expected to have my first child at twenty-three, just like she did. So at eighteen, instead of going off to college and imagining the raucous times to be had there, I was thinking that I had only three years to find a husband and settle in to a life. Her life. At eighteen, I was project-ing forward to twenty-eight and seeing my mother. By twenty-eight, she'd been married for seven years; she'd already had two children and would soon become pregnant with her third. Strong, yes. Inde-pendent, yes. But settled is mostly how I saw her. Awfully settled. And at eighteen, that life seemed safe, if not entirely glamorous. At eighteen, I assumed that ten years—a decade!—would bring great change. I believed that I, too, would be married by twenty-eight, that I'd have children by twenty-eight, and that I would most cer-tainly be settled by twenty-eight—in a house, with a car, saddled by the corresponding mortgage, car payments, rather dowdy wardrobe, regular 401(k) investments, the works.

Shortly before turning twenty-eight, I realized (oh) how the mighty had fallen. In la-la love with a new boyfriend (the kind you're not in yet but know you will be in short order—that spell of early love when you actively make out in public, despite think-ing it's repulsive when other people do, when it escapes your no-tice that he wears sunglasses indoors, when you misinterpret, then reinterpret, every little thing he says), I decided to introduce him to Dan, my most fiercely protective brother, who happened to be passing through town. During the course of our brief conversation over drinks at a neighborhood bar, Dan and I started discussing a mutual friend's wedding we were to attend the following week-end, about which neither of us was excited.

"I hate weddings," my boyfriend said with some degree of exas-peration. "In fact, I'm convinced that weddings are passé for our generation. I don't even know why people bother, given how high the divorce rate is. Just look at my parents."

"Just look at ours," Dan replied (our parents of the still-happily-married minority).

"Yeah, I guess. But I'm sure as hell never getting married, and I can't imagine that any of my friends will, either."

"I don't understand," Dan said. "So you're just going to live with someone forever? What about the kids?"

"Ugh," he groaned. "Kids? Are you kidding? I hate kids! I've never met a kid who didn't totally slow the pace. Even on the off chance that I decide to get married someday, I can assure you that I will never, ever have kids."

Dan, four years my junior, left shortly thereafter. When I returned home, he was waiting up for me at the kitchen table, all but foaming at the mouth. He told me that he'd thought my boyfriend was fine up until that pronouncement, after which he despised him immensely. "What kind of a man doesn't want a family? I mean, he basically told me that he's using my sister. That he has no honorable intentions whatsoever." I tried to explain that we'd been dating for such a short time, that Dan shouldn't judge him on that alone, all the while reeling from the shock myself. The idea of those dreams being taken off the table so quickly, so fiercely, had been overwhelming. Dan asked me what I wanted without giving me a chance to respond, going on to say that if this was it—this wasteland of dating without purpose, of mating without ever tying the proverbial knot—then that was fine. But even saying so, he looked disgusted. Such a life was not for him; not for someone raised in our family. To be honest, it was the first time I realized that I wasn't quite sure what I wanted out of life, let alone my boyfriend. Just the same, Dan's argument festered inside me, and I ended things with my boyfriend less than two weeks later without ever making my reasons for doing so entirely clear.

That fundamental idea—that I was not destined so much as actively trying to become my mother—has informed the way that I've behaved with other men over the years. The notion that I would be married, mothered, settled by twenty-eight led me to sift through men in an exacting, inelegant manner. I've spent years analyzing men instead of dating them, with the intention of saving time and energy once I had (immediately, within five minutes) deemed them unacceptable as a life partner. A life partner! At eighteen! Twenty-one! Twenty-five! If I couldn't imagine rocking away with him behind the white picket fence, he didn't make it to the second date, which, I saw far too late, doesn't make any sense and hasn't produced any viable results. My longest relationship lasted seven months. My best lasted a scant three before I decided we were never going to make it long-term and convinced myself to get rid of him. He told me recently that I have too many rules for people. He has no idea how many rules I have for myself, or how those same rules doomed the us of he and I.

Rules—broken ones—were all I had to think about the day after the party. Without my cell phone or any numbers beyond my parents' (the curse of cell-phone culture), my day was spent walking around my neighborhood, buzzing my apartment, buzzing their apartment, sitting with my friend at the bar, and thinking. Unlimited time to think is the worst commodity on any morning after a fall, whether literal or figurative (in my case, both). I berated myself more with each passing hour. Why did I go to the party? Why was I still spending time with my ex? Why didn't he send me home before I got out of hand? And how the hell did I get those bruises? I became a walking embodiment of disappointment and displeasure. By the time someone finally answered the door, I couldn't even look him in the eye. As one of the hosts handed me my purse and asked if I'd made it home okay the night before, I said yes. Then no. Then, as I turned to walk down the stairs, I looked up and said, "Sorry. For. My bad behavior." It was belabored and inarticulate. He looked awkward, yelled after me as I kept walking, "No, you were fine. It was fine." But I didn't feel fine. I felt like an idiot. Like an oversize child.

Rules also defined my wacked search for love. With my thoughts so tempered by the quality of a man's character, his steadfastness, his commitment to providing a quality education for children we didn't have, his loyalty to people I didn't know, his love of family I'd never meet, I became totally oblivious to the short-term factors that typically define good relationships: whether he'd pay for dinner, whether he'd be good in bed. Passing the test for me became passing the two-week mark, the three-date mark. One date was always enough for me to tell if he would provide enough of a challenge. If he was smart enough to quip back. If he was capable of keeping up. After two dates, I had a very clear sense of who was in and who was out. And after three? They so rarely got to three that it's hard to know for sure what the rule for three was. Still, even those who fit the royal flush of good man, good partner, and good prospect had trouble getting past me. One extremely solid man I knew, who will surely suffocate some willing girl with love and affection, once sat me down for a wee chat during which he presented himself with all the characteristics I'd supposedly been looking for, before going on to suggest the ways in which I might change to fit his needs. He offered a five-point plan for improvement. The first was that I would never achieve anything without discipline, a characteristic I was sorely lacking. The second was that I had to take myself and my writing more seriously. The third was to date him. The fourth and fifth are now lost to me, given the shock. Suffice it to say I moved out of that room and out of his life as quickly as I could.

So where did such fastidiousness get me? Such single-minded precision? Where am I—actually—at twenty-eight? Far from the idealized life I'd imagined, I am single, without children, in an apartment (with two roommates, no less), without a car, with a budget more interested in clothes and cocktails than retirement accounts. At twenty-eight, instead of living the life I'd imagined for myself at eighteen, I am living the life I probably wanted to— or thought I was—living at eighteen. Which, once I stopped to think about it, was a fairly exciting revelation.

*   *   *

The morning of my twenty-eighth birthday, I was assured by several colleagues over coffee and almond croissants that twenty-eight was one of the good years. The best years. Later that evening, once the coffee had turned to beer and the croissants to burgers, one male friend said with some degree of certainty that I was lucky. "My ex," he began, "had such, I don't know, expectations." "Expectations" was strung out comically, though perhaps not purposefully so. "I mean, she was thirty-one, so it was all tick-tock, you know? But twenty-eight, that's a different story. That's the perfect age. Just before desperation sets in. You know?" I knew. Or thought I did. At the very least, I knew it was a pretty funny statement coming from a pretty arrogant kid. I mean, what did this twenty-five-year-old guy know about being a twenty-eight-year-old woman?

Still, I believed him. I believed them all. I didn't feel desperate. I felt great! Different, somehow, than at twenty-seven. Upon turning twenty-seven, I declared myself still twenty-five in thought and feeling. But at twenty-eight, I felt twenty-eight. And it felt good. I was confident. I was happy. I was very much my own person and proud of who that person had become. I was assuming responsibility for and in my own life.

Roughly two weeks after said birthday, I RSVP'd successfully to a very exclusive party that was to be attended by several celebrity authors, writers whom I admired and had always wanted to meet. Scads of friends responded to the same party, but for some reason I was the only one placed on the list, a list that did not allow for plus-ones. I was slightly nervous about attending on my own, but I thought, I'm twenty-eight years old. I am a confident and independent woman. I can do this! I'll meet lots of great people, make amazing connections. I stopped just short of declaring myself belle of the ball. It wasn't until I walked through the door that I felt my confidence wither. When the idea of chatting up the entire room fell to meeting three new people—just three!—I soldiered through the line at the bar and, armed with a vodka tonic, made my way into the crowd. But the crowd was full of twosomes and threesomes, no one looked familiar, and every time I moved toward a group with a smile as top-shelf as the vodka, they seemed to turn inward. I wondered how they'd gotten all of their friends in; more than that, I wondered why I'd chosen to wear such obvious clothing. The flouncy pink skirt that had been deemed adorable so many times that summer suddenly seemed altogether too conspicuous, and I imagined that many of the guests on the balcony, caught by its unusual shape and color, would be watching its wearer standing in place all night. Alone. So I moved through the crowd. "Weaved" would be a better word. Snaked my way this way and that, ate cold cuts, returned to the bar. By the time I'd caught sight of those literary luminaries, my spirit was broken. I knew that I could saunter over and talk to them and that they'd be polite and respond. I knew that once I started speaking, I'd have lots of intelligent things to say. After all, I'd read all of their books. I'd admired them for years, convinced friends to buy each new novel. But in that moment I couldn't think of a single thing to say except "I've had a crush on you ever since *The Intuitionist*." And somehow I didn't think that would be enough to break my lonesome spell. So I watched as the authors took the stage behind the band, was smiled at (pityingly, I thought) by a famous poet, and left as soon as I could get out the door.

For all of my bluster, I was reduced instantly to an insecure kid, feeling the familiar strains of that confident-on-the-outside, confused-as-hell-on-the-inside eighteen-year-old girl I'd been ten years earlier and thought—really thought—I'd left behind. As I headed for the subway, I put on my headphones, turned my iPod to an earsplitting volume, and laughed hysterically while walking down the street. In that instant, I didn't care who saw me, I didn't care how I looked, I was simultaneously eighteen and twenty-eight—quite possibly the best of both worlds. After all, weren't there advantages to being both a child on the brink of adulthood and an adult still checked by her youthful impulses?

While it may not be the twenty-eight I'd imagined myself working toward, it is certainly the twenty-eight I've actually been working toward. I graduated from college. I went to graduate school. I've had two full-time jobs in completely different industries. I have a career, am independent, self-confident, and having a pretty fantastic time. When a friend from grad school with whom I'd been out of touch for several years asked how I was, I said happy. I am happy. I live in a neighborhood that I love, in one of the best cities I can imagine. I have good friends and lots of them. I don't have to answer to anyone. I don't even have to answer my phone. I can throw a great cocktail party or host a great dinner party. And I cook because I like to cook, not because I think it will make me more attractive to men or prepare me for a life I've yet to live.

So there you have it. I've supposedly reached that moment when it all comes together. When each brick combines to form a house. The house of me. Another lie, I figured out.

One night I went out to dinner with a few close friends, the brother of one of those friends, and some of his friends. When my friend attempted to take all introductions upon herself, she did it Bridget Jones–style, with polite mini-bios as precursors to the inevitable wan smile and weak handshake. While introducing her brother, she said, "This is Beau. He's a rocket scientist. He has his Ph.D. in astrophysics, discovers craters, publishes in *Nature* magazine." And when she got to me, she said, "Shannon got her MFA, and now she writes really great e-mails." Everyone started to laugh, so my sweet, sweet friend carried on, wanting the full weight of her belief in me to be felt. "No, seriously. One time

I was breaking up with this guy, and I was so angry that I couldn't get anything coherent down, so she wrote the break-up e-mail for me, and it was so mean." The crowd looked embarrassed as my friend lumbered on, "But he was really mean, so it was perfect." Introductions finished. Reputations in flux. Taken together, I'm an overeducated bitch who writes really great e-mails. I suppose there are worse things.

Around that time, I realized that every action doesn't need to have an equal reaction in order to be important. Having my MFA didn't mean I had to write the great American novel, and I didn't have to impress a group of rocket scientists. Isn't that why they're rocket scientists—to impress people? The experience itself was as worthwhile as any potential result. How could I know, for instance, that I'd leave grad school with my degree and one of the best friends I'll ever have? You can't plan for the truly significant moments in life. They're moments. They happen. They creep up unexpectedly and defy reason. And that's what I have to remember about life on a larger scale: Accumulating experience is nine tenths of living, so I should stop trying so hard to create myself and spend more time being myself. I should let myself make mistakes, date the wrong men, drink too much, have moments that I'm not proud of, learn as I go along instead of deciding ahead of time how life is supposed to be lived. I should reconfigure the rules—not only the ones I have for the men I'm dating, but more importantly, the rules I place on myself. I should start focusing more on the plot and less on the denouement. After all, when is the resolution of any story truly satisfying?

Just as I'm starting to settle into my own skin, regardless of its age or imperfections, I am reminded that an entire decade has passed so quickly. The idea that I've achieved so much and so little, over the course of ten years, is astounding. And yet, when I try to imagine where I'll be at thirty-eight, do you want to know how I see myself? Married, mothered, settled. I guess I've got ten years to prove myself wrong. I should have plenty of opportunities to do so, given that everyone else I know is embroiled in a Quarter-life Crisis. Job, money, love: Nothing's ever right. My friends are preparing to move out of the city in search of something. In search of themselves—at twenty-three, twenty-five, twenty-eight, thirty-one. Me? I'm planning to stay. After all, I just figured out how.

A Thousand Times Yes

By Beth Lisick

It's always been my favorite word. There's nothing like a well-timed "yes" to get things started, keep them going, change their tack, switch them back, and guarantee you'll be asked for your answer again and again. Saying yes is like having a perpetual date with the world.

Ever since I was a little kid, I loved the part about how saying yes made things happen immediately. Yes, let's go catch moths in a jar—Yes, let's put on a neighborhood talent show—Yes, let's get in the car and pretend that we are two sisters smoking cigarettes and driving to Las Vegas to meet our boyfriends the real estate agents. Yours has blond hair, mine has brown hair. Yes meant trying and testing and experimenting. There was instantly movement, motion, something new. The only reason to say no was if you were scared, and I was never scared of much. It took me years before I realized that sometimes, when you say yes, you begin to experience the law of diminishing returns.

The first time I knew something big had changed in my life was when I turned down an offer to interview Yanni. Yes, Yanni the New Age sultan and former sexy manlover of *Dynasty*'s own Linda Evans. Because I wrote an arts and entertainment column, I was used to my e-mail in-box being a constant garden of electronically transmitted delights. For years I could reliably turn to it for laughs and distraction, the same way some people watch reality TV or read trashy magazines.

Imagine being greeted in the morning by publicists who keep their CAPS LOCK ON AT ALL TIMES and desperately want to tell you:

SHANNON DOHERTY TO REVEAL HER
FAVORITE CRISPY SNACK CRACKER

or

AVERAGE JOE RUNNER-UP
LAUNCHES BENEFIT BUNS CALENDAR

My eternal adolescent was thrilled with the knowledge that, at any time, I could contact someone to talk about these developing "news events." Basically, it was an invitation to make prank phone calls. I could pick up my phone and say, "Hi, Susie! I just got your message about Mr. T 'socking' it to the Red Sox fans on Friday night by endorsing the new Hanes Double Tough socks™ because he pities the fool who doesn't have a sock with a reinforced toe and heel to help prevent holes where they happen most. You said at the end of your e-mail that you would love to know what I thought, and I just wanted to call to say keep up the good work!"

The point of this being: There used to be nary an invitation or opportunity presented to me that I would turn down, especially if it was dumb and a complete waste of time. I loved the haphazardness, the opportunity to participate in something unexpected. I wanted to be part of a magical, mysterious butterfly effect. Instead of asking "Why?" I always asked "Why not?" How could you say no when you could be saying yes? I was addicted to giving up control in order to be propelled into a new experience. I liked not knowing what would happen next.

There might be a downside to being a yes lady, but first put on your hippie pants and think about how good it feels to say yes when you really mean it. Yes, I will go out for a drink with you. Yes, I'll quit my job and drive around the country for a few months. Yes, you can do that to me and see if I like it. Yes, I will play third base in your softball game wearing a *Star Trek* uniform. Yes, I want to learn how to surf. Yes, let's not sleep all night and then get a box of doughnuts and watch the sunrise from the roof. It is a fact that you will see more things and meet more people if you say yes with greater frequency than you say no. (This is when we start remembering that there are plenty of things we wish we'd never seen and people we are sorry we ever met.)

Because I was raised by decent parents and didn't have many boundary or self-esteem issues, I was quickly able to whittle down my yes answers throughout my early adulthood without harming myself but leaving my sense of adventure relatively intact. Oh, but there were some real doozies along the way. Some bad calls. There was the night when my "Yes, I would like to see your yurt" led to a forty-five-minute drive deep into the foggy Santa Cruz Mountains and ended with the question "But why do you have a pistol on your bed next to those restraints?" He didn't turn out to be a sociopath, and I'm glad for that. I was lucky. He was just your run-of-the-mill perv who was pissed that I took one look at his setup and made him get in the car and drive me all the way back into town. There was also the unsettling fact that when I walked in, Roxy Music's *Avalon* was playing, leading me to believe that he had put on the album before he came to pick me up and it had been repeating for the past four hours while we went to dinner and saw a movie. I found the fact that he had set up a scene before leaving his yurt-home completely retarded. Especially considering this was our first date. So he was bummed that I had said yes but was now saying, "Well, I guess I saw it. I said, 'Yes, I'll come see your yurt,' and there it is, isn't it? Now I gotta go."

But let's dissect this particular situation. Is there a lesson learned? Is it "never agree to check out a Mongolian tepee with a biophysics grad student who drives a car that smells like rancid peanuts"? It's not that I wanted to say no but ended up saying yes because I felt pressured into it. I really, really wanted to say yes. To my nineteen-year-old self, he seemed like a pretty cool guy. Looking back, I'm able to conjure a slight feeling of weirdness about him that I should have picked up on before I agreed to go back to his place. There was the way I felt him staring at me in the movie, something strange about his mouth. My instincts about people have definitely been honed throughout the years, but I can still feel, deep in my gut, the youthful excitement and curiosity that made me want to say, "Yes, let's see what happens." In this instance, especially because I never felt threatened, I'm glad that I said yes. Now, of course, I would have a hard time being enticed by anyone living in a yurt. Or at least I'd be smart enough to take my own car.

With certain types of questions, the more they're asked of you, the quicker you learn to stop saying yes. These are the questions for which your yes answer is like a tiny electric shock, where the voltage gets cranked up each time, until you find yourself with your head in your hands, weeping, "No, you cannot borrow five dollars until you get your paycheck next week. No, you can't crash on my couch for a while. No, I don't have time to read your screenplay. No, let's not put that on my credit card. No, I don't think it's a good idea to go to the liquor store for another bottle of tequila." In saying yes, you become one step closer to learning to say no.

By far, I've gotten the most out of my incessant yeses in regard to (what I can now barely refer to as) my career as a writer and performer. When I started writing and doing spoken-word performances at age twenty-four or so, I did every single gig that was offered to me. I performed in churches, schools, bars, cafés, tents, plazas, restaurants, street fairs, theaters, libraries, office buildings, private homes, and community-center rec rooms. I almost never got paid, but I didn't care. Sometimes there would be ten dollars, and that was great, a big surprise at the end of the night. I never expected to make money from writing or performing because I'd never met anyone else who had. I wrote in my spare time, went to the open mikes around town, and somehow showed up for work at eight A.M. One good thing about the $7.50-an-hour desk job is that you can always find another one.

Eventually, a local publisher heard me read and asked me to compile my writings for a book. I said yes. When the book came out, I took my savings, borrowed my dad's truck, and drove around the country for six weeks doing readings. I slept on floors, got a few write-ups, and came home 750 copies lighter. I even made about five hundred dollars from people passing a hat around for me. My career didn't exactly snowball—it still resembles more of a sno-cone: small, low-budget, and kinda fruity—but I met a lot of people that way. Thousands. I discovered that by saying yes over and over again on a very grassroots DIY level, you can go a lot of places that you might not by plugging away on some sort of pre-scribed career ladder. The world of opening yourself up to other people's questions is wild and random.

Sometimes I still do shows in exchange for beer, but now that I can't throw back a half-dozen pints like I used to, it's not as much of a deal. Plus, doing free shows is a hard habit to break. How do you turn down benefit shows after someone's house has caught fire, his band's gear has been stolen, or she's just been diagnosed with non-Hodgkins lymphoma? It can really suck saying no. It can make you feel like a bad human. I have a kid, so nowadays I've got to hire a babysitter to do a non-paying show (because my husband-man works nights), and I lose money to do it. Are there any other thirty-six-year-old moms out there still occasionally performing for liquor?

Being someone who has lived mostly in the moment, I never placed much stock in the importance of "turning thirty" or "getting married" or "having a baby." I wasn't even sure I'd ever do any of those. I've never kept a list of things I'd like to accomplish in my life and always laughed off the five-year plan as an unnecessary self-empowerment crutch for the non-spontaneous. I got enough satisfaction if I remembered to check my pockets for stray lipsticks before I did a load of wash. That seemed like an attainable goal. When I realized a few years ago that being a writer wasn't just some phase I was going through, life simultaneously became harder and easier. It was clear that I would never have a 401(k) plan or a benefits package or a steady paycheck. For the first time in my life, I acknowledged that if I wanted to write and perform for a living, if I didn't want to wind up with another desk job, I would have to make an effort to succeed on some level. More than that, because I was such a reactive person (and because my reaction was usually affirmative), I had to learn how to say no sometimes. It sounds easy enough, but when you've developed a habit of looking to the world to provide you with amusement, distraction, and even purpose, it's hard to turn the beat around. Now I had to put myself in charge of figuring out what was *worthwhile*, a task nearly impossible to do while in my twenties, because everything seemed worthwhile. If I hadn't done something yet, it was automatically a pretty intriguing idea.

So when I get an e-mail asking if I'd like to have some quality alone time with Yanni, I take a moment to think about how funny it would be to meet him. I try to imagine what we would talk about and what he would be wearing and what his hair would look like. I picture sending a JPEG to my family and friends with the note *Me and my new boyfriend!* Then I think about how much effort this will take, how much energy I will have to put out. I think of the other things I could do instead—really exciting things I don't have enough time to do, like reading a book or cooking a great meal or hanging out with my family—and then I stop thinking and just hit delete.

The Pursuit of Happiness

By Rebecca Traister

I wish I didn't feel like I was disappointing them every time I talk to them," said Allison, my first post-college roommate, hanging up the phone after talking to her parents. It used to seem like we had this conversation every other week or so in those first couple years after college: about the pressure we felt from our folks, the expectations we just could not seem to meet.

The disappointment Allison feared she was handing her parents had nothing to do with the fact that she was waitressing and taking modern-dance classes rather than working an office job; it had nothing to do with not having a serious boyfriend, or not having a savings account, or not having an advanced degree, or not having any real furniture, though all of those things were true. It wasn't about the fact that she'd moved from Tennessee to live in an expensive shared apartment in a city that seemed to be a rejection of everything her family stood for. No. These choices may not have been the ones her parents would have made, but they were eager to support their daughter in them. The way that Allison felt she was letting them down at twenty-three was much simpler: She wasn't happy.

I knew exactly how she felt. I was working a series of entry-level jobs, as the personal assistant to a high-profile actor and the assistant to a lower-profile editor; I performed bank-account acrobatics to pay my rent bills, take care of my cats, feed myself, keep up with the news, stay in touch with my family, and learn my way around New York City.

I slowly but surely tried to weed through all the people I met in New York. I made friends with whom I spent days at Coney Island and nights at dive bars; we'd scrimp to save up for Italian meals at a restaurant that made the best beet ravioli but was for special occasions only. We'd try to start homey traditions, like inviting everyone over for Sunday-night dinners, though we could never keep it up for very long.

I got along with roommates as well as anyone gets along with roommates; for a couple of years, I let my brother sleep on my couch after he dropped out of art school. I fell in love hard a couple of times with guys who were fun and with whom I watched movies and stayed out late and did stupid things, but with whom I did not have particularly healthy or mature relationships.

I kept my jobs; I did them well; my bosses liked me. And yet when I spoke to my parents, none of these markers—of survival, if not success—seemed to register with them. All they wanted to know was "Are you happy?"

It was the one thing I couldn't give them.

Had I been born a century or even a decade earlier, my twenties would likely have been spent trying to get married, or being married and trying to have babies, or raising babies. Had I been born with fewer advantages, that decade might have been spent working jobs that had nothing to do with personal interests or aspirations and everything to do with making ends meet.

There was a time not so long ago, and circumstances not so far away, when the first real decade of adulthood was a serious scramble to ensure financial and reproductive survival and success, to do well by the family who raised you, to lay the social and economic foundation for the family you would create.

But the world I was born into—though not a rich one, certainly one with many advantages—did not require that I get a Mrs. in college, or that I begin to support my family as soon as I was able. My parents were professors, lefties, members of the suburban middle class. Their requirements of me throughout my childhood were more than generous and less than rigorous: that I drink milk with every meal; that I wear my seat belt every time I got into the car; that I peed before we left on a road trip, even if I thought I didn't have to go. After I turned fifteen, I had to have a job—waitressing, scooping ice cream, working retail—during every summer and Christmas vacation. Still, even that was about expanding my horizons by teaching me responsibility and how to manage finances; it wasn't because I needed to make a contribution to the family's coffers or pull my weight in food.

No, my parents wanted nothing serious from me. I didn't need to have a graduate degree or a 401(k) when I got out of school; they weren't waiting for me to bring home a suitable mate of any particular race or religion; they didn't care if I made "the right sort" of friends; there was no expectation that I own my own apartment or that I formulate a ten-year plan. They wanted me to explore my options, consider the possibilities of what I could be, whom I could know, where I could live, what shape my life could take. They were from a generation that believed in raising children with respect and freedom; all they wanted from their offspring was the satisfaction of knowing that they had given them enough room and tools to discover themselves.

It's not that my life was underwritten by my folks. They weren't rich, and they couldn't subsidize my apartment or buy my clothes, though they loaned me a couple hundred bucks every once in a while. I had to get myself a job, rent myself an apartment, set up the electricity, find some furniture. I chose to do this in New York City. And I did okay.

But when my parents called, though they were pleased enough that I had a checking account or had successfully hauled a bureau

I'd found on the street up three flights of stairs, what they really wanted to know was about how I felt about my life, what I was learning, whether I was enjoying myself. For a good five years, I'd have to either flat-out lie or try to distract them to keep from telling them the truth.

"Is it fun?" they'd ask hopefully about my job as the personal assistant to the actor. How was I to tell them that what I did during the day was ferry take-out containers to the actor's favorite sushi restaurant, which was so fancy that it didn't deliver. I also made travel arrangements and took his cats to the vet.

"Are you having a good time?" they'd ask about my job as an editorial assistant at a glossy magazine. Good God, no! I was ordering car services and changing the coffee filters and fixing the Xerox machine. "You must be learning so much!" they'd say hopefully. Well, sure. About Xerox machines. But I could not in all honesty fulfill their fantasies by telling them that my days were spent discussing editorial content and trying to match the perfect journalist with the perfect assignment.

"Are you enjoying yourself?" was the question during my brief stint at a dot-com. No. In truth, I didn't have any idea what the company I worked for *did*. I'd been hired as an "assistant editor" for a company that was going to make "book videos"—like music videos, except for books—and my job mostly involved reading free books sent by publishers and helping the company's co-founder order furniture for the lofty downtown office. What I did there was completely immaterial. I came to work each day to collect a paycheck.

Even when I finally made a turn toward a fulfilling career, becoming a reporter for a newspaper at twenty-five, I couldn't quite pass the happiness test. I was getting there. But I was unsure that I would succeed, or ever please my demanding bosses, or ever earn more than $25,000 a year. I woke up with nightmares about having gotten facts wrong; I quavered in editorial meetings with the knowledge that my story pitches were not likely to pass muster. I hated not being sure of myself, not feeling confident that I was good at what I was doing.

My parents weren't the only ones who seemed to think my third decade was supposed to be like a ten-year trip to Great Adventure. My older colleagues seemed to recall it as the slaphappiest time of their lives. "You're so young; I'm so jealous," my thirtysomething bosses would opine. "That's the best time to be in New York. You have so much energy, you recover so quickly, you have everything out in front of you, every choice still available to you. Appreciate it! Also, could you order me a turkey sandwich on rye?"

I wanted to appreciate it, I really did. But those choices, all out in front of me, weren't so much thrilling as they were terrifying. Didn't these chipper nostalgics remember what that meant? Having everything in front of you may look pretty good in retrospect, but in reality, it can be paralyzing. I may have had relationships and great jobs and better money all just over the horizon. But I didn't have the faintest notion of how to get to them.

So, no. I was not happy. I wasn't miserable, either. I was scraping by, living, going about the business of growing up. But not rolling around on the urban sidewalks, savoring my carefree sex life and alcohol-soaked bacchanals. Here's what those early years felt like:

Often they were lonely. I had gone to college in the Midwest and moved east with only Allison in tow. We used to sit at home night after night, having literally scraped together (like, from the bottom of our purses) the money for Chinese takeout. We'd eat spicy pork dumplings and ask each other, "How do people make friends?"

I had felt very ready to be done with college, and yet to my surprise, I found myself missing it so much that it sometimes hurt to think about. I missed the feeling of popping into a local bar and knowing that there would be familiar faces inside, the assurance that walking down the street would turn up friends in cafés and bookstores. I missed the community, the sense of shared purpose. I missed having crushes, drinking buddies, the assuredness of knowing where and how I fit in.

Of course, as the years went by, Allison and I did make friends. But when you're making friends as an embryonic adult who's had a lot of the collegiate swagger knocked out of her step by tight budgets and low-rung jobs and no idea of who she is or where she belongs, social stability doesn't gel as quickly as it used to. The early friendships I made in New York were born of an almost desperate desire to create a social structure where there was none, and at their start, they felt performative: "We are going to get a meal and go to a bar because that's what friends do and I so desperately want a friend." Some of those relationships have lasted, but only because they deepened, because time made them real.

As for the men, I know many people who had lasting and rich romantic lives during their twenties, who enjoyed either casual sex or monogamy with a partner before the pressures of children came to bear. I happened to have neither of these experiences but, rather, invested myself fully in a couple of relationships that sucked my lifeblood. "I love you," I'd say to a man I didn't really love, desperate to hear it back from him, not because it would make the relationship better but because it would make the relationship sound better. "We had such a great weekend," I'd manage to enthuse to my mother about a relationship I knew was unconsciously going south. As with friendship, I performed love and sex. What was important was that the audience—my parents, my peers—believed I was having a good time.

I was also very broke. The anxiety of paying my bills each month—from rent to electricity to the accursed credit card I'd picked up in college—was so great that it nearly eclipsed all my pleasures. I still writhe at memories of trying to get money to pay my share of a girls-night-out dinner only to be told that I had no funds, of having my credit card rejected again and again, of bouncing checks. When a colleague would buy new clothes, I'd burn with shame and a healthy dollop of jealousy. New clothes were not possible. A couch was not possible. And the damage that was done in those years to my credit is still being undone now, at thirty, when I am finally comfortable enough, if not to buy a new couch, at least to not worry about bouncing checks.

I was not professionally fulfilled. There was nothing rewarding about any job that I had until I was in my late twenties, even though they sounded like fun. Entry-level jobs, no matter how glamorous the company is that they require you to keep, are designed to be done by well-trained monkeys. I got coffee. I answered phones. Sometimes I ordered lunches. Yes, I did have a strong brain and an expensive education. Yes, I did have ambitions—though my inability to define them gnawed at me miserably—but none of them had anything to do with how I was spending my days.

All this whining is not to say that I was miserable—actually, far from it. I was alive; I was in New York City; I had all the luck that the Western world can offer a young woman beginning her adult life, and I knew it. What I'm saying is that I wasn't *satisfied*, and that was the feeling that I felt pressure to experience.

But satisfaction is not what our twenties are about. They are years for striving and worrying and self-doubt, for experimentation—social or political or sexual or professional—that may result in pleasure or in disappointment. What I had was determination and curiosity and some kind of belief that this stuff was going to work itself out.

I am incredibly grateful to have had the advantages I was given. I wouldn't give back any of it. The truth is, I'm sure that had I found contentment at twenty-three, I would not have advanced much. It was the grinding energy and friction provided by my dissatisfactions that fueled my will to keep going to work each day, to keep trying to make things better. The personal fulfillment that my parents wanted for me, that my colleagues expected me to be experiencing, was as elusive and unachievable a goal as any I could have set for myself in my twenties.

Even back then, when Allison and I stayed in and watched *The X Files* for the sixth night in a row, we'd laugh about how easy it would be to forget how hard this had all been. "I bet we'll romanticize this someday," we'd tell each other. And it's true. I have to smile now when I think of the spicy pork dumplings, the gofer jobs, and the shaky beginnings of friendships.

I am determined not to betray my twenty-three-year-old self, who resented the pressure to be fulfilled when she was merely responsible, to be joyful when she was daunted, to have a ball when she was just plain scared. But if I could, I would send her this message from the future: While the tight budgets and self-doubt and broken hearts don't disappear, just over the border at thirty, I can honestly say that I am pretty happy.

Lie #4

*"I'll have satisfying
relationships, great sex,
and fabulous friends"*

The Best-Laid Plans

By Jennifer O'Connell

This is it, I remember thinking as I moved into my first-floor apartment. The white stucco walls were blank, the living room empty, and the kitchen cabinets bare, but that didn't faze me. We were going to fill the walls with fabulous prints, not the Pink Floyd posters we'd tacked to the wall in college, and scatter the living room with comfy but cool starter furniture (I already had my eye on a blue-and-white awning-striped couch). I wasn't too concerned about the kitchen cabinets; I didn't cook. There was really only one thing missing in that one-bedroom apartment: my boyfriend. The person who would share the fabulous apartment with the turquoise pool and the view of the cactus-covered mountains. Joe. And in two short weeks, he would join me in our new home, and we'd begin our lives together. The four years we'd spent as a couple were just practice.

I was twenty-two, freshly minted college diploma in hand, when I left Boston and moved out west to put my plan into action. I had it all figured out—get a great job, meet new friends, cohabitate with my longtime boyfriend, and start my "real life." So what if I wasn't making as much money as I wanted, or that a broken alternator delayed Joe's cross-country trip. The anticipation of his arrival kept me giddy, hopeful that once he arrived, I'd have what I'd been waiting for. Once he did arrive, it all seemed to be going according to plan: Joe moved in, I got a job as director of publications for an international firm, was about to embark on my first transcontinental business trip, and even made two fabulous friends at work. I toasted myself from the plush leather of my first-class seat as I soared above the Atlantic Ocean. Life was good. I had big things ahead of me. Everything was going according to plan.

Well, maybe not. In London, my boss cornered me and attempted to stick his Scotch-soaked tongue down my throat. Back on American soil, I promptly quit, convinced I could rebound from this slight deviation in plan. I took a temporary job pumping frozen yogurt at the Cultured Cow and babysat. Even though my grand plan was beginning to resemble the employment history of a high school sophomore, I was optimistic.

I had love. Joe and I were doing exactly what we said we'd do— ditch New England for some sun and fun two time zones away from where we met. We slowly filled up the empty rooms with the awning-striped sofa and love seat, divvied up the closet space, and shared the toothbrush rack on the bathroom counter. Even if my college futon was flanked by a matching pair of milk-crate night tables, walking through the front door and seeing the pale wood of our new dining table distracted me from the fact that our underwear was tucked away in a particle-board dresser.

Joe worked at a liquor store while he looked for a job (who knew all those years doing beer bongs at the fraternity would count as on-the-job-experience). I wanted to believe that this was how everyone started out, that we couldn't climb the corporate ladder until we'd paid our dues, but there was no way to ignore the fact that our college diplomas were becoming less symbols of our accomplishments and more reminders of our underachievement. During the day, Joe would scour the want ads while I baby-sat three kids, and at night he'd head to the liquor store while I'd go dip extra-large cones in rainbow sprinkles.

Sometime during the week we'd meet up in our now-furnished

living room and talk about all the great things ahead of us. With few friends and no money, we didn't have much else to do. Our social life consisted of lying on the couch together, watching TV movies. One Saturday night, while an old black-and-white horror movie played on the TV, we reclined on the sofa together in silence, my head resting on his chest, a smooth chest that was now tan from the sun. It was so familiar, so eerily similar to the night years earlier when I'd told Joe I was at last ready to be his girlfriend.

I hadn't always been ready. For months Joe and I spent time together while I contemplated breaking up with my high school boyfriend. Finally, I ended my relationship and showed up in Joe's room one night unannounced. We sat among the tapestry-covered walls and Led Zeppelin posters and figured it out. Figured us out. After talking, we lay down on his couch, and I fell asleep on his chest. We stayed like that for hours, my head resting on him, the chest of someone who was now my boyfriend. Later, he told me that he was awake the entire time, just holding me and watching me sleep.

Now the couch we lay on was and ours (so what if I'd paid for it, everything felt like ours). When I cracked an offhand joke about the blob monster on TV, he laughed and told me, "I want to marry you." And I believed him. I needed to.

We celebrated Christmas with a party that included frozen hors d'oeuvres from Costco and my two friends. Joe decided to christen the holy night by puking all over our bathroom walls after too many Jägermeister shots, and I spent the rest of the evening wishing Santa had left a mop in my stocking. But the stains running down the shower walls didn't matter at the time; the next morning we'd wake up and share the meager little presents under our Charlie Brown tree. Our first *real* Christmas together. Morning breath and all.

Fast-forward three months, and not much changed. We paid

our rent by selling Budweisers and strawberry-banana smoothies. My friends crank-called the Cultured Cow, asking me to recite the night's flavors. You'd think after a few weeks I would have recognized the foreign accents they used to disguise their voices, but when it's nine o'clock on a Tuesday night and you're sitting on a stool upholstered with cowhide, you're thankful for the conversation. And the laughs. Because if there was one thing Joe and I were having too little of at that point, it was fun.

We'd made the leap to live together, so why did it feel as if everything that followed was less like a leap and more like a baby step? No, make that a *backward* step. We'd talked about the future, and when we did, it always extended out into time. I'll always remember a Halloween party the year before we moved in together, how I'd held my breath when a Dracula-attired partygoer asked Joe the question that seemed to be hanging over our heads like a bubble in a cartoon strip: "So, are you two going to get married?" I stood there in my black spandex outfit, my cat tail paused behind me, my cat ears standing at attention as I waited to hear Joe's response, waited for even the slightest hint of uncertainty or hesitation. But there was none. "Yeah," he told Dracula. I looked at him then, my boyfriend with the large M on his chest, the red cape hanging from his shoulders and the large gray mouse ears secured to his head, and I smiled. Mighty Mouse had said yes. The fact that I was dressed as a cat and he as a mouse is ironic now, but I didn't see it then, standing in some stranger's kitchen drinking keg beer and eating Doritos. I saw two people who had their future figured out. Two people who'd be there for each other. Forever.

Living together was supposed to be the beginning of something bigger, something better, the starting line we needed to cross to keep moving forward. And I wanted to move forward. I constantly wondered what was next. There was supposed to be a next, right? Wasn't that what living together was all about?

"First comes love, then comes marriage . . ." So what if the old-fashioned rhyme needed to be augmented to include "cohabitation." The message was the same. Love was supposed to lead somewhere. But the only place our love had led us was a place of stagnant careers, few friends, and a growing sense of restlessness. The euphoria of being in a new place had given way to dissatisfaction with a situation that didn't seem to be getting any better. Our lack of career prospects and friends only seemed to highlight our lack of fun. We were stuck.

Instead of moving toward something together, we felt like we were standing still. What happened to the all-night conversations we used to have? The silly moments we'd call each other Tweedledee and Tweedledum because it was us against the world? Or the times he'd tell me "I lurgle you," because he said the word "love" wasn't strong enough to describe how he felt? If we could just take care of our relationship, everything else would fall into place. I was sure of it. I had to be. Because if moving in together hadn't solidified our relationship, hadn't brought us closer to the finish line, then what would?

A friend's sister's wedding invitation brought me renewed optimism. Joe and I donned our best clothes and went to celebrate. There was cake, there was an open bar, there was hope. And after the reception, Joe had a surprise for me—an announcement. Was this it? Had he decided that it was time to move forward, to take the next step: marriage? No. He told me he wanted to be with his friends—in Boston.

But *I* was his friend. He'd told me I was his *best* friend. And to prove it, I had letters and postcards and enough Hallmark cards to reconstitute a small forest. The words reverberated in my brain. My stomach contracted as if I'd been kicked in the gut. He wanted to be with his friends? What the hell was that supposed to mean? I'd left my friends behind, too. I was also three thousand miles away from all that was familiar. He wasn't the only one who had given up things to put our plan into action. So why was he the only one bailing out?

My mind raced to find a solution, a way to fix this. I was the queen of problem solving, and this was just another setback that needed to be resolved. He needed friends, we'd find him friends. I'd find him so many goddamn friends, he'd be the social toast of the town. I knew he couldn't be serious about leaving. Nobody picks up his life and drives three thousand miles from home with a four-foot-tall ficus in the backseat just to break up with his girlfriend a mere four months later.

But apparently, there was someone who'd do just that. And I was living with him.

Oh, the tears, the pain, the ruined plan. Surely there was a way to fix this. Surely this was just another bump in the road. Surely the man needed psychological counseling—I know I definitely needed someone with a degree on her wall to tell me I was right. So I forked over a hundred dollars (the Cow may have been Cultured, but it didn't offer health insurance), and we went to see a professional.

I wanted the satisfaction that could come only from an explanation and Joe's realization that he was making a huge mistake. I cried, I pointed out all the reasons he was wrong, and I handed over the money to someone who told me I was probably better off without him. Even though I'd fought it, even though I thought I could single-handedly fix what was wrong with us, I knew she was right.

So I made another plan. I'd move back to Boston to be near my best friend. I arranged to have my furniture shipped and stored, rented a U-Haul, and started packing. There was no question who got what—for two people who'd supposedly shared a life, we shared very little. My name was on the phone bill that arrived in our mailbox every month. I'd paid for all the furniture and invested in all the things we'd needed to make a home. The sofa, the coffee table, the futon we'd slept on every night, they were all mine to keep. He had his ficus. We were going our separate ways.

Until my verging-on-ex-boyfriend totaled his car. Did I tell him tough luck and peel out in my U-Haul? No. I let him hitch a ride with me. The guy who had taken four years of my life and ultimately decided he'd rather do keg stands with his friends was going to share my front seat for three days and three thousand miles.

I'll admit there was a part of me that thought maybe a cross-country trip together was exactly what we needed to sort things out. We'd have hours of driving and the seemingly never-ending state of Texas to talk and remember the good times. While one part of me wanted to smack him silly, there was another that thought that if I was on my best behavior, maybe, just maybe . . .

It didn't happen. We talked, but the result wasn't a deeper understanding of each other. We laughed, but they weren't inside jokes we shared. We even had the obligatory breakup sex in the Motel 6s we stopped in along the way, but in the end, the ride was just a sixty-five-mile-an-hour countdown. Every mile added to the odometer, every landmark we passed, every time that U-Haul jerked to the left and shook me back to reality, I knew it would come to an end. I-90 couldn't go on forever. And no matter how much I thought I wanted it, neither could we.

Years later, I'm still amazed that I let him ride with me. I'm not that nice. But wasn't that the point? To prove I wasn't the bitch he wanted to move out on, to show I was the nice person who let him share her U-Haul? I wanted him to remember that I was still the girl he fell in love with his sophomore year, the one he once thought he could spend his life with. *Remember that afternoon at the Quabbin Reservoir, where we spent hours picnicking on the grass?* I wanted to ask him. *Don't you remember writing all those letters, sending me all those obscene cards with stuffed animals splayed out in various sexual positions?*

I wanted him to remember. Period. The night we met. The day we drove to Ensenada and drank Coronas on the beach. The

funny thing was, the majority of the things I wanted him to remember—the things *I* remembered—were memories made in
the first few years of our relationship. In hindsight, that wasn't so
funny. That I was so hell-bent on remembering who we were, as
opposed to seeing the people we'd become, was actually part of
the problem. The fact was, we'd changed. Both of us. He was just
brave enough to walk away first. And I was just scared enough to
keep holding on.

He wasn't my first love, but he was my first *real* love. And boy,
did I love him. It wasn't always easy, and there were times when
it seemed like more pain than it was worth, but I really thought
he was The One. So what if our fights had included clothes tossed
out third-floor windows (my clothes, his tossing), a drunken fist
that resulted in a broken finger and a cracked tooth (my finger,
his tooth), or that our friends thought we were the relationship
equivalent of a category-three hurricane? Even if we'd had our
problems, I was convinced that everything would fall into place
once we entered the real world. But even if college wasn't the
real world, we were still in a real relationship, and the things that
were wrong with us couldn't be solved by sharing appliances and
a mailbox. In the end, a history was all we shared. And even with
the best-laid plan, that wasn't enough.

I didn't recognize the guy who left me, and I don't think he recognized the girl he left. I didn't understand what he meant when
he told me he wanted to leave, but now I do. He wasn't ready
to buy in to my version of the future, my idea of the way things
should be. And that's exactly what it was. My idea. My plan. My
attempt at taking an unsure future and making at least one thing a
sure thing, no matter how uncertain we were.

As I look back from years later, I see that those months after returning to Boston were the best thing that could have happened
to me. I was single for the first time in years. I was by myself. I was
(gulp) alone. Alone—never could a word make you feel, well, so

lonely. But I was also on my own for the first time in my life, and there was something nice about that. I got a contract consulting job that paid well enough for me to support myself, even if it was guaranteed for only a few months. I sublet a friend's apartment for the summer, a huge four-bedroom apartment that was just temporary. I didn't think beyond the short lease, beyond the end of my employment contract. I learned to enjoy each day as it came.

It's never the time I spent living with my boyfriend that I miss, it's the time I spent alone in my first apartment. The nights I'd watch TV, convinced that every other person in the city—including an ex-boyfriend who shall remain nameless—was out having fun. I miss the weekends I could spend in silence with no one to answer to but myself, and the mornings I'd wake up without knowing what I'd do, without a single plan in place.

The day I dropped Joe off at his friend's house in Boston, it had all come full circle. I was right back where I'd started nine months before. It wasn't what I expected, and it definitely wasn't what I bargained for. When I remember how completely lost I felt, pulling away from the curb, how I glanced up into the rearview mirror one last time, I wish I were there to tell that twenty-three-year-old that maybe life wasn't about having a mapped-out plan. Maybe it's about the dead ends, missed turns, and wrong roads that eventually get us where we're going. Because all of a sudden, I had everything I owned in a U-Haul and no idea where I was headed. While, at the time, the idea was scary, I wish I'd known that it could also be the most exhilarating feeling in the world.

I Can't Have Sex with You

By Pamela Ribon

Confession: I am not a slut.

I've just reached thirty. Newly thirty. Still have the new-thirty smell. I got married just a few months before that milestone. For most of my twenties, I was single but attached. I was constantly with a boyfriend. Now that I think about it, I realize that one of those men is my husband, the other was my last boyfriend, and then the boyfriend before that was my boyfriend for the first two years of my twenties.

So. One decade. Three people. I guess I thought I'd have more experiences before I got married. When we were together, my last ex used to comment that I should have had more sexual partners. In fact, he mentioned it frequently enough that it started sounding like he was suggesting I cheat on him so he wouldn't feel like he was with a woman who had no idea how great she had it. But I was a busy girl, busy being responsible with a good day job that paid the bills. At night I was following my dream—performing comedy in a bar. After years of watching all of my actor friends date each other until they were miserable, I wasn't about to fall into that trap by dating comics (who are already miserable) until everybody hated everybody. So I was the one who listened and gave advice and stayed everybody's friend. But I am starting to think it's possible that I missed out on something important. That ex-boyfriend might have known what he was talking about.

Was I supposed to have a lot more sex in my twenties? Pardon the pun, but did I fuck up?

In my near-virginal defense, I was brought up to think that sex was the most terrifying, incredibly important, life-altering, monumental event. I went through school in the time when AIDS education was first being taught, back when they weren't sure how you got it. I also spent those formative years in the Deep South, where you can legally marry someone at fourteen, and many kids drop out of school to have their own kids before they hit the tenth grade. Because of this, my parents made sure to doubly scare me about sex. My memorable "sex talk" with my father concluded with him telling me that men don't know the difference between a vagina, a hand with some lubricant, or a rubber doll. Try getting hot for a boy after that little tidbit of info.

By the time I was old enough to start experimenting, I was convinced that having sex with someone changed everything, as if by letting someone be that intimate with me, I had to let him alter my DNA. He'd be a part of my *permanent record*. I'm the kind of girl who couldn't handle getting a B-minus on a report card. You think I want a one-night stand just hanging out there for everyone to see?

Another confession: I am not a prude.

I like sex. I like thinking about sex, writing about sex, writing about thinking about sex, having sex while thinking about sex, and thinking about sex I plan on having. Right, right. "Some of my best friends have sex!" I get it; I'm not exactly making a case for myself.

Look. Recently, I've become jealous of the girls on *The Real World* and their drunken, cigarette-laden hookups. This is crazy. I should have nothing but absolute pity for these girls. But I don't, because they don't remind me of me. I can't look at them and go, "Honey, I've been there. Now finish puking that tequila, crawl into bed, and forget about him. And for God's sake, put on some panties. America's watching."

Since I'm already publicly embarrassing myself, let me paint a picture for you. Me in high school. I think if you know this story about me, you'll understand how I was both obsessed and terrified of sex and then became a serial monogamist before I ever had that crucial Spring Break or Bust time in college when body shots lead to body slamming.

In high school, I had one of those sweet, perfect love affairs. We were cute-in-love, which is when you draw pictures for each other and act like little kids with lots of hand-holding and kissing and buying each other flowers. We were sixteen, and every song from the fifties had been written about our love. All innocence and candy. We were good kids, so nobody worried about us doing anything potentially life-ruining, like me getting pregnant. We were such good kids, in fact, that we were terrified we'd somehow accidentally get me pregnant, and therefore never had sex. Never even came close.

When his mother bought us a box of condoms because we were sixteen and in love and she knew we were good, responsible kids, instead of being flattered or stoked that Awesome Mom gave us a box of Trojans, we freaked out. We *freaked out*. They thought we were going to have sex! What did that say about us? What did that say about *me*?

Have I mentioned we were kind of nerds? I suppose I no longer have to mention that. What gave it away—the part where we drew pictures for each other, or the part where the box of condoms made us have a mental breakdown? Dorks.

Anyway, what we did, because we were too scared to have actual sex, was we created a Sex Drawer that we used like a piggy bank for sex-related items. Jesus, I can't believe I'm telling you this. But we had a drawer . . . Okay, it was the glove compartment in his car. And now that memory serves, it was called . . . the Sex Pot. *NERDS*. So we'd put spare cash into the Sex Pot, and whenever we got thirty dollars or whatever, we'd . . . Oh, man. We'd go to the bookstore and buy one of those *Joy of Sex* books to read about other people having sex, because we weren't going to. Sometimes we'd splurge on some Anaïs Nin or Henry Miller to read to each other. I recall one time we bought a pair of handcuffs. But with our sex life, as many times as we hit a triple, we never stole home.

Here's something I've never done. I've never met a man—a stranger, at a bar—walked up to him, sat down next to him, and started a conversation with the single intention of going to a second location with him for a wild night of body tangling. An important episode of *Oprah* once taught me that if you don't want to be killed by a kidnapper, it's important to never let the attacker take you to a second location. Once you go to the second location, you rarely survive. So unless we're going to slam ourselves into each other in a bathroom or the alley behind the bar, my fight-or-flight keeps me from ever imagining getting in his car or a cab or my own car and going to his place or my place or wherever it is that he will inevitably find a blunt and/or sharp object and stab me in the throat until I bleed to death. And yes, I'm sure if I had a one-night stand, it would end in me getting stabbed in the throat. When you don't have sex in your teens, you watch a lot of bad impressionable television. And when does the virgin not get killed on her first lay? Never.

So, I've never had a one-night stand.

Another confession: I haven't done enough traveling.

Until this year, I never even had a passport. This means I've never woken up in Barcelona and walked down the streets (are they cobbled? Doesn't it feel like all foreign cities have cobbled stones where a breathtaking man with dark hair grabs your hand

and saves you before you tumble into a ditch?) until a dark-haired man grabs my hand and saves me from tumbling into a ditch. We lock eyes, and I only sort of learn his name before he invites me to his favorite café, where we drink coffee until we're so jittery we must go back to his place to open a bottle of wine he's been saving "for a special day." The wine is so good and the sunset is so incredible and the day is suddenly so special that we have to take off our clothes, swim briefly in the pond or lake or river or whatever that flows across his property, until we collapse into his bed that has only one flimsy white sheet and we don't leave that bed until my flight's about to take off. My girlfriends are waiting for me at the airport, and they are pissed. I'm the only one without a tan, but I'm the one with the seemingly permanent glow.

This has never happened to me.

Confession Number Four: Back to the thought keeping me up lately. "Shit. Did I waste my twenties with monogamy? Dammit, why didn't I skank around a little?"

Our parents were usually coupled up and done with their sex lives by the time they were in their mid-twenties. But they grew up all Age of Aquarius and had frequent entanglements that started on disco floors or houses filled with pot smoke. They had just started taking the Pill, and everything was just groovy, man. Anything goes, right? Our parents were such sluts. They invented the concept of sowing wild oats, so why did they get us so scared? Why did they make us feel that sex was the very last thing you did with a person? This is why I've had many kissing partners, and run more bases with boys than some professionals in Major League Baseball, but I've had sex with four people.

Confession Five: Yeah, four. I know. That's not a lot, is it? Some of you are shaking your heads right now. I can feel it. "Only four? And married? Yikes."

Because, yeah. I think about it. Now. Not before. Not when I dated my husband for four years, not when I put on the ring, not when I was planning a wedding, not after I said "I do." Only now, when the thank-you notes have gone out and I'm a homeowner and my husband is exactly the kind of man I was supposed to marry. He really is The One. This is not about whether I married the wrong man. This is about the very notion that perhaps I was supposed to have way more sex before I got married, because I'm not going to have any more sex.

No more sex. Isn't this what men are supposed to struggle with? I'm a successful, independent, working, happy, happily married woman. I've got a house, a job, a loving husband, and a ridiculous number of cats. Done. American Dream? Living it. So why do I sometimes fantasize about pouncing on the man who refills my water glass at a Mexican restaurant?

There must be something wrong with me. It can't be that just the fact that I've never started dancing with a man in the middle of a club and he put his hand on the small of my back and his mouth on my earlobe and made me feel the music deep in my hips until we were pretty much having sex upright in the middle of a hot, sweaty crowd while the booze went to my head and this man's tongue went to my throat until we were stumbling toward a private (second!) location long enough to hitch our jeans low enough to become one being and was panting and he was grunting and I still hadn't asked him his name and he would never learn mine because I just wanted to get off and go home, alone, makeup smeared across my eyes and my hair telling everyone I'm a dirty, dirty whore until I passed out on my couch and woke up still in my clothes to the sound of my phone ringing and it was my best friend asking me with that tone in her voice, "So, how was *your* night?"

This cannot be what I was supposed to do sometime in my twenties just to feel like I lived them correctly. And if not, why did I easily come up with that scenario? Why did it flow out of me like something that *did* happen to me when I don't even know anyone that it happened to? See what I mean? Did I mess up? And if I did—when?

I am not responsible for the choices I made in my teens. Not really. Of course, I threw myself at the unattainable. And pined. And wrote bad poetry. A lot of bad poetry. And short stories and love letters that hopefully only I saw. I wrote a boy's initials on a notebook over and over until it became a Wiccan spell for him to fall in love with me. I stalked a boy's route home, casually and repeatedly strolling past his house, hoping he'd walk out and see me, start talking to me, ask me my name. I made a fool out of myself because I knew that boy with the dark hair and darker eyes in my biology class was The One. He should not only take my virginity, he should make babies with me and marry me and grow old with me and one day hold my hand in that hospital as I slipped off this earth and nobody would ever be loved the way I loved him.

Actually? I was right. I would never love a boy the way I loved a boy in high school. I would never again be able to invest that much emotion, passion, lust, and energy into one single obsession. In my early teens, there was no job, no rent due, no ex-boyfriend dating my best friend, driving me absolutely batshit. When I was sixteen, there was only me, that boy, and the perfect mix tape I made for him that I really, really needed him to listen to so that he understood my heart.

But once I hit twenty, the world opened. It opened wide. I could go anywhere. More importantly, I could drink anything. Sure, I had college, but not for long. And then this planet was mine, baby. Anything I wanted, anyone I wanted. No longer that self-conscious teen, I was my own person. Shit, I even owned a car. Let's go!

But see, what I did was I went and got myself a couple of jobs, threw myself into school, and found a nice boy who helped pay the bills, who liked playing Scrabble with me late into the night. We saw every movie together, went to concerts together, and moved apartments together. We got some cats. We were so grown up. So adult. Just two twentysomethings making the right decisions early on. Our retirement funds were going to be so awesome!

So I never had random sex, casual sex, get-back-together sex, same-sex sex, or pity sex. I've never fallen in love with someone purely because he's amazing in bed. I've never had sex with a teacher, preacher, politician, celebrity, rock star, athlete, model, architect, photographer, bartender, doctor, fisherman, circus acrobat, or Matt Damon. I've never been with the older guy, the married guy, the vegan, the apathetic bassist, the pothead, or the crybaby.

Last confession: I don't care.

Okay, one more confession: Obviously, I care, because I wrote all this, and even if I hadn't thought about it before, I must have some issues when it comes to all the sex I'll never have.

It's complicated. We're supposed to find one person and be completely satisfied with that one person forever. And while you can understand it on a romantic, intellectual level, there's still something inside our bodies that goes, "No fair!"

But this is it. This guy. He's all my sex, forever. That's what I promised. And here's why it's going to be okay. Here's why I'm not pissing myself with regret. When we're sitting at a dark restaurant together, candlelight dancing between us, and I look into his eyes, I can see what he sees in me. I'm his wife, his girlfriend, his mistress, his teacher, his naughty schoolgirl, his German exchange student, and his Charlize Theron. On a good night, I can be his Pilates instructor, his trapeze artist, and his desperate stripper. I'm his woman, and I'm his whore. Nice to know my acting degree's going toward something, right?

Our sexual experiences take us down a path from one entanglement to the next, as we learn how we want to treat others and how we ourselves want to be treated. I'm getting all *Oprah* on you again, I know. But it's the time in the essay where we come to the big conclusion, and right now I think I've proved that getting married turns you into a big ball of horn-dog worries. That's all this is. I know. I didn't get cold feet right before I got married. I never even stopped to consider what it meant in terms of my sexuality. That's because I have a great sex life. But seven months later, when someone asked me to sit still and write about sex in my twenties and I realized that not only are my twenties over, but my sexual identity is firmly tied to one person, I had a bit of a freak-out. Right here, in this document. So I thought about it and then asked a lot of my friends what they thought about it. And now that every person in my life is worried I'm about to have an affair, I can tell you my honest conclusion.

No confession, just the truth.

Maybe I didn't have a lot of wild nights and short-term relationships that taught me about heartbreak and how people can use each other. But in those ten years, I met three men, three special men. One man taught me physical intimacy, how bodies work together, what feels good to me and what doesn't. He taught me not to be afraid of my own body, and the power it can have against another. The second man taught me about respecting myself, about asserting not only what I want but what I need. I learned not to be ashamed of my desires or whatever weird thing I wanted to try.

But that last one—he put it all together and made it all make sense. As with the satisfaction of putting the last piece in the puzzle, our bodies clicked, and there was never a need for any more lessons. *Bam*. That's it. You and me, kid. Fireworks and shooting stars and all the clichés that go into two people fitting together.

So he has my body. He has my heart. He has my soul. But I'm married, not dead. My brain can turn him into anybody I want him to be. And this week I might just make him an Australian surfer boy who needs a place to practice his layback.

And that's okay. I've come a long way since adding five-dollar bills to that Sex Pot. But in the end, I'm still a nerd putting all her faith in a boy who hopefully won't break her heart or stab her in the throat while she sleeps. And isn't that what we're all looking for?

No? Just me? Yeah, I thought so.

Twentysomething Seeks Same for Friendship

By Leah Stewart

When I was in my early twenties, living in Boston and working as a secretary at Harvard, I wrote an e-mail to a college friend in the form of an application letter. *Dear Mr. Bechtel, I am writing to apply for the position of Friend, Level 3 (posting #345665). I am a recent graduate of a master of fine arts program at the University of Michigan, with many interesting things to say about the state of American letters today. With subscriptions to both* The New Yorker *and* Entertainment Weekly, *I am fully versed in high and pop culture and can take part in any level of discourse.* I listed my qualifications: my history of friendship with a diversity of people; my grasp of crucial friendship skills, such as asking encouraging questions, returning phone calls, and offering advice only when asked. Detail- and deadline-oriented, I'd remember my friend's birthday; a self-starter, I'd take the initiative in calling, writing, and expressing my affection through small gifts. I closed with: *I am extremely interested in sports (baseball), music (Bruce Springsteen), the broad and hilarious comedy stylings of Chris Farley, and what makes a clever and fascinating person like you tick. I think you and I would be a very good match, and I look forward to the day when I might address you as Mark.*

Almost ten years later, the joke remains obvious: A friendship is not a position you apply for but one you achieve through a process too mysterious to be quantified, the alchemy of love.

And yet. The other day, looking at www.craigslist.com, I noticed the heading "Strictly Platonic" in the personals. I clicked on the link, and what I saw surprised me, perhaps, more than it should have. People, most of them in their twenties, were advertising for friends.

I might not have written an ad like this myself, but I recognized the loneliness that inspired them. I knew what those people were missing; I knew that desire for intimacy and connection, the longing to be perfectly understood. I'd had those things when I lived in Boston. I was twenty-two, twenty-three, not yet ready for a family created by marriage and children, so I created one out of a group of friends, people I talked to almost every day. When my boyfriend Matt and I decided, at twenty-four, to move to Chapel Hill, I had no idea how lucky I'd been to have those friends, how much I'd regret leaving them behind. I was focused on the advantages of Chapel Hill over Boston: Matt's brother was there, and they planned to form a band, a long-held ambition. There would be no blizzards in April. For less money than we'd paid for our dump of an apartment in Cambridge, we rented a fifteen-hundred-square-foot house on two acres of land. The daughter of an air force officer, I'd been the new kid all my life. I knew I'd miss my friends, but I was also certain I'd make new ones. How could I fail to, after all the practice I'd had?

Here's what I learned when I moved to Chapel Hill: Making friends in a new town when you're twenty-four isn't the same as making friends in school. Unlike, say, college, where dorms are the platonic equivalent of singles bars, where every freshman is looking for a friend, the people in your new town might already have filled their quota. Unlike, say, in junior high, the people in your new town of similar age and experiences don't gather at a central place to look you over and decide whether to know you.

The absence of a school cafeteria turns out to make your life harder than you ever could have suspected back in seventh grade, standing alone clutching your tray, hoping that someone would wave you over.

Matt and I compounded the problem of knowing no one by taking jobs where we were unlikely to meet people our age. I was a cataloger in a used-book store, where I sat between two white-haired men. Matt worked temp jobs at the University of North Carolina, in offices full of middle-aged women. He did encounter one woman not much older than we were, but she once assigned him to go outside and comb the grounds for pinecones in order to make centerpieces for a dinner party. She was not a candidate for friendship.

In my loneliness, I found myself smiling too broadly at women on the street who looked like my old friends. I turned over and over in my mind my memory snapshots of them. I saw myself drinking cup after cup of coffee with Caroline upstairs in the dark Mediterranean café in Harvard Square, smoking her cigarettes and complaining about our jobs. Walking from Cambridge into Boston with Terry and rewarding ourselves for the long hike with chocolate-chip bagels. Meeting Samantha at the Spanish restaurant for tapas and too much sangria. Dancing with Shivika at a bar that had "mod night," admiring the go-go girls in their Twiggy dresses, white eye shadow, and glossy knee-high boots. I still talked to all of those women on the phone, but I wanted someone physically present, someone who would meet me at our favorite restaurant, someone who would share my love of *Buffy the Vampire Slayer* and come over every week to watch it. I wanted to do and see the same things as someone else and then talk about them with her later—that mutual experience, and processing of experience, of which friendship is made.

I tried to make friends. I went to the gym, I went to yoga class, but I had no idea how to progress from casual chitchat with an-

other woman in workout clothes to a suggestion that we get coffee. There was a woman about my age whom I saw regularly at the
yoga studio. I heard her talking about her volunteer work with
a local film festival, and she struck me as someone with whom I
might share interests, someone I could like. I considered how I
might befriend her: Should I put my mat next to hers and try to
strike up a conversation? Should I hang back after class? Should
I be direct and ask if she wanted to go get lunch? In the end, she
caught me looking at her a little too often, and the smile she gave
me became a nervous one. Horribly embarrassed, I avoided her
eye, never making any further attempt. It seemed to me it would
be easier to meet people I was looking to date. A single person in
a bar is prepared for, perhaps even expecting, someone attractive
to sidle up. But a woman looking only for friendship doesn't walk
up to a tableful of women and say, "Mind if I join you?"

Matt's brother had not seemed at first a likely conduit to friendship with other women: He was a senior in college, and at the
time, the gulf between being a college kid and being a working
twenty-four-year-old seemed huge. But then it dawned on him
that he knew a woman my age, from his part-time job at an art
gallery, and he decided to set us up on a blind date of sorts. Kathleen and I met for dinner. She radiated the assurance of a woman
practiced at being cool and pretty. Her hair was long, dark, and
sleek. Her lips were red, her smile knowing. Her nails were buffed
and polished into perfection. The way she talked, on subjects from
local bands to gourmet cooking, implied an immediate, knowing
intimacy, a mutuality of opinion. Like the girls who'd befriended
me when I was the new kid growing up—Karla, in England, with
her frilly dresses and British accent; Michelle, in Kansas, with
her horses and cowboy boots; Nicole, in Virginia, with her feath-
ered hair and obsession with Duran Duran; Kim, in New Mexico,
with her pickup truck and church youth group—Kathleen decided to take me under her wing.

My friendship with Kathleen was my attempt at being a party girl, a scenester. This was not the sort of person I was, and I knew it. But I was in a new place, and as a veteran of many cross-country moves, I considered myself infinitely adaptable. I was willing to try on a new identity every now and then. Before we went out, I'd go to Kathleen's house and let her make me up with eye shadow and blush. I felt like the styling doll I'd had as a child, a disembodied Barbie head mounted on a plastic base, eyes wide, smile broad, ready for her close-up. I went to parties with Kathleen at a series of hipster apartments in old houses decorated with thrift-store furniture and homemade art, where the music came from a record player and almost all the conversation was banter. I saw some of the same people over and over: an olive-skinned woman with an abundance of dark curly hair who painted fantastical pictures of cats and women with almond eyes; a boy with square glasses who talked earnestly about our policies toward Cuba; a pale, skinny girl in fifties-style dresses who turned out to be a schoolteacher. I don't know what these people had in common, but whatever it was, I didn't share it. I couldn't make friends with any of them, though I persisted in the attempt for a while, going out again and again with Kathleen.

One night, maybe Halloween, I went with Kathleen and another woman to a bar called the Local 506. There was a band. The place was packed. You had to shout to be heard. Smoke hung in the air. I threw myself into the experience. I drank a lot of Maker's Mark straight. I danced with Kathleen and the other woman in a stripper cage. For a while I had a great time. And then somehow I got separated from Kathleen, and as I fought my way through the crowd of strangers, looking for her, I felt with a sudden intensity that this was the last place I wanted to be.

There was an essential problem in my social life with Kathleen, active as it was: I didn't like it. I didn't want to go to bars and then after-closing parties that lasted until six A.M. and shout inane comments over music and watch some guitar player flirt with Kathleen and have a headache the whole next day. I wanted to go to the movies, then get a cup of coffee and discuss the movie. I wanted to be at home having a small dinner party. I wanted to talk. I was no longer, it seemed, infinitely adaptable, and that night at the 506, I faced the fact that I couldn't make myself into a person suitable to being Kathleen's friend.

In the meantime, Kathleen had introduced us to some of her other friends, in particular two men she'd gone to college with and their girlfriends. These people were scenesters, too—two of them had radio shows at the Duke station; one had owned a small record shop before he started to work as a bartender; one had once worked as a photographer—but they had lifestyles much more akin to our own. We had dinners at each other's houses and met for drinks and went to the movies. But still we couldn't seem to get past a certain level of acquaintance. We didn't talk on the phone. If we didn't see one another for a month or two, it didn't seem to matter. I liked them. I knew if I had a party, they would come. But we weren't friends in the way I'd always understood the term. We weren't intimate. We didn't seem to need each other. If Matt and I moved away, I wasn't sure they would miss us when we were gone.

I complained about this lack of intimacy to an old friend, and he said, "Welcome to the world of adult friendships." I thought about that statement for months whenever I saw these new friends. Maybe he was right. Maybe we had outgrown the kinds of friendships I'd had in school and in Boston. Coupled off, with pets and jobs, our identities largely formed, maybe we just didn't have the same need. Matt said, "It's because we don't get really fucked up together," which was perhaps another way of saying the same thing. I considered, too, the possibility that I wasn't available to new friendships, given the amount of time I still invested in maintaining my old ones. Maybe I was like someone who claims to be dating new people but spends all her time on the phone with her ex.

But then I met Annie. I'd gotten a job working for a literary magazine, and she was the managing editor. Annie was about ten years older than I was. She had a quick wit, a loud laugh. She was a poet who'd gone to graduate school at Iowa, which had the most highly regarded program in the country, and then decided she wouldn't try to publish but would write only for herself. I'd met people who made this claim before, but no one who actually meant it. Desperate to publish, I admired her casual, unpretentious commitment to art for art's sake. I developed an instant girl crush on her. I wanted her to like me, so in her presence, I became shy and awkward and said inane things that, in a horrible self-torture, replayed again and again after I said them.

Here it was, the chemistry, the instant sense of connection I'd wanted, but I had no idea how to make it mutual. Like a lovesick teenager, I made excuses to go into her office and chat with her. I thought of clever things to say. And here's where the mysterious part of friendship comes in, because although I certainly made an effort, would have filled out an application to be Annie's friend, I have no idea how I finally achieved the post. I can't remember the first time we did something together outside the office. I don't know whether it was at my suggestion, or whether Annie asked if I wanted to see a movie and in so doing told me what we always want to hear: that she liked me back.

In finding Annie, I found the sort of intimacy I wanted in a friendship. But I came up against a new difficulty. Annie was so busy, so overwhelmed with her job and her marriage and her two elementary-age children and her preexisting social life, that it was hard to schedule outings with her, and after we both left the magazine, I saw her less and less often. When we did have plans, she often had to cancel at the last minute because her husband had to work late, or she did.

About a year after I met Annie, one of my old friends, Sarah, decided to move to the area. I was thrilled. Lucky her, she arrived equipped with friends. Not only was I there, so was her best friend from college, and Sarah stayed with her best friend and her best friend's husband for the first three months after her move. Once she found her own house, she decided to have a party. She invited everyone she'd met: people from work, a guy who worked at Whole Foods, her yoga instructor. Alas for the party, this diverse group didn't connect in the way Sarah probably imagined. Instead, there were factions—a group of people from Sarah's job at a university press playing a game called Dictionary in one room, a gang of drummers holding an impromptu concert in another. Sarah managed to get some living room dancing going, but the drum leader turned the music off so that a woman in a cardigan with blond braids could perform some slam poetry while he accompanied her on bongos. It was a terrible poem, and the party wasn't much better.

At the time I was baffled, even annoyed, by this party and Sarah's need to have it. In me and her college best friend, she had exactly the sort of intimate friends I'd been missing. Why weren't we enough for her? Now I think I understand. Her college friend was married, and I might as well have been. Regular companionship was a given in our lives, taken for granted, and perhaps I was on the lookout for friends as much as I was because I wasn't on the lookout for a man. Maybe, being single, Sarah wanted friends who were single, too. Maybe, being single, she wanted to meet some men. We'd run into this problem again and again during the years she lived here; I'd want her to come over, she'd want to go out. And then she dated a man I didn't like, and for a while I hardly saw her at all. From her I learned again the lesson I'd learned with Annie—what you're asking for from a friend is her time, and as we head into our late twenties and early thirties, that's in increasingly short supply.

Still, I'm reminded that, even as we acquire jobs and spouses and children, we are lonely without friends. Last summer I had lunch with a long-distance friend I don't often see. She'd recently moved to a new city, and as she gave me her impressions of the place, I tried to frame a question I wanted to ask so that it wouldn't sound as though she'd just finished her first day of kindergarten. Finally, I said, "I don't know how else to put this. Have you made any friends?"

She paused. When she said no, she hadn't made any friends, I could tell that the lack was weighing on her. She was a writer also, working at home, with two small children, and her life was too busy for joining gyms or taking art classes. She was hoping to meet some compatible mothers when her eldest started preschool.

So perhaps as we enter our thirties, the preschool or the playground is the next meeting place. I discovered the truth of this when I had my own baby. Remember the women I liked but didn't feel close to? One of them had a baby the year before I did, and after my daughter arrived, she was at my door with advice, support, and, most importantly, dinner. Now I talk to her almost every day, a turn of events that reminds me how an intense mutual experience can create an intimacy that would take years and years of casual encounters to establish. She shares my frustrations, my worries, my joys. What do you know—she's my friend.

The F-word

By Caprice Crane

> Harry: No man can be friends with a woman he finds attrac-
> tive. He always wants to have sex with her.
> Sally: So you are saying that a man can be friends with a woman
> he finds unattractive?
> Harry: No, you pretty much want to nail them, too.
> —*When Harry Met Sally*

When I landed my first *real* job in New York, my circle consisted of an alcoholic boyfriend, a friend or two left over from college, and a couple of cordial neighbors (one a compulsive liar and
another who may or may not have been a call girl). In the high
school–like atmosphere of the place—rife with cliques, insecurities, power trips, and gossip—I quickly found a sympathetic soul
in Danny, who worked a few doors down from me.

There was early friendship-building, but because he was (and still
is) a man, it got hazy. Was this getting-to-know-you stuff or flirting—
palaver or a probing of the defenses? Hard to tell, but since I had a
boyfriend, I figured it had to be innocent. Like me, apparently.

What to call Danny, my non-boyfriend boyfriend? What are
these friendships that plateau at platonic? It's so sanitizing to
speak of a relationship that way—as a "philosophical contempla-
tion and appreciation of another's mind" as opposed to her (or

his) behind. Not to mention dishonest: What guy would deny that among the things he's contemplating is your cleavage? And what guy with amorous intentions (hidden or not) doesn't cringe when he gets called that dreaded f-word—"friend"?

What's more, in the thin lexicon of male friendship, or men-ship, I've never found a single substitute for the term "date." I'm always at great pains when out with a male friend to insist to any curious on-lookers, "It's not a date," but I'll be damned if I know what it is.

So for the first of our non-dates, Danny asked if I'd go with him to an Elvis Costello concert. I didn't respond at the time he asked (even though I loved Costello) because it seemed too datelike, so he placed my ticket in an envelope on my desk and left the office. (Pretty slick, huh?) I guess I was going. I was a whore for good music (if not a whore for Danny), and I figured I could clear up any misunderstandings by simply explaining the situation to any-body we happened to meet that night. ("Excuse me, Mr. Costello? This is not technically a date, you know. Could you please play 'Pump It Up' for me and my FRIEND Danny?")

Danny and I ended up having a great time at the show, get-ting drinks at the Royalton afterward and bonding over music and books and practically everything. It was pretty much a perfect first [insert appropriate term here]. Or would have been, had I not al-ready had a boyfriend, who was probably passed out somewhere. It was a particular quality of my decision making in my early twen-ties that drew me to not so much rejects as *projects*. Guys who needed fixing up. And I'm always faithful—even to a train wreck.

That night came the first of what would lead to years of awk-ward goodbyes with Danny. You'd think after the first thirty-seven partings, you'd get used to it, but sadly, that's not the case. I nor-mally hug and kiss friends on the cheek without thinking twice about it. (I have one friend who is the exact opposite. If she wants to express affection to a guy, she'll poke him, and usually with a sharp object, like a pencil.)

But every time Danny and I said goodbye, we had the awkward moment. The which-cheek-are-we-going-for, is-he-going-to-try-to-kiss-me, shouldn't-we-have-the-hang-of-this-by-now moment. And yes, we'd had the talk. The uncomfortable I-have-feelings-for-you talk. But we'd also established that we were just friends.

And that's where male-female (let's call them MF) friendships get sticky. If I knew he had feelings for me and I allowed it to continue, was I really a friend or more a point of frustration? If he knew I had a boyfriend and kept hanging around, waiting for me to dump him so he could take his place, was *he* really being a friend or a vulture waiting to feast on the decaying corpse of my terminal relationship? Each of us rationalized it, but over time we were driving each other a little bit crazy. Danny and I were David and Maddie from *Moonlighting*. A great show—that went to hell as soon as they had sex. All the more reason, in my eyes, for us not to.

I was never actually taught how to be friends with the opposite sex. We have a treasure trove of books and movies that teach us what to do—and not do—with boyfriends. But what about friends who are boys? And let's be clear here—gay male friends do not count. I mean, they're important. No woman over twenty-one should be without at least one gay male with whom she can consort, cackle, and watch the Oscars. But my gay male friends function pretty much like girlfriends (better, in a way, since they won't steal my boyfriends—probably).

Neither am I talking about friendships with guys who are clearly unsuitable as romantic partners due to a massive age discrepancy, a massive waistline, or a massive SUV to shuttle around the wife and kids. After all, there are general rules of engagement in the dating world. For instance, people partner up in roughly the same band of physical attractiveness. Which is to say that if you're an eight, you can pal around with a guy who's a four, and it's reasonable to expect that things will be staying on the friendship tip indefinitely. Keep in mind, though, even if he's a nine and you're a five, he will still be thinking about sex with you every time you drink from a straw or drop a pen on the ground. I didn't make up these rules, and of course there are the exceptions, but that's the general system.

Where I have often looked up from an uncomfortable laugh or a touch that lingered too long, only to find myself standing on the corner of Sexual Tension Street and Awkward Avenue, is in friendships with men who are straight, in my age range, and funny/smart/unrepulsive enough to at least be considered dating material. It's the difference between trying to stay on a diet while locked in a vegetable crisper and staying on that same diet while locked in a Dunkin' Donuts.

My confusion on the matter was first expressed in the form of me crawling under my desk in the second grade to declare my friendship for Marc Sampson by kissing him on the knee. The only person less pleased than Marc by my unsolicited knee affection was my eighty-year-old teacher, Ms. Murphy, who tapped her foot and waited, with a nightmare-inducing scowl on her cracked face, for me to emerge from underneath the desk.

Sure, I was young and innocent and for some reason incredibly drawn to his knee, but even then I instinctively wanted males as friends. And as I grew up, I would learn I wasn't alone.

In that odd stretch of relationship real estate that our twenties form between school, a serious career, full-time marriage and/or momming, most women find the male friend indispensable—pre-husband, inter-boyfriend, post-crush. And yes, most guys want to have sex with their female pals, and most girls want their male friends to act like neutered boyfriends until they find a real one.

But I've had more than my share of close male friends. Though someone perhaps a little more cynical might divide the majority of men we encounter into just two camps—those who have already had the privilege, and those who are still trying to bury the bone—I tend to take a more benign view of things.

Why shouldn't I be able to have a fuck buddy without the fuck, a really close friend who doesn't take advantage of the proximity to attempt any inserting, a soul mate who isn't interested in mating? Think of it: We'll get together, have a good time, I'll see things through his eyes and he through mine.

My guy friends say that they can let down their macho guard around their women friends and open up in a way they can't with their male friends. Plus, their male friends don't have boobs, which make everything better. And when we joke about thinly veiled things (or not so thinly veiled, like when my friend Jim announces that it's his birthday, and in his family, there's a long-lived tradition in which the males must receive blow jobs on their birthdays), I know it's because we're over the sexual tension. Way past that.

My girlfriends say guys are a good way to get the male perspective, the kind they can't get from girlfriends. Also, it's hard to reach high-up places. And change tires. Not to mention the need for the occasional wedding date. So it would appear that yes, guys and girls can be friends, as long as they've already had sex or there is virtually no interest on either side. (Of course, excluding any desert-island scenarios.)

So while Danny was clearly my non-boyfriend boyfriend, my actual boyfriend was still very much in tune with his inner caveman. He wanted to perform the modern-day equivalent of bashing Danny over the head with the jawbone of an ass so that he could drag me by my hair back to the cave for sex as God intended it.

Point being, most guys don't like it when their girlfriends have straight male friends on the side. Chris Rock once referred to these platonic pals as a "dick in a glass box." In case of emergency, break the glass. It's true. Some women have been known to turn the underlying and frequently undying sexual tension into a contingency plan, transforming the non-boyfriend boyfriend into the aforementioned "in case of emergency" guy, like one of those fire hoses behind glass that you're supposed to break if your life is going up in flames. String a guy along just in case, and if neither of us has found anyone by the time we hit X age, we're getting married.

Some male-female friends legitimately have no ulterior motives, either because they've been through that underpass already or because they just never felt the spark. Some will claim to have a strictly platonic, drama-free friendship. But even in those, if one party (read: the girl) was drunk and/or horny and intimated that to the guy, you could count the seconds before he'd be out the door, calling behind him to ask if she prefers lubricated or non-lubricated condoms. (Tip: always lubricated.)

It didn't matter to my boyfriend that I was completely, utterly, homicidally faithful—he wanted to know what the hell the deal was with the Dick in a Box. Was I keeping Danny on simmer so that I had a premade next boyfriend in the event of my current boyfriend's likely intoxi-carceration?

No. I just wanted Danny's friendship. It was comforting and safe. He knew me better than I knew myself. And I didn't keep it a secret from my boyfriend, which caused no small amount of ruckus on the home front.

Eventually, the drunk boyfriend faded from the picture, and everyone at the office assumed that Danny and I were now an item. We ended up spending every waking moment together. When you're in a close relationship with someone of the opposite sex, people think one of two things: You *are* dating or you should be dating. People noted how cute we looked together, and if I was ever seen (gasp) alone, I was immediately asked, "Where's Danny?"

Danny and I *were* cute together. We had more inside jokes than a married couple of twenty years. I'd call him as soon as I got home from anywhere, and vice versa; we'd e-mail if we weren't on the phone, and we'd instant-message when we were too lazy to walk six feet down the hall. I'd search high and low for an out-of-print record that he wanted so I could surprise him on his birthday, and he'd track down a long-lost episode of my father's TV show to surprise me on mine. It was friendship perfection, the model non-marriage. Except every now and then he'd say something to me like "I want to brag to the world about my amazing girlfriend, but all I can legitimately show off is an awesome record collection." Those words would stab me in my heart. And when I fell in love with a new alcoholic, it would shatter his.

Of course, the history of romance is riddled with examples of a patient suitor overcoming a lady's indifference—or open hostility—through sheer persistence ("I do believe I'm falling for that royal pain in the ass!"), so Danny hung around, biding his time. But while the suspense of waiting is great entertainment, let's be honest about what happens to the ratings when the girl gives in. Crash.

When it comes to the sacred temple, too many men discover all too late, it's better to travel hopefully than to arrive. Where do men think the verb "to screw up" comes from? Why fuck up a relationship by fucking? Besides, while I've heard people say that you can never have too many friends, I have yet to hear the same about sex partners (except Birthday Blow-job Jim).

In the case of Danny and me, it wasn't until he started having relationships that everything drastically changed. His new girl-friends would be jealous of me and insist that he and I cut off all ties. Devastated, I'd comply. Then they'd break up and I was expected to once again be the surrogate, and I would be. For a time. We'd get back into the swing of things, but then one or both of us would get into another relationship, and things would change.

Early in our friendship, I'd bought Danny a dachshund Beanie Baby and, for obvious reasons, named him Weenis. The little guy sort of became our mascot. Once, Danny took Weenis on a trip to Los Angeles. When they returned, I received a photo travelogue, complete with pictures of Hollywood-bound Weenis on the plane with headphones on and LL Cool J's biography in his lap, Weenis sunbathing, in a sauna, driving on Melrose, standing on Burt Reynolds's star on the Hollywood Walk of Fame. Who wouldn't love it? Then Danny got another girlfriend, and she demanded he end our friendship. For real.

I took it badly. And I did something awful. I kidnapped Weenis. This is the first Danny will learn of it. I'd planned on returning the fuzzy little sausage after snapping shots of him on the Eiffel Tower, in the Vatican, perhaps working the slots in Reno. I was just waiting out the current relationship to reunite Danny with a well-traveled Weenis. But he stayed with the girl for two years. Something dawned on me at last: The whole thing had gone too far. I was too ashamed to admit what I had done. I'd stolen his Weenis. And I no longer had a way to give it back.

My good fortune with good friends who were male started in high school with Ryan and Ben, two friends with whom I'm close to this day. Ryan and I wrote screenplays full of fantastic dialogue and empty of plot. Ben was the loyal compadre who ratted out my alcoholic high school boyfriend when he was cheating. (Happy-ending sidebar: Yes, I finally reversed that misguided pattern and no longer date alcoholics. One day at a time.) Ben later crossed the country to visit me at college, sleeping with me in my cramped single bed, treating me like the sister I am to him.

Still, things don't always run so smoothly. Sometimes I've known the sexual tension to veer toward tantrums. The vein popping out in the middle of the forehead as they've tried to contain the vein popping out elsewhere. In college, my off-and-on friend Todd would cycle between occasionally professing his love for me and then bailing out of our friendship if I wouldn't be his real girlfriend (instead of his non-girlfriend girlfriend). Naturally, I'd be hurt, because I felt I had a lot to offer as a friend and a human being. And if all he was looking for was sex, then screw him.

Yet, angry as I was, I'd miss my friend and beg him to come back. Eventually, he would. His frat-boy friends hated me because of the anguish I caused him by not giving it up. So they took matters into their own hands, punishing me in the form of a three A.M. delivery of groceries I didn't order. On a winter night when I was in bed with a raging fever, I buzzed up a delivery boy whose package was: a can of ALPO dog food (didn't own a dog), Slim-Fast (so, I'm a fat dog?), and tampons (a fat dog on the rag?). Then Ex-Lax. I see. Apparently, I'm a constipated fat dog on the rag. Todd would later apologize, and I would later forgive him.

If it seems I wasn't taking his feelings into consideration or at least bending a little, know that I was, and I did. When he had called it quits for the third time, I was so distraught over losing Todd that I decided to give "it" a try. The pain of losing my friend felt like breakup pain. Didn't that imply that I had feelings for him? So I showed up at his apartment late one night and made out with him. I stopped short of sex (that was a little more bending than I was willing to do), and we had a fun-filled few days. But after that, it was he who decided our romance was a dead end. That rejection was what ultimately allowed him to be friends with me.

Do MF friendships occur in nature devoid of sexual tension? Yes. They can. That's my situation with Charlie—over ten years without an awkward pause, misconstrued glance, or innuendo. Can they survive a healthy dose of it, unconcealed but also tightly sealed in a container of mutual respect? Yes. That's been Jim, a divorced dad who's one of my closest friends now. We get along great—share the same sense of humor, see movies and concerts together—and I adore his kids. And we've never had sex. He is completely comfortable being just friends. Granted, he'd be the first to admit that if I ever made that late-night phone call, he'd be all about it. Especially if it was his birthday.

I just have to keep reminding myself, the Battle of the Sexes is traditionally fought wearing blindfolds. Men and women will never really understand each other completely, and that's fine.

All I know is, every time the opportunity to cross over from friendship arises, I will confront the dilemma as if for the first time: Do I leave it at a handshake and a hug, or relent and forever alter the arrangement? Because sex is easy to find. But a good friendship? Now, *that's* something worth protecting. I've spent my twenties learning that same lesson over and over. What do I have to show for it? Some lifelong friends, but also a can of ALPO and a man's Weenis. And Danny, if you're listening, I can't tell you how sorry I am about that.

I Hate You. Let's Be Friends!

By Deanna Kizis

I'm sitting on the floor in my living room, yanking Hefty bags out of the closet. Bag after bag, each one stuffed to bursting like Santa's rucksack. Most coat closets are filled with snowboards, puffy winter jackets, and unplayed guitars; I have piles of stretched-out brownish-greenish plastic—occasionally ripped—that contain debris from the Land of Lost Relationships. In one, there's a Pez dispenser an ex-boyfriend gave me because it resembled my dog. In another, I find directions to an ex-boyfriend's house, which I wrote down on a notepad on the day of our first date. After emptying out yet another, I unball a cocktail napkin scribbled with the words *You know you love it.* I sit here amid play programs (hopefully clean), lingerie, boyfriend T-shirts I once slept in, a clear plastic bowl, broken seashells, ripped-up photographs, Valentine's teddy bears, birthday jewelry, and a visor from Hawaii that says BITE ME. Occasionally, I pull out something really special, like the note that reads *IRA: I NEED MY BOOK MANUSCRIPT BACK (ALL COPIES). AND MY JOURNAL ENTRY BACK. YOU HAVE NO RIGHT TO IT. *ANYTHING I GAVE YOU THAT YOU DON'T WANT, THROW IT IN THE TRASH.*

These are my bitter bags of stuff.

The bitter bag of stuff is a tradition that began as I stumbled through my twenties, when I found myself constantly breaking up with boyfriends. No, let me self-disclose: When I found myself constantly getting *dumped* by my boyfriends. When this would happen—which it did at least once a year when I was between the ages of twenty-one and twenty-nine—I'd sweep the house like the FBI, cram anything that reminded me of him into a Hefty, and drive to his place, crying so hard it was as though there were a hurricane inside my own eyelids. My intention would be to dump it all on his front doorstep. This was pathetic, I knew. I didn't care. The contents of the bitter bag of stuff would say what I could not: *Look here, you foul beast. You've hurt me so much that everything we've ever touched has become relationship roadkill.* But then sometime between heaving the bag off the front seat and ringing the doorbell, I'd turn around. I'd stuff the bag back in the car. I'd drive home, chuck the Hefty into the closet—where it would give a plastic sigh beside the growing pile—and call my best friend, Eve.

"It's over," I'd say. "But I kept all the crap."

"That's good," she'd say. "At least you still have your dignity."

She. Was. *Lying*.

Flash forward to my post-twenties life. Today I peruse my bitter bags of stuff, toss my hair, and laugh. For I am no longer a member of the Hefty set. I am something else altogether different. I am, to sum it up in one word, adored.

It's true. Where men are concerned, I'm fussed over, coddled, taken to dinner, and given thoughtful presents—not just for birthdays, mind you, but "just because." My calls are returned in a timely manner, and when I send a one-line e-mail, I get two pages back. I'm offered free U2 tickets, the extra seat on a chartered yacht, and chicken soup when I'm sick. I get all this from not one but nine eligible men. All of them are attractive, intelligent, hilarious, and successful. (Not to mention heterosexual, I assure you.) I am utterly irreplaceable in each of their lives.

"But," you stammer, "not long ago, you were a pathetic psycho loser. Where did you come from, divine creature? Are you a rules girl now?"

"Please," I say. "I'm not above a tearful middle-of-the-night 'Don't leave me' panic attack. And I recently told the man I've been dating that if he didn't propose soon, I would choke on my own tongue. Precious little has changed."

"Then you've been holding out on us," you say. "You are a supermodel who's given up the psycho crack drugs and emerged more in control and beautiful than ever."

"Not even close!" I say. "I'm five foot four, have a huge bump on my nose, and since I quit smoking, I've gained so much weight that some skinny bi-atch at American Apparel recently directed me to their new stretch thermal line because she thought I was pregnant!"

Now you are in awe. "Who, nay, *what* have you become?" you ask.

I reply in a whisper: "*I am the woman with nine ex-boyfriend friends.*"

Nine ex-boyfriend friends, all of whom moved to supposedly greener pastures back in the day. All of whom worship me now. In fact, I am loved so much—so much!—that I couldn't possibly get dumped by anyone else: I simply don't have room in my schedule for more fancy dinners, and I have so many mix CDs filled with sweet songs I might like that I don't have time to listen to them all.

The transformation from Pathetic Psycho Loser to Beloved Goddess of All She Surveys was slow. Painful. Seemingly senseless. For a decade I was held prisoner by my twenties, a time when I could smoke cigarettes all day without having imagined lung freak-outs; thought of a tuna-fish sandwich with bacon and sprouts as healthy; and dated everyone in Los Angeles who had a valid driver's license. (It was heartbreaking to rule out the ones who didn't, but you can't go anywhere in L.A. without a car.)

Where men were concerned, the problem, if hindsight serves me well, was that I usually went out with guys I should have been friends with in the first place. These were cool dudes, but most of them (all of them?) were wrong for me. Back then I liked two types of guys: funny, good-looking, mean, and commitment-obsessed; or funny, good-looking, nice, and commitment-phobic. Either sort would do. As long as there was no way the relationship could have a happy ending, I was in there. (Psych 101 break: Because *I* was unconsciously commitment-phobic, I chose men who would never get close enough to challenge my own fears. You have at least three friends like this, and it'll take them approximately ten years to work it out, so let's move on.)

If I was attracted to a guy, I had to have him as my leading man. I'd turn into Gollum from *The Lord of the Rings* and scheme to get my precious, becoming more charming and infinitely less demanding in his presence than I really was. I played the ingenue: alluring, spontaneous, and quick with compliments. I could be easygoing, sweet, and sexually deviant, but in a marriage-material kind of way (or so I preferred to think). If I had to sum up the persona I conjured in one word, I'd say it was—please forgive the terrible cheesiness—sparkly.

But I couldn't sparkle forever. By the time I had said leading man in my clutches, I was tired, dulled, chipped. The ingenue mask would crack with wear, and I'd start to look disturbingly like a person. A person who at times could be bitchy, stressed out, and overworked. A person who refused to take the bad seat in a restaurant and never offered to drive. A person who was not always complimentary. (A favorite story of Eve's involves my braying at a boyfriend's birthday party when everyone was arriving late: "Dude? Do you *have* friends? I mean, are they just, like, blowing off your birthday or what?") In my own defense, I don't think I would have misrepresented myself—would have sparkled so falsely—if he'd been the right guy. The problem was, in my twenties, I believed *every* guy was the right guy.

When he realized we weren't a perfect match, he'd stomp me. And I'd be so upset about said stomping that I, like many women I know, would throw out the friendship with the boyfriend.

Everyone knew when I was in the midst of another relationship crash-and-burn. My dry cleaner would take pity on me when I'd go to pick up clean clothes, offering me the stiff tissue she used to wrap pressed shirts. The guy who delivered Italian food from Michaelangelo's around the corner would arrive with an extra bag of rolls. Even the handyman knew. When he showed up one morning to fix the sink, I was in the same cocktail dress I'd been wearing the night before, my false eyelashes dropping at the corners, making me look like Bambi's Gothic nightmare.

"He leave?" the handyman asked, getting out his toolbox.

I nodded and curled up in the sink, hoping his work would distract me from my miserable state. "He'll be back," I said, sniffing.

The handyman tilted his head and sized me up for a moment before he got down on his knees and said, "Ya think?"

I got jilted so often, I had two systems to deal with it: the Easy Way (cry, drink alone, take up jogging again, get life back together) or the Hard Way (beg for a reconciliation, call and hang up two hundred times, stalk him at parties, horrify friends, cry, drink alone, take up jogging again, get life back together).

When I turned thirty, I was single. I had dated everyone I'd ever met. I was out of prospects and dejected in spirit. Then a miracle: Shortly after I blew out my birthday cake, aflame in candles, the ex-boyfriends started to come back. Just like I'd told the handyman, that disbelieving pipe dweller. This happened slowly yet all at once, like those videos where you can see grass growing after it's been sped up six thousand times. Sometimes the boyfriend's return took months; one time it took five years. Eventually, I'd get a cautious e-mail asking how I was. ("Does this address still work?" an ex would say.) Or there would be a voice-mail message. ("I know we haven't talked in forever, but . . .") Or he'd approach at a party. ("I was *wondering* if you'd be here . . .") It turned out they were not calling, writing, saying hello to get back together. Invariably, these men were approaching me because they wanted to be friends.

The first time this happened, I was a bit taken aback. Dave—who got in so deep, I wrote a whole novel about our breakup—once took me out to dinner for my birthday to make amends. When I found out it was because he wanted to be "just friends," and not because the life was slowly draining out of him since we'd split, leaving him lying on the kitchen floor with his mouth moving in slow gasps like a dying fish, I threw down my napkin, chucked in his direction the stack of cautiously wrapped birthday CDs he'd brought for me, and ran hysterically out of the restaurant into a rainstorm, where I proceeded to— You know what? Let's just say I didn't take it well.

Still, over the years, being just friends got easier. It was a combination of maturity, moving on, and forgiveness, which, I've determined, is the essential key to happiness. There was something about these guys I liked, I realized. And a certain way they made me feel about myself that I enjoyed—in the beginning, at least. If I could stop being in love with them, I could be in serious like with them. Like, forever.

So. My nine ex-boyfriend friends are my biggest fans, my staunchest supporters, my dearest confidants. Whenever I see one of these guys, I look great, I feel great. They tell me I look beautiful; I feel even better. Harry still calls me "sweetheart" and drives me around Silver Lake Reservoir while blasting Cheap Trick with all the windows down. Matthew still tries to convince me I can drink him under the table and laughs when I can no longer feel my own feet. Probably the closest ex-boyfriend friend is Dave, who no longer cowers in fear when we bump into each other at Blockbuster. Just the opposite: He babysits my dog for me when I go out of town, and he lets me drink all his wine, provided I let him use my pie dish whenever he bakes.

However, a woman must be a real friend in order to be privy to such love, such devotion. I had to get through the bitter-bag phase. I had to stop spreading rumors that one of my exes had man boobs. I say nothing about the one who wanted me to buy a six-inch dildo—for his pleasure, not mine. Sure, those stories are 100 percent true, but these are my *friends* now. You gotta represent. Furthermore, as a friend, I do not roll my eyes when one of them asks whether I think he would get more girls if he used cellulite cream. I don't complain when another one—the British one—calls my voice mail and screams into the phone, "I have just shagged a music-video model! A. Music. Video. Model!" I applaud them when merited. I scold if deserved. I am often asked my opinion. If one of my exes breaks up with a girl, he calls me, his voice soggy with despair. "What did I do wrong with you?" he asks. So I tell him exactly, and at great length, what he did wrong with me. I am detailed. Dispassionate. Honest. The phone goes quiet. He listens, making no arguments, going, "Mm-hm, yep, mm-hm." The best part is when I'm done. When he agrees with me.

"Wow," he says. "I *was* being really selfish when I said I wanted to take Japanese lessons instead of being with you. I wish I had known a good thing when I saw it."

Or: "If only I knew then what I know now: Twenty-two-year-old virgins really aren't that great of conversationalists! You were right. You were so, so right."

Of course, there's a dark side. Having a stud corral of exes can be hard on a new relationship. I'm booked up months in advance. I've already promised to take ex-boyfriend number one to my best friend's birthday dinner (not that he ever would have attended when we were going out), and that time I went to Belize with an ex while I was dating someone else caused serious hysterical e-mail bombardment. I'm damned if I explain, damned if I don't; when I say these guys are just friends, my new boyfriend will carefully screen through every picture on my iBook, as men do, and notice that I happen to be playing tonsil tennis with most of them. When I come clean and introduce someone as an ex-boyfriend, my new boyfriend is tolerant, perhaps. Until we replay this awkward moment for the fourth, sixth, or ninth time. Then my new man starts to wonder aloud if I'm a slut. Whenever this happens, I open my mouth, turn my eyes up to the ceiling in search of some other plausible explanation, and say, "Well . . ."

I was once even asked to choose—by a boyfriend, I mean. Him or the Nine. I hemmed and I hawed. I made excuses. I tried to explain.

"They keep me in touch with the youthful me," I said. "But *you're* my everything."

When this didn't work, I said, "But I can't abandon these guys! They'll drop down dead! Like dying fish! They'll never survive the loss of me!"

"What do they have," he demanded, "that I don't have?"

Then he stormed out of the house.

Then he called from his cell phone.

Then he dumped me.

I cried and cried.

We didn't speak for a year.

The funny thing is, he called the other day. He wanted to know if we could have dinner sometime. He's realized he's still in love with me, poor thing.

"I'd *love* to have dinner!" I said.

We set a time. We picked a place. But, I told him, there was one teensy little problem.

I really just want to be friends.

Back to the Pacific Beach Café

By Hollis Gillespie

First I want to make it clear I wasn't shocked to learn that Becky was fucking our boss. Everybody was fucking everybody at this place. My own roommate, Melissa, was fucking the "manager," a big Hawaiian guy named Richard who occasionally referred vaguely to a wife and kids in some faraway place. I never got that straight and always thought Richard had fabricated his family to serve as a Teflon buffer that would keep chicks from sticking to him. Still, he was a hundred years old (or thirty-five, at least) and heavy, with a face like a pail of paste, and even though I knew Melissa was as picky about her prospects as a rooster pecking out winners on a racing form, it still disgusted me that she balled this guy, often while sober, even, and often while wearing lingerie she borrowed from me without asking. A few years later, when I was working at another restaurant, Richard once showed up in my section, and I was all set to pretend like I'd never met him if not for the fact that he apologized to me, in front of his dinner companion, for ripping the crotch out of my pink satin camisole set.

But back to the Pacific Beach Café. I turned twenty while working there, probably marking my lowest point in this personal decade. The only person who worked there who wasn't fucking someone else who worked there was my sister, Cheryl, who was still busy fucking the busboy from the restaurant we'd worked at prior to this one, a windowless steak house patronized solely by wealthy men. There, the waitresses were required to wear leotards, stiletto heels, and skirts so short they could barely clear the tiny aprons we wore around our waist. I lied about my age to get that job, too. I was always lying about my age back then. There were just not a lot of decent-paying jobs for seventeen-year-olds with a college tuition and a cocaine habit to support, not to mention rent.

But back to the Pacific Beach Café. I myself was fucking the assistant sous chef, as well as dating—but not fucking—the bartender, who of course (and this was always the case regarding restaurant staff) was also the resident coke dealer. The assistant sous chef's name was Lars, and we never had sex, like, in the kitchen or anything, though once I stuck my hands down his pants while he was trying to concentrate on making my order. It was not hard to break Lars's concentration, because he was borderline retarded, but God, he was hot—a blond surfer with a body carved out of marble. It just goes to show that when it comes to being a decent whore, I am pretty bad at it. Looking back, I realize that if I'd been the get-ahead kind of whore like Melissa, I would have been sleeping with the bartender, whose brother was the other owner of the place. It would not have been as advantageous as sleeping with the actual owner, like Becky was, but it would have been a better move careerwise than my habitual hide-the-sausage jaunts with the sweet, dumb, and adorable Lars. At the very least, my cocaine would have been free.

It must be something that runs through the women in my family, this whole aversion to whoring your way ahead. My own mother married an alcoholic traveling trailer salesman. She herself was a mathematician who had to become a missile scientist to support the family. I was nine before I figured out not all mothers made bombs for a living. I was riding my bike to school with a friend, and we stopped by another friend's house on the way to see if she'd join us. She met us at her fence and declined. The reason, she explained, was because she had not finished having breakfast with her family.

I recall my wonderment as I pedaled away. "Why doesn't her mother just leave her a bowl of Halloween candy on the kitchen table before leaving for work in the morning?" I asked, and it was explained to me then that some mothers don't work, or at least not the kind of work that takes them away in the morning before their kids wake up and returns them later that night with a badge clipped to their lapel that reads TOP SECURITY CLEARANCE and deposits them, exhausted, in the Barcalounger in the living room, where they'll sit with their wigs askew, smoking their Salem menthols, while their kids are in the kitchen melting down an entire stick of butter to pour over the popcorn they made themselves for dinner that night.

But back to the Pacific Beach Café. Again, I cannot say I was shocked that Becky was fucking the boss. It's just that I was surprised. She was freakishly pretty, for one. She did not need to work for a living with looks like hers, not as a waitress, anyway. She could have whored up a really nice life for herself just using sex as a currency, even by California standards. She had long blond hair that shone as if she were lit from within, eyes as blue as blowtorch flames, and skin the color of creamed coffee. Plus, she was kind of quiet and didn't ever get drunk and pass out in the parking lot. Once she came to work with her right arm bandaged because she'd been hit by a car. It happened while she was riding her bike, and she just got up, brushed herself off, assured the driver she was fine, and went on her way.

"Are you kidding?" I shrieked. "You should have sued the ever-lovin' shit out of that guy!" She just shrugged me off, saying something about how she didn't want that "coming back to her." She didn't tell me expressly that she believed in God, but it was evident she believed in something—something that promulgated her being a good person. I shook my head in bewilderment. My mother was an atheist, and for the better part of my childhood, I was not allowed to go to church. Curiously, we still had one of those big illustrated children's Bibles hanging around in our house. It probably came from my father, who was not an atheist, but still he didn't want his daughters getting a God habit that would require him to drive us to church each week, thereby cutting into his Sunday beer time at the local tavern. Sometimes, though, he'd come home drunk and read us a few passages in his serious James Earl Jones voice until my mother rescued us by distracting him with the sound of air escaping from an opened can of Budweiser.

I liked the pictures in the children's Bible, especially those of Satan. I had no idea who Satan was, just that he had hair like Lyle Waggoner, really white teeth, and a perpetual sunburn. Bummer about that cloven hoof, but other than that, I thought Satan was fairly hot. My favorite picture was the one where Jesus pushed Satan off a cliff, and Satan's red satin robes billowed about him as he looked back at Jesus in midair, mildly perturbed. Yes, I was seven and I had a crush on Satan, and I even told my mother I'd marry him when I grew up. I remember she looked at me levelly after hearing this. "Kid," she said, pointing at me with her lit cigarette, "whatever you do, don't get married."

But back to the Pacific Beach Café. Jesus, talk about your opposites—here Becky was, all beautiful and too nice to sue the man who *hit her with his car*, yet she was fucking Cromwell, the owner of the restaurant where she worked, a man who built his whole empire from the proceeds of a lawsuit involving a car accident. Years earlier, he'd been just walking down the street, he told me once, and someone went and ran him down. "Lucky you," I told him. "Not really," he said. "No, really," I countered. I mean, sure, he walked with a limp sometimes, but boo-fucking-hoo. This paltry suffering served as the seed money that germinated into what would become, over time, four popular beachfront restaurants. Not only that, but he was a smallish gimp who got to surround himself with beautiful women, some of whom actually fucked him. He was married, five hundred years old (or at least forty), smelly, hairy, psoriasis-flecked, and he forbade his waitresses to wear bras, for chrissakes. He was such a sea urchin, seriously, that when he was telling me his story about being hit by a car, I could have sworn he was trying to weasel a sympathy fuck out of *me*.

Call it intuition or upbringing or both—call it anything but firsthand experience—but the stone-cold fact is this: I knew before going in that fucking the boss was always gonna be a bad business move. Take Melissa. Richard eventually put her up in an empty apartment near the beach, but she still had to pay half the rent, work her cocktail shifts, *and*—let me emphasize here that this is the most odious part—she had to continue to fuck Richard. Show me the equity in that.

Even today I have a friend who is fucking her boss; she believes she's "climbing the corporate ladder" when really all she's climbing is the sweaty, crass, married ass of a pockmarked, balding bag of bacon fat with, like, a clipboard or whatever it is that midlevel corporate suck-ups wave around these days to exude a false air of importance.

"Are you insane? Are you a drooling, booger-eating idiot?" I ask her. "If you don't wise up, your ass is so canned."

But she doesn't listen to me. She's got that infuriating, faraway look in her eyes, as if she's remembering the bionic blow job she gave her boss before meeting me for coffee. Jesus God, how do you talk sense into someone like that? She thinks she is securing her future, she thinks she is distinguishing herself from the rest of the turd pellets in the pile, when little does she know that her shelf life is already eroding. My guess is that she has a few weeks, tops, before that selfish diaper wipe dumps her like a load of toxic waste. He's a *guy*, after all, and most guys formulate excuses to bolt long before they have the actual sex. Guys will make up early-morning squash matches during the appetizer course, thus eliminating the obligation for any cuddle time should their date decide to copulate with them after dinner. So, c'mon, what guy is gonna want to hang out forty hours a week with somebody he's balling?

"Canned," I reiterated to my friend, "like a truckload of tuna."

But back to the Pacific Beach Café. Oddly, as I mentioned earlier, I don't speak from experience. I mean, of all the wrong moves I've made in my life, you'd think boss humping would easily be among them, and as I said, I was never the corporate-climber type. One time, though, Richard took me aside and informed me that the restaurant was firing half the staff, but I could ensure my position if I partook in acrobatic sex with him on the table in the break room right then.

"Let me get this straight," I said. "If I lay you, I get to keep my crap-ass job?" Then I laughed so hard I nearly coughed up the pitcher of margaritas I had drunk by the pool before showing up for work that day. I didn't screw him and he didn't fire me, but he did can the cocktail waitress who *was* sleeping with him. I'll never forget the sight of Melissa throwing her drink on him, then throwing other people's drinks on him, then screaming at him all the way out the door. Believe me, it is not an unpleasant memory.

Becky is a different story, though. She should not have been fucked, and I mean that in every sense of the word. Though she was beautiful, she was the kind of person who wore chunky heels when stilettos were in style. I remember she served us all after work one night when my coworkers and I were sousing ourselves at the bar, everybody young and grandstanding about their designs on life, especially me, because I'd just been accepted to a program to study literature at a university in Oxford, England, and I had plans for myself.

"I'm climbing out of this tar pit, people." I laughed, clinking cocktails in celebration with my waitstaff friends, each with big dreams, too. I remember Becky was widely despised by then, an inevitable by-product of sleeping with the boss, who was absent that night, but Becky weathered the sneers anyway. She was not much older than me but had a young daughter who lived far away with relatives. "I want to own my own place," Becky chimed in, "have my own business."

We toasted to her dream but almost broke our eyeballs rolling them at one another afterward. "'Have my own business,'" we mimicked the minute she turned her back to go fetch another round. It didn't occur to me then that she probably had that dream because it insured her against having to sleep with the boss to climb ahead.

A few days later, Becky got fired, and a few days after that, I didn't show up for my shift and never went back. I used to attribute it to luck that I decided way back then—offhand and all of a sudden—to quit working at a place where the people used one another like toilet seats. I used to look back in gratitude and say to myself, "Whew! Who knows where I'd be now if not for that impulse to ditch my job at the Pacific Beach Café!" But I recognize now that it was less luck than it was an inner uneasiness over the choices I saw for myself if I stayed on that path, a foreboding brought on not by watching what happened to people like Melissa, who deserved to get fucked, but by watching people like Becky, who did not.

Now, every time I hear of someone sleeping with the boss, I am brought back to the Pacific Beach Café, to the sight of Becky sitting in her relic of a Celica, her forehead sitting on her steering wheel as she sobbed. I remember watching her from the window of the restaurant, as did nearly the rest of the floor staff on duty that day. We all stood there, none of us having ever really needed a job before, none of us with a little girl we were trying to become worthy enough to raise, none of us trapped in a mess we thought we could climb out of by balling the boss. We all stood there, watching Becky cry, and none of us went to her.

My Own Mr. Big

By Kristin Harmel

Okay, confession time: I admit to a *slightly* unhealthy obsession with Carrie Bradshaw, of *Sex and the City* fame.

I covet her shoes. I've gone into credit-card debt emulating her character's sense of style. I've even met the "real" Aidan (actor John Corbett) and gone into overdrive fantasyland maybe-I'm-really-Carrie-after-all confusion as he talked to me with that cute Aidan smile and those gentle Aidan eyes.

For a while, I couldn't figure out why I was so transfixed. Or why millions of seemingly intelligent, sensible twentysomethings like me sat mesmerized, week after week, to see what our thirtysomething fictional counterparts were up to. Or why even today I and the legions of *Sex and the City* fans across the country insist upon reliving Carrie's pain on an endless loop with the help of the show's DVDs.

I had liked lots of television shows before, but my interest had never been this deep. Growing up, it was *Mister Rogers* and *Sesame Street*, but I never yearned to visit the Neighborhood of Make-Believe or hang with Oscar in his can. Later on, it was reruns of *I Dream of Jeannie*, but I never dreamed of hopping into a pink harem costume and blinking my way into the heart of an astronaut. *Saved by the Bell* didn't make me long to serve detention with Mr. Belding alongside the yummy Zack Morris.

But *Sex and the City* is different and always has been. Even knowing how it all turns out in the end, I practically salivate every time I turn on an episode, as if it will impart some vital truth that I've never been privy to before, despite having seen each episode numerous times.

Just last year, I finally figured out why:

I am Carrie Bradshaw.

Okay, so I'm not *exactly* Carrie Bradshaw. Actually, I'm still in my twenties, have never worn a Manolo Blahnik (too expensive!), and don't look nearly as glamorous as she does when I'm writing from home. In fact, even as I write this, I'm not adorably perched at my windowsill or sprawled out on my bed; I'm sitting amid a towering pile of clutter in the kitchen nook that I call an office.

But when it comes to dating, somehow my life has been nearly a carbon copy of hers. Before you start getting all suspicious and suggesting that perhaps I've unconsciously emulated Carrie's dating mishaps—no, I was a walking romantic disaster long before I started watching the back episodes on DVD. (Yes, that's right, I couldn't afford HBO during the years that the show aired. Budgeting on a meager twentysomething income is no fun, is it?)

My Carrie Bradshaw–like streak began with my own Mr. Big, a larger-than-life, emotionally unavailable man with whom I fell hopelessly in love despite the myriad obvious reasons not to.

I met him when I was twenty-four. Much like Carrie's first encounter with Mr. Big on a Manhattan sidewalk, my first run-in with Christopher* was a brief one, a fleeting moment that somehow blossomed into more. Our eyes met as we passed in a crowded hallway, we exchanged smiles, and that was it. We were like ships—or *Sex and the City* characters, if you will—passing in the night.

---

*Names and places have been changed to protect the not-so-innocent.

That same night, dressed up in a new red dress and new silver stilettos, I was out for a night on the town with three of my girlfriends, when I saw him in the corner of the bar we had happened upon. Like a scene cut straight from a *Sex and the City* episode, our eyes met over the noisy Saturday-night crowd, and he smiled at me, that slow, lazy, confident smile that I eventually grew to love.

I felt like my heart had stopped. Not only because he was smiling at me and because I'd implausibly seen this man twice in one day (à la Carrie and Big) but because I'd simultaneously noticed that he was signing autographs for a gaggle of giggling girls, which meant that, unless the girls had lost their minds, he likely wasn't just some random guy from the street; he was some sort of celebrity. I suppose if my pop-culture knowledge hadn't been so painfully out of date, I would have recognized him as a musician from a band that had a few hits on the radio at the time. But I didn't— until my friends helpfully clued me in.

And just as Carrie's friend Samantha points out her Mr. Big and is impressed with his status as "the next Donald Trump," my friends were busy gawking at Christopher and apparently impressed that he was staring in our general direction. I, on the other hand, was blushing, embarrassed, and completely shocked that he seemed to be looking directly at *me*.

Just as Carrie was more or less unfazed by Mr. Big's millionaire status, I couldn't have cared less that Christopher was in a band. Truth be told, I would have preferred him not to be. But I couldn't ignore the electricity in the air or the way my heart was pounding in my chest. I had never experienced anything like it before, and I haven't since.

To this day, I wonder if that's what love at first sight feels like.

"It's you," Christopher said softly once he had made his way over to me, smiling that crooked, confident smile.

"Hey," I said back, no doubt blushing furiously. It was pure magic.

Later that night, my friends politely drifted away, and he joined me for a drink. I suppose this constituted our first date, since we spent the rest of the evening sitting with each other, deep in conversation, until the bar closed. Then, after a feverishly paced make-out marathon, which finally ceased at about five A.M., we spent the next five hours talking. Just talking. About everything you could possibly imagine.

We spent the next night together, too, talking until the sun came up, and by Monday morning, I was thoroughly exhausted, both emotionally and physically. But I had no idea what would happen between us from there. He was leaving that morning to fly back to Los Angeles. And I was stuck in—of all places—Orlando, Florida. I wondered if perhaps, in his mind, the connection we had shared was simply a temporary one, a fun few days away from reality. But as with Carrie and Mr. Big, it turned out to be real, beautifully, unbelievably real. Or so I thought.

Over the next few months, Christopher called me every night. We'd talk for hours, although neither of us were phone people; somehow we always had something to say to each other. I learned what I thought were the most intimate details of his life, the innermost secrets of his heart. In return, I told him mine. I was swept away by what I thought we had, by what appeared to be perfection.

Christopher was Mr. Big in every way. I used to torture myself by jealously reading on chat boards what his female fans were saying about him after shows. He was charismatic, sometimes aloof, sometimes untouchable. And just as Carrie soon learned that Mr. Big had an ex-wife, I eventually learned that Christopher had an ex-girlfriend—we'll call her Gertrude simply because this is my story and I can call her whatever I want—with whom he had lived for several years. Like Carrie, I was haunted and bothered by this piece of his past. Mr. Big tells Carrie that he will never marry again, at which point she should have seen the writing on the wall. Like Carrie, I brushed it aside when Christopher mumbled something about not being ready to dive back into a relationship. And as for Carrie, the revelation would come back to haunt me.

Christopher and I started seeing each other once every three or four weeks. He would fly to see me, or I would fly to see him. He moved back east, to New York, and we saw each other more frequently, although we were still miles away from each other. I thought we were growing closer. We had never really said the words, but, like Carrie, I assumed he was my boyfriend, that we didn't need to say so, because what else could we be if we spent hours on the phone with each other every night, talked several times during the day, and flew to see each other frequently? I thought we were going somewhere. I thought I knew Christopher inside and out.

It was a long time before I realized I never really knew him at all.

I don't know exactly when things changed, but there was a turning point in our relationship, maybe four months in, when I started to notice an almost imperceptible shift. Whereas he had called me every night, I suddenly seemed to be initiating many of the calls. While our conversations were still warm, open, and often deeply personal, I began to sense a reticence in him. Something was off. But instead of backing off, like someone logical and self-respecting, I plowed ahead, convinced that if I just tried hard enough, everything would feel normal again. After all, I loved him. And I thought he loved me. What else could matter? Just as Carrie overlooked Mr. Big's commitment phobia time and time again and instead focused on the undeniable connection they had when they were together, I did the same with Christopher. I was operating under the theory that if I refused to see the problems between us, they didn't exist. Admittedly, this was not the best logic.

Christopher's commitment phobia was growing more apparent

by the day. I knew he cared about me deeply; there was never any doubt about that, and to this day, I still believe it. But the closer Christopher got, the more scared he seemed to become. I was apparently terrifying. The harder Carrie pushed, the more Mr. Big withdrew. She coaxed him into saying "I love you." She made him spend time with her friends. She left things in his apartment to try to make herself more of a permanent fixture in his life.

I did the same. I accidentally-on-purpose said "I love you" before he did. When he flew down to see me, I bent over backward to put him together with my friends, in the desperate hope that they would bond and adore one another, solidifying his role in my life. When I flew up to visit him, I tricked myself into feeling like I belonged in his life, falling in love with his dog, pretending to like and admire his rock-star lifestyle that should have, in retrospect, been a sign to me of his inability to grow up and commit.

I failed to see that while I had made my life an open book for him, he had kept his life all but closed to me. I was lucky to be getting through the first chapter.

Carrie's relationship with Big ended when he neglected to tell her that his job was sending him to Paris for six months and that he didn't expect her to go with him. Mine with Christopher ended when he went to Australia on tour and didn't inform me that his ex-live-in-girlfriend Gertrude would be going with him. I may have never known, had I not called to wish him luck with his gig and instead heard her voice on the phone in his hotel room.

"Did I ever really love Big?" Carrie wonders in the episode in which Big leaves for Paris. "Or was I addicted to the pain, the exquisite pain, of wanting someone so unattainable?"

I sometimes wonder the same thing about Christopher. I don't doubt that I loved him. In fact, I still do, a little bit, in a masochistic corner of my heart. But when I look back on it now, his unattainability was so obvious. I thought that I could change him, that it would become as clear to him as it was to me that we were a perfect fit. But was I chasing after something I knew I could never have?

Like Carrie, I had led myself down a path of fantasy, believing that the man I loved was along for the ride, whereas in reality, much of the relationship may well have been in my head. That's a tough thing to come to terms with, which may be one of the many reasons I've felt such a kinship with the fictional Carrie since then. It's a whole lot easier for me to recognize the mistakes she's making with Mr. Big than it is to take a good, hard look at myself and see all the ways in which I went wrong.

Of course, Carrie's story with Mr. Big continues. When he leaves for Paris, it's toward the end of the show's second year. In year six, they reunite; he's finally ready to grow up and be with her, for real this time.

But life is not a TV show. My life isn't anything like the show's finale. There will be no happy reunion with Christopher. We won't live happily ever after in the wake of some grand romantic gesture, because in real life, the men who hurt us don't come back to sweep us off our feet.

It's been two and a half years since Christopher and I met, which I figure puts me squarely in the middle of season three of my story line with him, so who knows how it will all turn out? I don't think I could ever date my Mr. Big again. I'm not addicted to the pain. I don't want to hurt that way again. And I try to be at least a little bit logical. Life would be so easy if we could follow our hearts and trust them to lead us down the right paths. I've learned the hard way that logic has to kick in somewhere, unfortunately. Otherwise, our hearts have the disturbing tendency to lead us cheerfully down the path to destruction.

I haven't had a post–Mr. Big Aidan yet. (Darn it, it's my season three . . . where *is* he?) But I've dated other guys since Christopher and I parted ways. I've discovered that it's hard to shake the shadow of my Mr. Big, because he still lingers in my mind and in many aspects of my life. There's something sadly addictive about loving someone who can't or isn't willing to love you back.

Had it not been for *Sex and the City*, I would have wondered more if something was wrong with me. But seeing Carrie torture herself in the same ways I did with Christopher made me feel an odd sense of peace with the whole situation. Fortunately, I had gotten hooked on the show about two months before Christopher and I parted ways—just in time for it to become a vital post-breakup safety net. It went beautifully with the countless cartons of Blue Bell mint-chocolate-chip ice cream I depressively scarfed while blowing my nose through a record number of tissues.

As I coast on in the post-Christopher episodes of my own life, after watching each of the *Sex and the City* DVDs numerous times, I've realized that there's more to the show than post-breakup comfort. Oddly, it's become sort of an inspiration for how to live my twenties. No, I don't mean going out and getting laid on a constant basis, like Samantha, or, at times, Carrie. What I mean is that the show is about fumbling our way through life—work, friendship, love, everything—and stumbling here and there but making it through okay. My relationship with Christopher hurt like hell, but I'm still here. It didn't kill me. Frankly, I think I'm a better, stronger person because of it.

True, my post-Big dating life isn't as glamorous as Carrie's, although there are lots of bizarre parallels. I've been out on a few dates with a young rookie from the Atlanta Braves; akin to the post-Big "New Yankee." I had another writer who was, to some extent, my Jack Berger (although he didn't break up with me on a Post-it note, thank goodness). I had a Ray King (although mine was a photographer, not a jazz musician with ADHD). I had a Bill Kelley (although in truth, the only similarity was that he, too, was a politician; thankfully, he never asked me for a golden shower). I've even chatted about film scripts with Matthew McConaughey, as Carrie once did in L.A. I've had my own versions of many of the guys I've watched on *Sex and the City*. Truth be told, my dating life in Orlando is far more likely to be filled with strange guys with bad pickup lines ("Hey, you're kinda short" is a personal favorite) and lots of baggage ("It doesn't bother you that I've been divorced twice, does it?" asked one particularly promising twenty-nine-year-old). But in the end, aren't I better off than I was when I was sitting by the phone, waiting for my Mr. Big to love me back?

Now I'm happily single. I appreciate and adore my girlfriends. I love my life. And I'm learning to be comfortable in my own skin, which, as you might have guessed, is a lot easier when I'm not trying desperately to make a man like Christopher love me.

I've realized something else as well. Our twenties—in fact, our lives as women—aren't about finding the perfect shoe, the perfect job, or even the perfect guy to complete us. They're about finding the most perfect version of ourselves—and about discovering, and accepting, that this person will always be imperfect. And sometimes that imperfection will lead us into very misguided choices about whom we chose to give our hearts to.

No, I'm not Carrie Bradshaw. Or not entirely, at least. But I feel that becoming a little bit more introspective and self-aware, like Carrie, is probably a step in the direction of becoming a better version of me. Flaws and all, Carrie learned through the course of the series to love and value herself and to stand on her own. It is perhaps the most important lesson one can learn as a twenty-something.

In the last episode of the show, Carrie says something that struck a chord with me: "The most exciting, challenging, and significant relationship of all is the one you have with yourself. And if you find someone to love the you *you* love, well, that's just fabulous."

As I move toward thirty and beyond, I'm looking forward to having an exciting, challenging, and significant relationship with myself, too. I've promised myself that I'm never again going to get involved with someone who lacks the capacity to love me. I'm even looking forward to more heartbreaks and failures, because they make me who I am. My season four is just around the corner. I'm looking forward to the whole journey.

I hope you are, too. It's a beautiful one, even when the path to happiness is littered with Mr. Bigs.

Knot Tied Up in a Bow

By Laurie Graff

I've been thinking about you." Philip's voice spoke cautiously into my cell phone. "Remember that New Year's Eve? When I was in med school? I still think about that. Do you remember?" He didn't wait for a response. "That was incredible. In the morning you wore my burgundy robe, and the scent of your perfume stayed on it. Whenever I missed you, I would smell the robe to remember."

I still could remember. Me in his bed, in the morning, in the robe. Looking at Philip and brushing my hair.

"I've been dreaming about you, too, Laurie. The last six months."

"What do you dream?" It was a sticky summer Sunday on New York's Upper West Side. I had wanted to go the beach, but the forecast was iffy. I was running errands when my cell phone rang. Philip had grabbed my attention, so I took a seat on the steps of a brownstone, sipping iced coffee while I listened and waited.

He paused. It seemed difficult to say.

"Tell me. It's safe," I said.

"Okay." Philip took a breath. "We're in bed. It's great. It's passionate. We're having a lot of sex, and . . . Well, we're having a really great time."

"How old are we? In your dream."

"In our twenties," said Philip without missing a beat. "I haven't had that in a long time, you know. Not in twenty years."

Twenty years is the time that Philip has been married to Sharon. Twenty-one years was the last time Philip was with me.

Philip's phone call was not out of the blue. But his admission was. He's stayed in touch. A call once or twice a year. A card at Christmas or my birthday. I have met Sharon, I've met his kids. He's happy. Philip makes sure to tell me that each and every time I see him. Each and every time we talk.

"Sharon is great. We're good partners. Good friends," he'll tell me, talking fast, repeating the words as if they're a mantra. "She makes me laugh, but . . ."

"But?"

"It's not passionate. It never was. I try. It's just not there. I miss that."

Why would Philip, a passionate man, choose a woman with whom he had no passion? It was a question I had wondered. A question I had asked. And a question I was never able to understand the answer to when I was in my twenties.

I viewed my twenties as the beginning. Everything was new, and everything lay ahead. There was time, and I intended to exploit it. I had struck pay dirt at the beginning of my acting career, landing a role in a Broadway show and being seen and heard plugging everything from fast foods to phone services in commercials. The headiest day was when I shot my first commercial playing a college student with a foot-deodorizing problem by day; at night arriving at the theater in time to be the beauty-school dropout in a long-running hit musical.

I had dates and boyfriends. It was wonderful when a blind date would come to pick me up at the stage door. And I spent several years in a relationship with a sweet wannabe actor. Though I cared for him, I ultimately didn't feel we were a match meant to be. Letting go was very, very hard, but I felt I had to. I went on.

There were always highs and there were definitely lows, but there was no rush. Things would fall into place in their own good time.

But not everyone felt as I did.

The last night I had spent with Philip was in an apartment on Walnut Street in Philadelphia. I was in a play, and the theater company had put me up there for four months. Philip had come to town for a medical conference. He had seen the show and taken me to dinner. We went back to my place and went to bed.

"That was wonderful," he said, trying to sit up soon after it was over. I had a loft bed. The ceiling was quite low, and Philip bumped his head. "I want to talk to you," he said, lying back down. Well, what choice did he have? "Come here." He reached his arms around to hold me close.

In bed, we could always make each other feel good. That arena, for us, was easy. I felt warm toward Philip. But he looked serious. Pensive.

"You know I like you," Philip began.

Uh-oh. I got a little nervous. I didn't think he would break up with me—but I thought he might propose!

"I feel it's time for me to wed," he said.

I shot up in bed. At five foot one, I just missed the ceiling.

"And I think I met someone I'm going to marry."

What?

How dare he tell me something like that, like this! I thought. I wanted him to want me, but I knew we had some basic differences that had not been reconciled. A wave of relief and rejection rolled right through me.

His internship was finishing up down south, and he had met a girl at a crafts fair. She would follow him wherever his career took him. She would be happy to put her dreams on the back burner and do whatever Philip needed. She would be a doctor's wife. He was going to do his residency in Ohio. He thought they might even settle there.

"You wouldn't want to give up your career for mine."

"Why is it a choice, Philip? Why couldn't I be married to you and also act? If you married someone with an MBA, you wouldn't think twice about whether or not she worked."

"I know you wouldn't want to leave New York."

He had me there. But it turned out that Philip was also offered a residency at Columbia. In the heart of New York City. I asked him to take it. To give us a try.

"What could be so bad?" I asked. "You'd have New York City, money, and me."

But his mind was made up. "Look, if things go as planned, I know I'll be able to marry Sharon. But if I go to New York and things with us don't work out, I'd be starting all over again. And then what? I need to have my first child by thirty. I need to stay on track."

My, my. How romantic!

The pressure Philip felt in his twenties was one he had put on himself. But it was not a pressure I would allow to be put on me. I let him go. He married Sharon. He sent me a postcard from his honeymoon in Aruba. *Having a wonderful time . . .*

Wish you were here, wish you were here.

Philip became a cardiologist, keeping the affairs of his heart all clinical. It was the opposite of how I lived. Not just personally, professionally, too. It wasn't that Philip objected to me being an actor; he just objected to his wife being one.

I had tried to explain that, unlike a woman with a nine-to-five job, I could create my own schedule around auditions, gigs, and classes. There was time, sometimes too much, between jobs that could allow one to take care of a house or child during the day. Inevitably, compromises would have been made. But Philip, in his twenties, could see only *what* I was, not *who* I was. He felt hardpressed to make a decision. It all felt so urgent.

What are you going to be when you grow up? was something I needed to know. When it came to work, it was easy for interests and talents to be the guide. But *Who are you going to be when you grow up?* was the deeper question, and the one that would bond us to another person. Or not.

Thanksgiving is a time to be grateful for what you have. This year on the holiday, I received an e-mail from another beau from my twenties who had realized two decades later that he hadn't been grateful for what he'd had when he had it.

I have been writing fiction books about frogs. Not in the scientific sense, although I've discovered some biological traits of amphibians that are shared with the human male, causing me to wonder about men's socialization when it comes to dating women. Anyway, in the fluky ways of the Internet, somehow or other, Allen came across an e-mail promoting my book as part of a list of nationwide singles events. He recognized my name and did a search that led him to my website. To my absolute shock, I received an e-mail from my old boyfriend, who signed off by saying, *This frog apologizes. Ribbit.*

Long-forgotten memories of Allen took hold. Also studying to be a doctor, he'd been extremely sleep-deprived, spending most of our yearlong relationship asleep, if not in a coma. He had been so closed off emotionally, so shut down physically, so unattainable. So what did I find attractive? you may wonder. His potential. It was clear and, I thought, within reach. Coming from a close-knit, loving family, I felt sure that if I remained patient, loving, and caring toward Allen, all of that would come back to me. In my twenties, I fell hard for potential, because when I was in my twenties, I thought it was everyone's goal to have their potential realized.

I hung on through some awful times. Despite his silences, detachment, and withdrawals, I cheered Allen on in the relationship ring, certain he would knock out his demons and be declared a champion. But Allen only sulked and skulked until I let him slither away.

I would not commit to shoving a square peg into a round hole, but I did commit to constantly trimming and rounding off its edges, surprised for a very long time that the peg still did not fit.

"What are you getting out of this?" a therapist had asked when I went to talk about breaking away from Allen.

"It's what I *will* be getting," I would answer. "How good I know it could be, if only . . ."

Like a lost and found, I had a list of things that were missing, and I was sure I was the one who would find them.

"But what if this is it?" the therapist would ask. "What if Allen is only as deep as what you see now? What if this is as good as it gets?"

I could not fathom that concept in my twenties. Didn't we all want to be better? Admittedly, Allen was unhappy. So wouldn't he do something, anything, to change that? I would. But I also could. I was unable to accept that Allen could not.

Finally, I let go. I stopped seeing Allen. I thought the painful feelings would never subside. Eventually, they slid away. Time is a great healer, and I never even thought about him. Then, last Thanksgiving, there he was. In an e-mail!

We exchanged a few notes, and Allen, now in his forties, told me everything I had hoped and prayed to hear when we were in our twenties. He spoke of life lessons and karma. Coincidence, growth, and timing. On the day I knew Allen was to call, the same hopes I'd had for us back in my twenties soared.

"Hi!" I said into the phone, talking to a man, a surgeon, but in my mind's eye remembering the face of a much younger boy. "I remember your voice; you sound great," I said, listening intently. Listening to everything, to all of the words, spoken and not.

Allen had become much more communicative. But that was all. After reading his e-mails, I had expected to find a man who'd found himself and was at last ready to bond with another. Instead, I found a more mature version of the same unhappy intern.

"I'm about forty pounds heavier than when you last saw me," Allen told me, munching on something as he spoke. "I've been on depression medication, but I don't like going to therapy. I'm trying to see if I can figure it out on my own. The HMOs were a burnout. I stopped work for a bit, though I will be going back. Sadly, I feel I've failed at every interpersonal relationship I've ever had. I thought then that I was just too young. That even though you were great, there would be women even better. But I've never met anyone else like you. If I only knew then what I know now—"

His voice trailed off. I waited.

"If I had just made a decision," he continued. "Maybe if I had just said yes then, I'd be in better shape now. Maybe we'd have grown together."

We'd have grown, all right. Into a fungus. One whose single cell split off into a variety of yeasts, molds, and smuts, creating a trail that led straight to divorce court. Allen could have no more committed to me than Philip could. And with so many missing ingredients, I was unable to commit to either of them. As lasting relationships, they were only recipes for disasters.

Yet I felt I had explored the possibilities with each of those men as far as I was able to go. And when the growth stopped, so did I. I moved on. Okay, not without a little drama and not without some tears, but I let my heart lead, and when the relationship was clearly not meant to be, my slate was clean for whoever was next.

But Allen and Philip shared something else in regard to me. For completely opposite reasons, the men experienced something I never did. Regret. Of all the feelings I had, that one did not make it on my list.

When I was dating, I was cultivating a relationship in the present, instead of resisting it in favor of a fictional future. If the present was lived to its fullest, the steps to the future would present themselves. The future would have to write itself. It was not set in a preconceived template.

At a recent family function, I saw my cousin's daughter, Dale. Twenty-two, she had just moved to New York without her boyfriend to begin a career in advertising.

"I really loved Billy, but I felt he would hold me back if I were to get a really great job," she said, anxiously picking at the fried potatoes she was fearful would put on pounds.

"But do you want to be with him now?" I asked. I'd found a real connection to be more than a little elusive, and it made me sad to think she'd let go of someone she might have loved.

"Yes, but I don't think that's good enough. I have to think about my future. What if he's right for now but not for later? Wouldn't it just be harder to break up?"

I couldn't answer her question, so I listened. There was no right answer, but there was no wrong one, either.

She was pining for Billy now. They were not separated because of the present. They were separated because of the unknown future. If Dale allowed herself to explore that relationship now, without worry, she would know in her heart whether it was something that would work for her. But, too afraid of *what would happen if*, she chose to go it on her own. One day Dale might look back and feel she had made the right choice. But she might just as easily look back with regret for not having seen it through the first time around. Especially when she was so young.

Being in your twenties is being young, though it doesn't feel that way until you're older. Forty will be young when you look back from sixty. How do you blend the desperation of getting ahead as fast as you can with the luxury of time? But is there another choice that would offer an option of happiness?

We'll never get to go down the same road two different ways. When I have to make a choice, I can only hope I'm making the best one. I've found I do better when I at least feel as if I can do anything. The more permission I give myself to do and feel what I want, the more I will reel myself in. Tell me I can eat the whole cake, I'll want only a slice. Tell me I can stay in bed all day, I'll get up and go to the gym. Tell me I can sleep with him, I'll have to see how I feel. But tell me I can't? Well . . . Then I wind up indulging the wrong feelings and embracing the no. That, I feel, is what many of the men in my life have done.

Recently, I saw yet another man I knew in my twenties. I was a waitress in a restaurant he then owned, and he was married. I was free, he was chained. And he wanted to have an affair. I liked him, and I confess I indulged my feelings. But only platonically. I wouldn't become involved with a married man.

Will lived in the suburbs and drove his convertible to the city for work. I'd often find him sitting outside my gym, waiting for me with the top down, picking me up after an acting class, or driving past my apartment building on a weeknight. Even then I was high on my indulgence theory, so I tried it out on him.

It worked. He left his wife.

I didn't feel guilty. I hadn't created his problems, nor had I exacerbated them. I'll admit to a little flirtation and a lot of fuel to his fire to find out what was making him so unhappy and to take a stand.

I received the call on a Saturday night as I was headed out the door to meet my friends and see a fellow actor in a play.

"Skip it and have dinner with me."

Will had wooed a bit too late for my taste. "I already have plans," I had said.

"Cancel them. I'm free," he replied.

"Exactly. You're not a married man sneaking around. You can call me up in advance and make a proper date."

He wouldn't. He dated another waitress. Eight months later, he went back to his wife. Years and years have gone by. On occasion he will still call. Only weeks ago, my doorbell rang at eleven A.M. on a Sunday morning.

"It's Will," I heard through the intercom. "Can I take you out for breakfast?"

Will felt the time that he had allowed himself away from his marriage only made it stronger when he returned. They've been together over forty years, so they must be doing something right.

"Do me a favor," said Will as he said goodbye to me on my corner. "If you ever run into Beverly, don't tell her I sometimes see you. I don't think it would be cool."

I assured him I would not, and chuckled as I walked away. Will was in his sixties. Still cute, still wearing jeans, and still driving around in search of some excitement. In my twenties, I remember feeling surprised by Will's midlife confusion. It was hard to grasp that he could be questioning things the same way I was, the same as my friends in our twenties. I remember feeling proud of him when he explored his feelings, and happy that they led him back home feeling renewed. I find it fun when I get that random call from sixtysomething Will now.

But I learned something from him that I have carried through in my romantic life. While we may age, while we may grow wiser, while we may develop reference points that make us choose a different route, when it comes to romance, we will always remain young. And the more we allow ourselves our true feelings, the younger we will always feel.

"I can't stop thinking *what if*."

It was the end of my conversation with Philip. He expressed that to me finally, and with great sadness.

"Oh, Philip," I said, sighing. For the first time in all these years, I felt it, too. Philip had held on so tight to his decision, his correct, right, practical decision to marry Sharon, that he would never acknowledge his feelings for me. I realized in the moment that I wanted him to.

"It won't hurt you, Philip," I coaxed. "Just say how you feel about me, how you feel about all this. Acknowledge the feelings you have. If you give in to them totally, I promise, it won't make you file for divorce. It won't make you cheat. I promise you'll be okay."

He was. Oh, it was a little teary. We had our moment.

A week later, I found a missed call on my cell. When I dialed the number, it belonged to Philip. I left a message saying hi. He didn't call me back. By giving in, he had let go.

He at last got to express himself in a way he hadn't been able to do in his twenties. But the twenties—what a great time to experiment! What could be better than to be young and independent? Having the luxury to stop and look around, to smell and rearrange the roses. Possibilities come our way as gifts. How great to open each one and experience it. No need to tie each package up in a bow; it might only wind up tying you up in knots!

I'm now in my forties. Because I haven't "settled down and married" traditionally, I've often felt my ribbons were untied, leaving all loose ends. But I notice I don't feel that way so much anymore. As I reach the end of this story, I am reminded of a poem I composed in a writing class I took my senior year of college.

> Packages
> inside me
> wait to be
> opened.

I took the class for fun. After all, I was a theater major, intent on becoming an actress. I did. I am. Yet these last three years, I find I have also become a professional writer. My hobby led the way. As for dating, well, I still do. For all I know, I may wake up one day and find myself married.

Embracing your own dreams and differences may lead you somewhere you never expected. No matter what your age, there's still time. Time for new gifts and new packages to open. I speak from experience when I say it's not so bad to be unbowed.

Lie #5

*"I'll be where I'm supposed
to be, doing what I'm
meant to be doing"*

Please Let's Speaking English

By Heather Swain

Exactly six weeks after I was married, I stood in a six-foot-by-six-foot bathroom next to a small Japanese man in bright blue toe socks. He spoke no English, and aside from a few polite but useless pleasantries, the sum total of my Japanese enabled me only to state with great enthusiasm, "I have green eyes!" Yet this man had been sent by my new employer, the Town of Sawara Board of Education, to teach me the art and science of working a Japanese *ofuro*, or bathtub, which, with its funny square shape and wooden lid, looked more like a giant rice cooker than a bathing device.

My husband, Dan, was back in Indiana, packing up his drum kit in sturdy black cases labeled FRAGILE and THIS SIDE UP. He and his drums would join me in another week to live for the next two years in our twenty-foot-by-ten-foot rectangular home that had straw tatami mats for floors and a trash can the size of a Big Gulp cup. It had taken me a while to convince Dan that we should move to Japan. "Think of the travel. We could go to Thailand!" "Haven't you ever wanted to learn another language?" "You love sushi!"

Really, I wanted to go to fulfill some romantic notion of starting our married life far from home in an exotic place where we knew nobody and could bask in the pleasure of each other. In the end, it was the incredible jazz scene in Tokyo that enticed him.

So when I landed a teaching job in a small farming town about an hour and a half outside Tokyo, we were both surprised, but agreed to take the plunge. Only months later, as I stood dumbfounded by my complete ineptitude with a Japanese tub, did I realize that my idyllic vision of solitary newlywed life halfway around the world was quickly slipping down the drain of domestic drudgeries such as learning how to bathe, cook, shop, and drive on the other side of the road, not to mention speaking, reading, or understanding the language in our new town.

Being a good midwestern gal, I wanted very much to please the Japanese man in front of me, who was by then sweating because it was at least 97 degrees outside and 104 degrees inside the tiny bathroom. I intently watched all the machinations he went through with the bathtub, and nodded as if I could comprehend even one word he uttered. First this knob. Then that switch. Next the red thingy. Not before the blue thingy. Then turn on the water, but don't forget the plug or . . . Here he mimicked what appeared to be an explosion and fire.

The thought that I could cook myself like some cannibal feast while trying to bathe made my bottom lip quiver. All I wanted was the tiniest comfort of home in my new apartment. I could live with the fact that all my neighbors would be ogling my American bras and panties drip-drying on the balcony, since there were no clothes dryers. Having no oven would be tougher to accept, since I loved to bake, but I had faith that I could learn to make brownies in a toaster oven. And I was genuinely growing fond of my futon that by day I had to roll up and shove into the closet in order to make enough room to walk around. But come on. Was it too much to ask for a shower with knobs for varying degrees of hot and cold water? I thought the Japanese were supposed to be so technologically advanced. I had imagined a completely automated apartment equipped with slick remote-control microwaves, fuzzy-logic washing machines, and my very own cleaning robot. Oh, dear God, I thought as I stood in that tiny sweltering bathroom on the verge of tears, please don't let me cry in front of this poor civil servant.

I wasn't exactly the most culturally sensitive person after five days in my new country. I knew the basics—how to bow and remove my shoes when entering a home—but usually, I felt like a Neanderthal stomping through a Victorian sitting room whenever I encountered Japanese people. I was certain that I offended at least one person on a daily basis with my sloppy American manners and overly expressive Western ways. In this situation, I had the horrible feeling that crying in front of a stranger in Japan could result in said stranger being forced to commit seppuku. Surely he would assume that he had greatly offended and troubled me if I were to become a blithering idiot in front of him. And over a bathtub, no less. Then again, it wasn't the bathtub that was bothering me. I realized as I towered over this man that I shouldn't have been in Japan, sweating and sniveling over the intricacies of plumbing. I should have been back in Indiana, where I belonged, happily married to my college sweetheart and finishing graduate school, like I'd been planning for years.

Although I was confident that Dan and I loved each other, and we'd always gotten along well, I realized in the minuscule bathroom that we'd never tested the boundaries of our life together. We'd had separate lives back in Indiana (me in graduate school and working, him traveling with a band), a situation that we believed helped keep our relationship fresh. But now, dear God, the two of us (plus an entire drum kit) would be crammed together in monk's quarters in a country where we were illiterate, dumb, and perpetually lost, with no one else to talk to. I could imagine sitting across from each other, night after night in that tiny apartment, bumping knees and complaining until frustration grew over us like a suffocating moss and we'd run screaming straight for a divorce before our newlywed life in Japan had a chance to begin.

Dan and I were married when we were twenty-six years old. We met during my senior year of college, when I was applying to doctoral programs in anthropology all over the country. I'd definitely noticed the dark-haired musician coming and going from the apartment below mine and thought he was cute, but otherwise, I was too busy focusing on my future as Dr. Swain, anthropologist extraordinaire, to pay him much attention. Then one day I walked into my bathroom to brush my teeth and heard him singing below me. He wasn't just singing. He was peeing and singing a jubilant song, and I thought, This is the kind of guy-for-me, someone who celebrates the simple things in life, like a good piss.

Although I would have been loath to admit it, being a feminist and all, after I fell in love, I didn't want to be separated from Dan. By the end of the school year, the happiness and fulfillment our relationship had brought to my life trumped the acceptances I'd received to Ph.D. programs in California, Chicago, and Texas. However, in my mind, throwing away a promising academic career for a relationship was the worst kind of muddled self-sacrifice a woman could make. If a friend had been going through the same thing, I would've counseled her to follow her career. I would've said things like "If the relationship is a good one, then it will endure the separation" and "If he loves you, he'll be supportive of you leaving" and "You never know how long a relationship will last, but a Ph.D. is forever."

Looking back, I realize that part of my drive to get a Ph.D. rather than a Mrs. was a yearning to distinguish myself from the girls I'd grown up with who finished college, then moved back to our small town for a life of wifedom and motherhood. Since high school, I'd been bucking and bridling against any path I perceived as leading me back home. Just what was so bad about my hometown? Well, nothing, really. It was a perfectly lovely place to grow up. Safe, familiar, cozy tree-lined streets where perfectly happy people greeted one another by name and secretly carried CIA-worthy mental portfolios of one another's lives. It would always be perfectly lovely and overly familiar but nothing more, which was the heart of the problem for me.

Some part of me feared that if I fell into such a life, my brain would atrophy, my midsection would expand, I would willingly wear polyester, make casseroles with canned soup, and talk about the lives of sitcom characters as if we were friends. Then someday I would wake up in my extra-large stretchy pants and look around, wondering how the hell I ended up in a split-level ranch house with a surly husband, ugly kids, and an ill-behaved yappy toy poodle. It was regret that I most feared, but not just any kind of regret. I could take it if I'd gone out into the world and failed, made mistakes, come back home licking my wounds, and admitting that life here wasn't so bad after all, but I could not accept the regret of complacency. Yet despite all the fears I had about choosing a man over a career, I couldn't quite imagine moving forward in my life without Dan. So, by some convoluted logic, I turned down all my acceptances to anthropology programs in other parts of the country and enrolled instead in a graduate program in philosophy at good ol' Indiana University in Bloomington, where Dan was finishing his undergraduate degree.

Dan and I quickly grew comfortable in our domestic bliss. We rented a sweet little house outside of campus with two bedrooms, a front porch, a backyard where I planted herbs and made a compost heap, and a basement where he practiced the drums and rehearsed with his band. By all accounts, we had a good life that could only get better in Indiana. So why, I asked myself as the Japanese man went through the motions of drawing me a bath yet again, had we chucked it all to live in the land of public squat toilets, overcrowded commuter trains, and fish bologna?

Up until then my experiences in Japan had consisted mainly of searching for food by dragging my dazed and delirious jet-lagged ass around the old part of town, where the streets were winding and indecipherable. One day I happened on a grocery store, but I lingered too long in front of the soy-sauce display and was elbowed out of the way and sneered at by old women bent over like question marks from years of working in the rice fields. I worked up the gumption to go into a ramen shop, where five men with leathery faces and smokers' hacks turned on their stools to stare unabashedly at me, then applauded and shouted "Beri good-o!" when I successfully used chopsticks. I even found an "American bakery" but couldn't quite bring myself to try the corn and spaghetti sandwiches or the deep-fried bun stuffed with hot dogs and rice topped with mayonnaise, on display in the front window. None of this fit the romantic vision I'd had of staring into Dan's eyes across a beautifully laid table while he fed me bits of silky raw fish with ancient lacquered chopsticks.

What the hell happened to me? I'd wonder after I'd find my way back to my apartment to devour yet another bag of seaweed-wrapped rice crackers. I used to be adventurous and spontaneous. The whole point of leaving Indiana was to experience new things, meet new people, expand my horizons, and create a lovely outpost for Dan and me to share at the beginning of our lives together. Now I was acting like the ugliest American, grousing and muttering about everything unfamiliar and inconvenient, rather than finding joy or amusement in all the weird and wonderful ways of the Orient.

The whole idea to move to Japan was mine, and in my interminable style, I badgered Dan until he agreed to get married, quit his band, sell most of our belongings, and move across the world so I could teach English as a second language to sullen Japanese middle-schoolers. It's not that teaching English was a dream of mine. Nor did I have any particular interest in Japan, but I'd made a Japanese friend in graduate school, and hearing about the life she'd left behind in a small rural town made me realize how much of the world I hadn't seen yet and would likely never see if I stayed the course I'd set at home. Before I was halfway through with graduate school, I'd begun to get fidgety in Indiana. I began to wonder if I had merely traded one version of a complacent domestic life (the one I feared re-creating in my hometown) for another (the one Dan and I were creating on our own in Bloomington).

Couldn't we have simply taken a great honeymoon, like normal people? This thought dawned on me as the Japanese man showed me how to work the tub yet again. I could tell by the weary tone of his voice and his slumping shoulders that he needed me to nod and pretend to understand so we could be done with the surreal game of bathtub charades. Couldn't I have been satisfied with a cruise or maybe even some sort of eco-tour in a South American jungle? Did I have to actually move to Japan, where my sole source of entertainment for a week had been watching strange, masochistic, semi-pornographic game shows on TV? Dumping anthropology for philosophy was one thing. Quitting my Ph.D. program another. But those reversals ultimately affected only me. Now I had committed the biggest about-face in my history, only this time I was dragging Dan with me in the name of romance.

The Japanese man looked at me hopefully as the bathtub filled with steamy water. I grimaced and nodded uncertainly, but I couldn't possibly ask him to show me how to do it again. Mostly because if either of us had stayed in that room for another minute, we'd have been dead from heat exhaustion. We shuffled out into the kitchen, mopping our brows, grateful for the slight breeze coming in through an open window the size of a manila envelope. Then someone knocked on my door. Fearing that the Board of Education had sent another unsuspecting soul to my apartment to show me how to turn on my stove and warn me about gas poisoning and more explosions, I hesitated. Another knock. The Japanese man motioned toward the door, as if perhaps, being American and all, I didn't understand the whole knocking-and-answering thing. To appease him, I opened the door and found Mr. Suzuki, my supervisor from the Board of Ed.

I bobbed and bowed, extremely grateful to see Suzuki-san because he spoke a little English and always carried a pocket-sized Japanese-to-English dictionary when he was with me. He removed his shoes and came into the kitchen, then spoke to the bathtub man, who sucked air against his teeth and shook his head apologetically. I could just imagine what he was saying: "I tried, I really truly tried, but she's an idiot." I offered a pathetic smile to Mr. Suzuki, who thanked the bathtub man and told him he could go.

Next Mr. Suzuki pulled out a piece of notebook paper and began to read to me. "Ah, Miss Heather," he said. "In one week you have the husband coming to live with you. The Board of Education believe this apartment maybe too small for you to live. We find bigger apartment. The rent is more expensive. I will take you there now to meet the landlord."

Although I wanted to throw my arms around the man's neck and hug him like a long-lost uncle, I knew better than to put my grubby American paws on him. Instead, I bowed deeply and said, "Onegaishimasu." Please.

The apartment was just a few blocks away, down a quiet street, tucked behind a large walled garden. It was huge compared to the place I'd been living. Two large tatami rooms with closets, a balcony, a separate kitchen, a room with a toilet, and get this, a shower with a digital thermometer. "We'll take it!" I said before he even told me the rent.

Next he took me to meet Mrs. Yanagimachi, the landlady. She answered her door in a traditional kimono and invited us in for tea and rice crackers. After we'd exchanged pleasantries in Japanese, she look squarely at me and said, "Please let's speaking English." I nearly melted into a teary puddle of appreciation. I had a glimmer of understanding then that all I'd needed over the past week was someone to talk to, to share my experiences with, to ask questions of, and to feel reassured by. Yanagimachi-san told me about the other American English teachers who lived in the town but were gone for summer holidays. She told me about the members of her women's club, who wanted to take English lessons with me. It also turned out that she taught lessons on the koto, a large traditional Japanese floor harp, so she knew several musicians in town and a possible practice space for Dan to rent.

I peppered her with questions. Where could I buy fresh fish? Why did the stoplights play "Edelweiss" whenever the light changed from red to green? Why did groups of little boys point at me, yell "Gaijin!" and run away laughing hysterically? How come I never saw women in the pachinko parlors? Why were some melons wrapped in gold tissue paper, and how come they cost nearly fifty dollars? Mrs. Yanagimachi and Mr. Suzuki smiled politely at all my questions and tried their best to answer. Eventually, I realized that I was making them uncomfortable and thanked them profusely, then shut up and sipped my tea.

When I left Mrs. Yanagimachi's house, I felt infinitely relieved. I couldn't wait to call Dan in Indiana and tell him about my day. I imagined him at home, out for a beer with friends who would question him about our new life in Japan and wonder why we would leave everything we had. By then I knew why. The next step for us in Indiana was more of the same. For me, it was finishing school in a subject I was uncertain about while working a job I was good at but not passionate about. For him, it was touring around with the same five guys in a van, playing the same music until the band either "made it" and had to tour more or got sick of one another and broke up. It would have been scraping the money together for a down payment on a house and then having a baby or two until we were so entrenched in our domestic lives that tossing everything aside to move halfway across the world would have been impossible. We were moving to Japan because we could, and that was romantic enough.

I couldn't wait for Dan to arrive in our new town. I couldn't wait to show him the vending machines that dispensed cold cans of sweet milky iced coffee, called BM. Or the snack I'd found at the convenience store called Colon that was shaped like little yellow tubes stuffed with some strange brown paste. To hold his hand while walking along the canal that passed three-hundred-year-old thatched-roof houses in the old town. To teach him the few rudimentary Japanese phrases I'd picked up, like the most useful *zen zen wakarimasen* ("I understand absolutely nothing you are saying to me") and the way to bow and how he could slip his shoes on and off at the door without using his hands. There was so much for us to learn and do and see.

For the first time, I realized that it wouldn't have mattered if our apartment was small or we couldn't work the bathtub. We'd figure it out and find humor in our circumstances. When we chose to leave everything familiar and start our married life with adventure, we set a precedent that would serve us well in the years ahead. We could've gone anywhere, really—New York, Nashville, Bangkok, and later, we would. The point was to break out of a life of familiarity and challenge ourselves before we settled happily into the sweet complacency of a couple who's content with the experience of their lives. Japan didn't have to be the most romantic place on earth to start a marriage. The romance would come from plunging ourselves into something new and carrying a lifetime of shared memories from our experiences together. Japan was a great place to start.

The Road Almost Taken

By Anna Jane Grossman

When I was a kid, my mother was fond of telling me how she could track every good thing in her life—her current husband, her job, me—to a series of banal events that took place when she was twenty-five. Had she not had a dentist's appointment one night after work, she would've gotten to the grocery before it closed and wouldn't have gone out for a quick dinner with her neighbor. Had she not gone to that particular restaurant that night, she wouldn't have been hit on by the man at the table next to hers, and she never would have ended up marrying him.

Sure, it was an unhappy marriage. Sure, she'd spend the next half decade glumly making casserole while her future ex-husband watched football and did the crossword puzzle she'd set aside for herself.

However, that marriage put her on the path to her current life. A life she likes.

It was something I found myself thinking about a lot in the few days right after I turned twenty-five—days I was spending on press junket in London to chronicle the city's best new restaurants for the *New York Post*.

I was turning every little decision into a question of destiny.

For instance, when I found I was running out of cash and didn't have enough to buy a day pass on the tube, the simple question of how to buy a ticket caused all kinds of reverb in my mind. Perhaps I could just plunk down enough for one ticket and walk the rest of the day? Maybe this would somehow lead to my finding a Prince Charming who'd take me around town in a chauffeured car? Or perhaps a day pass would be the better way to go? Could this decision mean the difference between happiness and misery? Health and sickness? Life and death? Blond and brunette?

Ticket or day pass . . . Day pass! No, no . . . ticket. Or maybe . . .

Eh, screw it. I decided to walk.

My afternoon stop was high tea with a hotel publicist and two other journalists from lifestyle magazines in California and Florida. One had just gotten married, and the other two were in the midst of planning their weddings. The women were all around my age, and I was looking forward to sharing our eatery finds when I realized it was going to be a long teatime.

"Have you considered releasing doves?"

"I'm a big fan of tulle."

"I'm just in love with the fondue set we got."

"I was hoping for a cushion-cut diamond, but in the end, he decided the marquise-cut in platinum suited me best . . ."

Such a wide world, and yet I'd come all the way to London only to find myself listening to the same conversation I'd been hearing from women day after day back home.

I slumped deep into my chair, wondering how long I could go without participating in their little chat before it'd be rude. For a never-married single person, it was a discussion in which I could hold my own. I was the founding editor of the wedding section of the New York Post. Before that, I'd spent two years writing the engagements section at The New York Observer. I'd written for more wedding magazines than I cared to admit—but it wasn't the sort of thing I wanted to discuss. I hadn't chosen the wedding-writing business as much as I'd stumbled into it.

Marriages, to me, had always been things to be observed from afar. Was a wedding something I'd always wanted? Yes. Had I thought as a kid that I'd be happily married by age twenty-five? Yes. But I was starting to think that maybe it wasn't in my blood. I always ended up with guys who would forget to call for weeks at a time, or who'd start conversations in bed like "One day when we break up . . ."

Just like I knew I could never be an Olympic gymnast or a Republican, I was starting to think that, as nice as marriage seemed in theory, it was my duty in life not to partake in it, but rather, to chronicle it from afar.

"Cushion cuts have great clarity. I'm also a fan of the Asscher diamonds, especially when they're VS1," I threw in for good measure—I didn't want to seem like I was ignoring them. If only I *could* ignore them.

Truth be told, I'd once been a bit wedding-crazy.

But then I turned five.

At three, I was a bride for Halloween. At four, my cousin called off her wedding, and I was crushed, since to me this meant mainly that I was never going to be a flower girl. Distressed, I asked my dad and his girlfriend if they could get married so I could show off the petal-spreading techniques I'd honed for so many months.

"We can't," she said. "I'm not divorced yet from my first husband."

"Have a divorce party!" I said. "I can throw down the petals and then stomp on them."

Later on that same year, the marital problems in my family entered the realm of legend: My great-grandpa Simon became the oldest man in the world ever to get divorced. He got his own entry in the *Guinness Book of World Records*. More impressive yet, he became a *Jeopardy!* question.

Yet where there's divorce, there's also hope—the initial hope that your union will work out, and then the later hope that there's something better out there than the person you are divorcing. Nevertheless, I hoped early on it would never happen to me. No one dreams of divorce. Just as poor children must fantasize about riches, I dreamed of white dresses and happily-ever-afters.

But my genes have never pointed in that direction.

My parents have been married a cumulative five times. They had their wedding in a local kosher luncheonette after dating on and off for three years. My mother, six months pregnant with me, wore maroon. My dad wore no underwear. They separated two years later.

It was a venture arguably more successful than my mother's aforementioned first marriage. In a family of four girls, she was the only one to trespass beyond twenty without a husband. So her father encouraged her to marry the first stable thing that came along, and she ended up with the guy at the next table at that restaurant that fateful day.

When Grandpa walked her down the aisle, he whispered words of encouragement in her ear: "Better you marry now and divorce in a few years than continue running around like a tramp."

His insistence on enforced coupling—happy or not—didn't stop with her, either.

There was only one question he used to ask me whenever he'd call: "Are you married yet?"

It would be asked playfully, but it still became rather irksome after a while. The answer was always roughly the same. "No, Grandpa! I'm only *eight!*"

When I was fifteen, my grandfather died, and I went seven years without being asked if I had an intended. I spent those years doing what most unmarried teenagers did. I smoked pot. I cried for no reason. I worried that I'd never have sex. I had sex. I had a boyfriend or two . . .

And no cared if I was married.

Then I entered my early twenties. I cried for no reason. I worried I'd never have sex again. I graduated from college. I had a one-night stand or two and a few boyfriends. I had bounced checks and full-time jobs, pregnancy scares and appendicitis. And, although my aunts did ask if the men I was dating were Jewish ("Nope! But he *is* circumcised"), no one asked me if I was married.

Then, at age twenty-two, while working at *The New York Observer*, I got assigned to write the engagement-announcements column, and every week I met and interviewed three or four couples—*happy* couples!—who were about to tie the proverbial knot. Every week at least one bride would need to ask the question: Are YOU married yet?

I know this was usually intended to mean:

"Have you been through all this before?"

"Do you understand the bliss we're going through right now?"

"You're asking us all about our relationship, so it's only polite that we ask about yours."

But when translated through my cortex, the words got mightily jumbled:

"Why aren't you married yet?"

"No guy has ever found you worthy?"

"Perhaps you have a body-odor problem?"

I disdained these women for being so happy, and envied them at the same time. Was the problem indeed in my blood? Perhaps I had unrealistically high standards? Or were their standards just super-low? Was I not as capable of being adored as these brides-to-be?

In short, I couldn't help but siphon all these comments into the simple conclusion: I will never find happiness, like no one in my family has.

The twenty-nine-year-old reporter who sat next to me at work—a frumpy woman who described her wardrobe as "Cambridge-shrink chic"—used to shake her head in wonder when I'd hang up after conducting a phone interview with one of the many moony couples I met during my tenure. "I don't know how you do it," she'd say. The answer was easy, at least in those first few months: I was only twenty-two.

Everyone I wrote about was older by at least a year or two, if not a decade or more. On the grand calendar in the sky, I was not yet behind schedule. I wasn't pleased with my romantic situation, but I also wasn't too freaked out.

That is, until something terrifying happened: I turned twenty-three. Suddenly, I was meeting people my age who were getting hitched; I started meeting engaged people who were—the horror!—even younger than me.

That summer my own cousin, born the same year as I, announced she was going to do the deed.

Where was my wedding? Where were my flower girls? Where was my cushion-cut diamond?

"Are *you* married?"

The women at tea in our fancy London hotel were looking up at me from over their crumpets; they'd finally noticed I'd escaped into reverie. No, I wasn't married. No, no one in my immediate family was, either. Yes, I did want to get married, even if the result would only be entering the brainless state that these women had entered. Brainless but happy.

Interestingly, these ladies didn't seem to care if I had a boyfriend, even though I did, sort of. I'd been unenthusiastically seeing a guy named Bill for several months. His fervor for me was equal to mine for him. He'd forget to call me for weeks at a time; he'd rarely pay when we went out for dinner. He didn't give me anything for my birthday. He often canceled dates because he was too busy cleaning his apartment. Much of the time I was unsure he really liked me very much. I was also unsure I liked him. Yet momentum had carried us through the fall and winter, the best cuddling months of the year.

In short, I was closer to unhappy than happy about my job, my apartment, my finances, Bill . . . Everything was seeming a little stuck in gear, with no signs of getting oiled anytime soon.

A husband, perhaps, was the best solution.

Short of that, a nap seemed like it'd do the trick. I excused myself from the ladies and scones and clotted cream and headed for my room.

A few hours later, at a cocktail party, I was stood up by a British girlfriend who was to be my dinner companion. The prospect of dining alone at an expense-account meal seemed grim. Grimmer still was the idea of inviting one of the other journalists on the junket and spending an evening discussing the possibility of orchid centerpieces. So, in a moment of extreme chutzpah, I approached a man standing alone by the bar. He was clean-cut and wore a sweater vest and had un-British teeth. His looks didn't matter much—what mattered was that he was there.

"Look, I know this is odd, and we don't know each other," I said. "But would you be interested in coming to dinner with me? My date just canceled, and I don't know anyone else here and I have a reservation for two."

He smiled and blushed. "I'd love to, but I can't. I'm waiting for my girlfriend," he said. "However, I'm here with a friend who has no plans. Maybe you could bring him?"

Another hour later, I was in that aforementioned chauffeured car, with a cashmere-clad, balding, but rather handsome forty-year-old by my side. His name was Lars.

"I feel like I'm Cinderella and you're Prince Charming, whisking me away," I said.

"Aren't you the one paying for dinner?" he countered.

Indeed I was. But he ended up completely orchestrating the evening. He was the owner of one of the city's top restaurants and knew the owner of the place where we were going. She sent us free nibbles the whole dinner, and he picked out the perfect wine for each course. We sat for hours, and he told me about his private planes and collection of fancy cars. He told me how he gladly supported his aged mother, whom he adored.

"Are you for real?" I couldn't help but ask.

Lars just smiled back. "Why would I lie?"

I know it sounds nutty, but the truth is, I believed him. I figured, Why not? I'd never see the man again after the meal, and if he was lying, his untruths were at least making for an interesting evening.

At two A.M., the restaurant closed, and we moved on to an after-hours club to continue our conversation. We ordered sidecars, and then he started kissing me. I wasn't feeling particularly attracted to him, but I'd had enough to drink that it didn't matter much.

"You're amazing," he kept telling me.

I hated to disagree; however, I had to point out that he didn't know me at all. In fact, he'd asked very few questions about me the entire evening, as far as I could remember.

But then the questions began.

"If I got you a job in London, do you know which paper you'd most like to work at?"

"If we wintered somewhere, would you prefer Brazil or Greece?"

"Have you ever considered getting married?"

Huh?

I started to feel freaked out. Flattered but freaked out. Was I being proposed to by a man I'd just met, or was this some kind of ploy to get me into bed? Was this how all those glossy, happy women I interviewed every day ended up with rings on their fingers?

Would I be crazy to even consider having this conversation, or would I be crazy not to?

Then I started thinking about Bill. We weren't meant to be. We probably wouldn't make it until the summer, and not just because he didn't have air-conditioning. Yet I did feel some loyalty to him. It didn't feel right to just blindly shirk off our months together in order to entertain a fantasy being had by this man I didn't even think I was attracted to.

"I think I need to get back to my hotel," I said. He kissed me hard and asked me if he could join me.

"No!" I said. His pleas continued during the ride back to the hotel. He put his cashmere scarf around my neck. He begged.

"We don't have to sleep together," he said.

"Thanks for letting me know I have an option," I said.

"I didn't mean it that way," he said. "I just don't want you to go. Please let me come with you. I want to be with you a little longer."

When I finally wrangled myself out of his grip and got up to the room, the phone was ringing, although it was almost four in the morning.

I picked up.

"Can I come around to take you to breakfast in the morning?" Lars asked.

"You know, you're starting to creep me out," I said.

He was silent for a good fifteen seconds. "Look, I know. I know I'm coming on very strong. It's just that I also know you're leaving tomorrow, and I really like you, so I'm trying to get my fill. Perhaps I could come visit you in New York next weekend?"

"Good night," I said.

Not four hours later, the phone was ringing again.

"I've figured it out," he said when I picked up. "You'll stay here the rest of this weekend. Skip your flight today. I'll pay for your return on Sunday. I'll spend the weekend showing you the city. It'll be wonderful. Please say yes."

I was dumbstruck.

Could I really do that? Was this guy a total psycho or just a nutty romantic?

I was leaning toward the psycho conclusion, and yet I was actually tempted—by the excitement of it all; by the spontaneity and the possibility of an escape from my life. Tempted because, really, would I ever be in this position again? I pictured myself mouthing the word "okay." How would that feel? Could I do it? "Oh . . ." I said. "Wow. That's quite an offer."

"Please say yes."

I pictured him coming back to get me in his Porsche convertible or his black Ferrari (he'd talked to me at length about both). I imagined him wrapping me in a cashmere blanket and feeding me chocolates while driving across the Thames.

I also pictured having to beg to get him to get me a ticket home; I pictured being raped and murdered and written up in the awful London papers.

But what about the chocolates? What about the cashmere?

"I can't," I said, digging my nails into my palms. "Thank you. But I can't."

"I promise I'm not a lunatic," he said. "I am what I say am. You can check! I'm on Google!"

"I can't," I said. "Thanks, but I just can't."

That afternoon on the flight home, I realized I could still change my mind and get a ticket back to London the following weekend.

I could still do a lot of things, in fact. I could be Lars's wife by year's end. I could have a big white wedding. I could never have to work again. I could become a kept woman. In that one moment on the phone with him, I could have changed the course of my life forever.

Then again, maybe it's possible to do that at any moment of any day?

I could also go home and not shower for a week and eat nothing but macaroni and cheese and have no husband to care one way or the other. I could go join the Peace Corps. I could trek naked through the Brazilian rain forests or decide to become a nun or sleep with a different man every night for the next year.

I was twenty-five, unmarried, and standing in a hallway of open doors. Behind every door lay the possibility to be happy, even if there was no fondue set or diamond involved.

Before I had even unpacked back home, my phone was ringing. I could see it was Lars on the caller ID.

As I held the phone in my hand, my brain flashed on what we'd look like together as a couple . . . what it would be like to move . . . what it would be like to not work . . . what it would be like to *not* write about happy couples all the time. Would I still be the same me? A me whom I actually maybe didn't hate so much to begin with?

If divorce is a form of hope of something better out there, then opting to not begin a relationship with someone—can't that be a form of hope, too?

My brain flashed on the corridor doors. This time, however, I was standing there with Lars, and a lot of those doors were closed.

Then the call went to voice mail, and I went on with a life I'd never been more excited to live.

Homesick for the Place You've Never Been

By Julianna Baggott

Whatever you do, don't fall in love with a poet." This was my mother's parting advice. She's Southern and believes in parting advice. And the advice wasn't bad, especially as I was twenty-two and heading off to grad school. In fact, I agreed with her. Of course I wouldn't fall in love with a poet. The poets I'd known in high school and college were pale boys who stood outside of the dances and bars wearing trench coats and eyeliner, looking teary. Sensitive and poignant though this may be, they weren't my type.

Plus, I wasn't going to grad school to meet men. I was going to write. I was tired of men. It's astonishing to me now how extremely tired of men you can be at twenty-two. But I was. I'd built a few from the ground up—teaching them emotions, a use of language, and eventually, some grunted manners. But I can't be too self-congratulatory. I'd ruined my share as well. In fact, I'd recently ruined someone's career at NASA, broken up someone else's engagement, and been blamed for a sizable car accident (no fatalities). I wanted to put the whole idea of men in the back of a sock drawer and forget about them like an aged baggy of disappointing weed.

In reality, my mother was probably at a loss about what parting advice to give. I was going off to graduate school in creative writing, of all things, and what could she say about that without shrugging? My family didn't have a background in literary arts. My father once won a safety-motto writing competition at Du-Pont, where he was a lawyer. The motto was published on #2 pencils, and no one exactly remembers it, though it had to do with driving in icy conditions. This was the extent of our experience in the world of publishing.

My parents did know the arts. My father has written down on an index card the name and location of every play he's ever seen. I'd seen full-frontal nudity in a production of *Hair* by the time I was nine (this was the seventies, when people did these kinds of things). By thirteen, I had an unruly crush on the playwright David Mamet.

By the time I'd packed up for grad school, my oldest sister had already been a struggling-actress-turned-director/producer for years, dating actors. This would eventually work to my advantage. There was only one thing worse than falling in love with a poet, and that was falling in love with an actor.

You know where I'm headed. The only question now is how quickly did I fall in love with a poet? There was a potluck before classes started. He was the first person I saw as I walked up to the house. He was talking to the host's kid, a towheaded third-grader. I didn't know he was a poet yet, but there were only two kinds of writers (poetry or fiction) at this party, so I had a fifty-fifty chance. He had shaggy hair and blue eyes with dark lashes—but no eyeliner. In lieu of the trench coat, he wore a pair of wrinkled khaki shorts and sandals. He had this smile. I loved how it worked its way onto his ruddy cheeks.

He said, "Hi," as if he'd been waiting for me and had just started to worry that I wasn't going to make it but was relieved I'd shown up.

I said, "Hi," back, as if I was sorry that I'd been running late, but, a little breathless, I was here now. He introduced himself. His name was Dave Scott.

I told him how I've always been suspicious of people with two first names. "It seems greedy—as if you're trying to avoid the way last names lend themselves to fourth-grade meanness—rhyming in singsong."

"What's your last name?"

"Baggott."

"Does Baggott rhyme with something?" This is funny, coming from a poet. This is like poetry stand-up. "I was called Dave Snot. Were you ever called Dave Snot?" he asked.

I'd never been called Dave Snot.

That night I remember the towhead and her brother lighting firecrackers that skittered across the pavement. It was dark. It was hard to tell if Dave was staring at me or not. Later, a lot of people piled into his shitty Honda, and when the radio accidentally hit an easy-listening station, I started belting out "Brandy." I'm this kind of unfortunate drunk. Despite this, we exchanged phone numbers on a fire escape.

From there—what? There was a dinner with friends. He offered to drive me home. I had ridden there on a gargantuan tank of a bicycle from the forties, when, I suppose, tanks were all the rage. It was a loaner from a nearby aunt. Dave walked my bike a few blocks to his car, nearly as far as my place. He shoved it into in the back of his Honda. But the Honda didn't start. He tried it a couple more times. Then we both sat there a minute.

"I know what's wrong," I said.

He looked at me, a little startled, overly hopeful. "You know cars?"

"Yes," I said. "This one doesn't make any noise when you turn the key. It needs to make noise."

He found this charming. I found it charming that he found it charming.

I remark on the fact that I'd sworn off men. Sure. Yes. But that seemed all at once like an antiquated notion, a lark, a ruse, like something that sounds good while on a bender, but now, in the sober light of day, is obviously preposterous—like trying to put on a full-scale production of *West Side Story* set at your local 7-Eleven. Who would tackle such an unnatural feat?

And so he walked me and my bike to my place. That was when I realized I didn't have my key. It was in my pocketbook, which I'd left at the dinner party. And so it went . . . Eventually, there was kissing.

Eventually, there was sex.

Do I have to get into the sex?

I'll say this: I think I'm as tired of writing about sex now as I was tired of men back then. Men were work. They took effort. They needed cajoling. They needed counseling and comfort. They were, by and large, talking sofas.

But not this one. This one fit. This one worked me. He counted syllables on my back after sex, and when he said beautiful things about me, the meter was perfect. I confessed my love of the color of blue rubber bands on broccoli, and he brought me just such a bunch in lieu of flowers. It was this kind of courtship. Sometimes I'd trip him on purpose when we were walking, and he'd understand that it was a kind of autistic tic I had for showing affection. And I got over it.

It was the early-morning racquetball dates that tipped my mother off. "Eight o'clock in the morning court time? Who is this guy?"

I broke it to her as gently as I could. "I have good news on that front," I said.

"What's that?"

"I'm not dating an actor."

This was before I found out that he wasn't *just* a poet.

He was, in fact, a Shriver poet.

He told me this when he invited me to a Shriver family reunion—on a two-hundred-acre Shetland pony farm just outside of Baltimore. We'd been eating beans and rice, gauging our wine on how badly it stained our teeth purple. I was caught off guard.

"As in Maria Shriver?" I asked. "And Sarge? And the tennis pro?"

He said that Aunt Hat and Uncle Holden, the hosts, had in fact been to Maria and Arnold's wedding.

"Do you think Maria and Arnold will be there?"

He shrugged. In all fairness, he didn't know. He hadn't been to the farm since he was a boy.

He was little help, and I was ill prepared. I'd only been to my own family reunions in West Virginia, where my sister the actress once won a new Sears blender in a husband-calling contest. What does one wear to a Shetland-pony-farm Shriver reunion? A hat? I'd heard rich people wore hats to horse-related events. And what would I say to Arnold, exactly, when we met? "You and your wife have excellent jawlines, perhaps the best jawlines of any couple in America"? Dave and I would be spending the night, and I wondered if I might bump into Arnold and Maria in the morning, after taking a bubble bath in some claw-footed marble tub. I wondered if they'd fly in via helicopter, touching down on a grassy lawn. I'd learned from watching *Dallas* that rich people had heliports in their backyards.

Now, don't get me wrong. I'm not the type to go for the money. I think that I've already established that: I was trying to become a writer. But as we drove up the coast in the Honda—seven hours with the heat on full blast to protect the engine—the prospect of a timely death of an elderly doting Shriver crossed my mind. I knew Dave had no money, but with Shrivers in the wings, how long would it be before a trust fund, a simple inheritance? I didn't dwell on it, but when two young writers get together, there is an unspoken argument that exists on a molecular level from the first instant. It's an argument about time, and arguments about time are usually arguments about money, lightly disguised. Imaginative by trade, we were both aware that if this were to work out long-term, we would be jockeying for housewife. Writers want to be at home, by and large, close to their own screen. Because I had no real sense of money—not wealth and not poverty—I thought about the future only abstractly.

I knew better than to tell my mother about the Shriver aspect of the reunion. Why orchestrate disappointment?

When we drove down the dirt driveway to the mansion, I was reminded of the fact that the rich are an unpredictable lot. We were greeted by about fifteen itchy dogs on the front porch, mangy dogs, more than one having a stump where a leg should be. There was a tree growing out of a crumbling chimney, a bird-shit-stained statue of Saint Francis, the yard spotted with noisy barking wild peacocks. Maria and Arnold were not there, and it was pretty obvious early on that they wouldn't be touching down. However, the guest list wasn't without its surprises: a Communist uncle and, if memory serves me correctly, a weasel-raising cousin. (Was that right? Do people raise weasels?)

But this was nothing once we got the full tour by our knowledgeable guide, the weasel raiser's mother. There was a small room devoted to thirty-some years of unopened mail, much of which was probably monthly payments of people who'd bought their little girls now-long-dead Shetland ponies.

In the upstairs bathroom, a sword hung on the wall next to a picture of a Shriver holding up the decapitated head of a native of someplace unidentifiable. There was a room for the sole purpose of dying, cleverly called "the death room." The walls were lined with pictures of famous people on their deathbeds, presidents, mostly. A fake bookcase led to a Prohibition-inspired hiding place. In one corner was an eight-legged formaldehyde-steeped calf in a glass case. The attic walls were covered in World War I posters and newspaper headlines, the ceiling decorated in a similar fashion for World War II. A ham hung from a beam, but the caretaker had been dead for years, so no one was sure how long the ham had been curing. The attic stretched on and on, room after little room, each filled with giant steamer trunks of God knows what. Silver? Shriveled hams? Shrunken heads? Impossible to say.

I was horrified, naturally. But I'd read some Flannery O'Connor by this time, some Márquez. Although I didn't know what to do with it, I knew an eroding literary landscape when I saw one. On some level, I understood all of this as a gift.

Dave was stunned by it all, too. He said, "I just remember the ponies. I was a kid, you know. Kids remember ponies."

The food was covered with flies, picked over by cats. I walked in on a caterer crying in the bathroom. Dave and I ended up splitting a Twix bar that he happened to find in the glove compartment. We were in this together.

We were shown to our room, next door to the death room. I was afraid to sleep on the sheets—it was all so deathly. Dave lay down, and I slept on top of him at first. Finally exhausted, I relented.

This is the point when the relationship should start to lose steam. Hadn't he misled me? Wasn't this oddness just a little too much to bear? But that isn't quite how it played out.

Oddly enough, our hosts, Aunt Hat and Uncle Holden, were endearing, holding hands as they greeted people from their wicker porch seats, which creaked like their own old bones. She wore a faded housedress. He was a retired banker with crusted mustard on his suit lapel and a droopy boutonniere. They rode around in golf carts. They were, in their own way, inspiringly romantic.

It was a landscape of stump-legged dogs and barking peacocks and golf carts, as foreign and fecund as a jungle. It was an estate rotting, yes, but from neglect of earthly possessions, an inability to part with the past, and a love of the living, a love that extended to ponies, strays, and even, or so it seemed, flies. This is where Dave and I would really fall in love.

In the morning, we brushed our teeth together for a long time.

Taken by this new image of being not one but two people, we looked at ourselves in the spotty mirror, spitting and rinsing, glancing from our own reflections to the other's and back again.

"Your nose is crooked," I said.

He leaned in to the mirror. "It just curves out on this side and dents in on the other. It's not crooked."

"By the time you're eighty, your nose will be in your ear."

"No, it won't," he said.

"Noses grow the length of lives." I had heard this on *Geraldo*. I was relieved that Dave didn't ask for my source. "I hate to tell you, but your nose is headed very definitely east."

Dave continued to brush and then responded, "My nose has, if anything, been sharpened, refined, in search of its element."

"Its element is obviously located in the East," I said. Dave, a little concerned, took a closer look at his nose. To make him feel better, I added, "Look, my nose is hooked under, the nostrils are tucked way up under there. You can't even see the nostrils what with the hooking."

We both looked at our noses, as if seeing them for the first time. And then Dave said, "So your nose will grow into your mouth. Everything you say will come out garbled." He paused. "But I'll only be able to hear half of it anyway, what with my nose in my ear."

With this, he pointed to our future together, what I realized in the moment that I wanted to believe: We would grow old together. It was the first small proposal in a series of small proposals.

I said that we would be great fun for the grandkids, perhaps they could even wheel us in for Show-and-Tell. That was how I accepted—a first small acceptance in a series of small acceptances. As if adding a bit of mood, a flake of the moldy ceiling drifted down and settled into the rusty sink like snow.

On one level, I didn't expect to fall in love. I saw this other future version of myself, a merciless, lonesome writer, banged up, brooding, bullying her way through life. But honestly, I also felt like this was the person I'd been waiting for. There was a feeling of relief—a feeling of *Oh, here you are, finally*. And this is what you look like. And this is what your voice sounds like. And this is the set of your childhood memories. I'd thought I'd been looking, but really, I was just waiting *for him* without knowing that I was waiting, without knowing that I missed him. I thought the ache was a restless lonesomeness, but it was more like homesickness for a place you haven't yet come to.

That's how the story begins. I was twenty-two and my mother said, "Don't fall in love with a poet," and I did and we've been together ever since.

Twenty-Nine-Year-Old Nomad Seeks Home

By Giselle Zado Wasfie

I am twenty-nine years old, it's fall 2005, and I have just moved back to California. As I unpack boxes in my new, empty studio flat nestled between the drag queens and dirty sidewalks of Hollywood Boulevard and the trendy trucker-hat boys and greenery of Los Feliz, I recite a familiar checklist: Need to buy a Hoover, go to IKEA for a new bed frame, should I even get a TV this time?

It's been a windy road back to the Golden State. From being a sheltered girl reared in mid-Michigan, during my twenties I've hauled my arse from New York to Santa Monica, Chicago to London, and now back west. It's come at a cost greater than mover fees, please believe.

Last year, in London, I applied for a job at my university. When the interviewer asked for my personal information, I had:

- a driver's license from Michigan
- a permanent address in Chicago
- a local address in the UK
- Job references from New York City

She shot me a quizzical look.
"I'm not on the run." I laughed.
She didn't.

(My humor never translated well across the pond.)

While my more "stable" friends have launched careers, birthed babies, and acquired mortgages, I've blazed a different gypsy trail. Or five. I've reinvented myself almost as much as my homestate pride, Madonna herself.

In New York City, I wore Manolo Blahniks and worked in editorial at *Glamour* magazine. I ate fancy salads in the multimillion-dollar Frank Gehry–designed Condé Nast cafeteria and gossiped about J.Lo (firsthand, mind you). I spent my nights drinking cheap alcohol with other creative types in Alphabet City. In fact, for one whole year, my friends and I would gather each Tuesday at Doc Holliday's on the corner of Ninth Street and Avenue A for all-you-can-drink-for-five-bucks Bud Light Nights. Hallelujah!

"Play 'You Can't Always Get What You Want'!" a patron would predictably yell across the smoky saloon. People love to hear that damn song when they're drunk (I'm no exception to the "reception").

Inevitably, "Dueling Banjos" would come on the jukebox, capping off the night with some slumming-from-the-Upper-East-Side ladies cowgirl-dancing on top of the bar. Those New York nights rarely disappointed my youthful (and yes, I am quoting Tom Cruise in *Top Gun* here) need for speed.

But after four years (my longest stint in one place so far), those happening New York days wore me out good. I decided the glamorous twenty-four/seven, $1,000-a-month shoe-box apartment, kitten heels and take-out food, magazine-editor lifestyle was not something I could see myself doing long-term. Apparently, my boss agreed. She fired me.

I decided the way to betray and bury my New York days was by moving to California, which real New Yawkers know is the ultimate sin and would never commit to unless they wanted to retire. But I pictured leisurely morning jogs by the ocean, a cute pad in some surfside town, screenwriting, wearing flip-flops year-round, warm winters, and my own kitchen without messy roommates who left dirty plates piled up for days. I was seduced by the antithesis of my East Coast years.

Be careful what you wish for was the theme for that year.

Before I knew it, the celebrity suckage was to draw me back into its vortex once again. My "romantic," "writerly" life in Santa Monica consisted of me spending most days alone, typing away on a novel, watching way too much TV (Food Network), going to a part-time screenwriting program in Westwood, and working part-time at a café in Malibu.

The café in Malibu was really the most undignified part. I'd taken the job to find out if I wanted to open my own bakery (I was disillusioned by the success of the hip Magnolia Bakery in New York and my own penchant for sweet stuff, like velveteen cake, which I was getting pretty crafty at making in my new apartment).

So I took the low-paying, thankless job and kept my head down to observe life as an ordinary worker. The likes of Pamela Anderson, Tobey Maguire, and Mira Sorvino graced us with their presence at the café. But no one beat local burnout Gary Busey, who would often storm in to swoop up a six-pack of fancy soda pop. He had such a creepy reputation that no one wanted to serve him. The first time I saw him, since I was a newbie, I got stuck with the job. Lucky me.

By the register, he shoved the bottles in front of me and stared at me with beady almond-shaped eyes, his skin pink and scaly.

I rang up the tab and went to bag his purchase.

"Two bags," he commanded in his gruff alto voice.

When I took his money and went to give him change, a quarter accidentally fell into the tip jar. My heart fell as I looked up to him.

His eyes bulged out of his head. "You owe me twenty-five cents," he seethed, reaching into the jar.

I was frozen. Watching this famous actor fish for some chump change was *amazing*.

I was horrified and sweating. After he fetched his precious coin and left, I knew I could never see *Point Break* again without shivering.

After a year in La-La Land, I decided I needed to move back to the land of normal, seemingly well-adjusted people: aka the Midwest. Though I'd escaped like a refugee from it five years earlier, I thought this time, after the hype of New York and L.A., I'd appreciate the unpretentiousness of Chicago.

I took a job this time in the arts, at a cool, contemporary museum where I solicited grants for exhibitions and projects. This felt much better. As if I was living my life with a higher purpose. And when I'd get home from work, I didn't have to slough off sleaze, like I'd had to in my last two celebrity-centric career incarnations.

But Chicago didn't inspire me. It was ho-hum. "Diversity" in that city meant being from Milwaukee or Indiana or Cleveland, Ohio. The fact that I'd already lived in New York (to which Chicago somewhat self-effacingly compares itself as the "Second City") and California almost made *me* a celebrity in that town, which was truly sad. It isolated me. So did the brutal winters of subzero temperatures. (L.A. had made me so soft).

Most of my midwestern friends had already moved on to starting families or moved on period, like to San Francisco or the East Coast, so my social life suffered. I wasn't into the pub crowd, and the frat scene had never done it for me. Plus, the locals adored Chicago, and I just couldn't get into that mind-set. Big-time disconnect there.

It didn't take long for me to realize that the Midwest and I were like two middle school friends who'd ended up in different high school cliques. So I made a plan to stretch my wings wider, to cast my net farther, and to apply to be a postgrad in London. Now, Europe, *that's* really romantic! Maybe I would never return. Maybe this was my destiny. A girl can dream.

I imagined an island full of witty, posh Hugh Grant types with nice shoes and fabulous haircuts. British men with worldly knowledge and cute accents who could wax poetic about Chelsea and Arsenal whilst debating Labour versus Tories in the next breath. Chaps who holidayed in Switzerland or the south of France. And who invited me to join.

And I got what I wanted again *or* what I thought I wanted *or* what I thought I wanted and actually wanted and then ended up not fullfilling my fantasies, which was becoming a trend around here.

Jesus, maybe I just needed therapy?

London partially redeemed my party-girl persona with my new post-graduate ambitions. My schoolmates and I spent our days discussing the Iraq War, frontline reporting, the Information Age, the Patriot Act, intro graphs, etc., and then blew off some steam drinking whiskey at the local Communist pub, Cuba Libre. The year was academic and alcohol-oriented. I delicately balanced intellect with booze.

I met many handsome boys who found American girls like me "sexy." (Or maybe they just think we're easy?) We'd make out in bars, exchange phone numbers, text-message, go out once or twice for lovely dates, and then they'd disappear, or I would. It was innocent enough, and my dalliances never went much past first base, but something was missing. Substance. My PG-rated romances fell flat.

Knowing that my student visa was to expire in one year gave me freedom but also put people off and kept me on guard. I wasn't stable or in it for the long haul. Or at least I wasn't sure I was and probably gave off a flaky vibe. And though I'd gotten that invite to go snowboarding in the Alps, it seemed a bit weird and sudden coming from a practical stranger, so I declined. Politely, of course. (We *were* in Britain, after all.)

I started questioning again: Did I feel right in London, or did I need to move on? How many more times could I do this without it becoming a joke or a real habit? Why was it that as soon as life calmed down, my mental restlessness went into overdrive? What had happened to my career, my passion, my focus, for chrissakes?

It's been said that those who wander aren't necessarily lost, but as I look back on recent years—while they've all been exciting and filled with travel and adventure and stories and independence— I see that I *have* been a bit lost, propelled by some force that I didn't understand. It's not particularly *bad*, but it is unstable, and I haven't had much time or space to cultivate friendships or put down some roots.

My mother wagered a guess and said I'd been "hiding." How dare she, I argued. How could she make such a judgment! The nerve!

After we'd hung up the phone, I realized she was right. I do feel like I've been hiding. I'm not sorry, but it's not something I want to keep doing. I want to be a part of life, not live on the outskirts of it or escape it all together. I want to exist.

This time I decided to move back to Los Angeles and try hard to give it a go. This meant not putting a time limit on how long I would stay, and it meant not investigating stints at language schools from South America to the Middle East, and it meant not deciding to transplant myself to another city like Austin or San Francisco when my fancy started getting fanciful and I got bored or frustrated, and golly gee, there's just so much to see in the world!

Noooooooooo.

It meant here is a city that I have a bit of familiarity with, where I don't have to make the same mistakes I made the first time around, where I feel employable, where I can rent a reasonable place, where I know some folks and can try to set up shop. Where my other dreams can come true—the ones that take time and patience and calm and being still. Who knows what could happen?

At the high cost of stability, deepened relationships, and a proper career model, my transplantation from Manhattan to Santa Monica, Chicago to England, and back around to the West Coast now, has given me some perspective on the often-envied snow bunny/odd job–havin'/freewheelin' lifestyle. It isn't particularly stress-free or all it's cracked up to be.

As my friends get promoted, hitched, happy 401(k)s, I get a new cell-phone number, transatlantic friendships, a well-stamped passport, worldly sophistication, and funny tales to tell friends living out a mostly peaceful, tranquil day-to-day life in cities or suburbs, and it's awesome. I'm cool, on the go, inspirational.

While I don't regret following my wanderlust thus far, I wonder if I'll get to settle down some. I envy my friends' homes and full lives and families. I want a bit of that—I said a bit.

My refusal to stay put and become a perennial student has meant many easygoing mornings of waking up at ten A.M., lying in my bed and staring at the ceiling, contemplating life while wind breezes through the orange curtains of my bedroom in a tiny corner of London. I've gotten to linger. And skip lectures. I've squandered my twenties, and I don't really care because, for me, that's just the way it's gone. I feel lucky about it.

I've been able to hit the gym at two P.M., when barely no one is there, and work out without being bothered by the busy after-work rush. I can chat with the counter worker who hands me a towel and ask her how she's doing that day, and have time to listen to her answer. It's been great to have space—that's so precious.

I could disappear for a few hours to see the Frida Kahlo exhibition at the Tate Modern on the Thames, when it isn't super-crowded. Or take a boat to Greenwich with my best mate and eat ice cream in front of the Cutty Sark and, later, stop by the pub for a late-afternoon whiskey on the rocks. I've felt all that freedom, and man, it feels so big.

Sometimes too big. Directionless. Frivolous.

Not many people notice if I am here or there, so while my disappearing act has been fun, it's also been quite lonely. Because if people don't notice me and we're not totally engaged, then they can't totally need me, and I'm not an integral part of their worlds. I'm just off in my own one.

I cannot say that I have any real roots at this point, that I've climbed any ladders, that I can afford a whirlwind weekend shopping spree or that I know my town so well that it actually feels like home. I've forgotten the feeling of home, of being stable, if I ever really knew it. I'm an immigrant, from Assyrian ancestry, a displaced ethnic minority without their own country who are often cited in historical texts as nomads.

I'm nomadic; it's in my blood to run (or walk, more likely, according to my leisurely lifestyle).

I can't remember what it's like to be good at my job and have a satisfied boss tell me so. I miss being able to have a stable bank account and see a more concrete future that I can build toward. Maybe with a partner, if I hang around long enough to finally get to know him.

Over the years, unplugging my life over and over again and living responsibility-free has meant space to create art, write, take my time, and be spontaneous. It's also meant a highly self-obsessed, isolated, marginalized me. I have been a satellite. Living by my own selfish whims. Hello, I've come this close to referring to myself in the third person!

But this is not a sad tune. It is just time to change stations and see what else is playing. As I sit on the edge of thirty, I have to wonder if it will be possible for me to hold on and challenge myself to find treasure on a daily basis and reconnect with my work and attempt to actually succeed in my field. Can I combine passion with consistency? Can I find magic and surprise without constantly overhauling my life and living deliberately out of sync?

Stay tuned, I remind myself as I unpack boxes in Hollywood.

About the Editor

EMILY FRANKLIN is the author of the novels *The Girls' Almanac* and *Liner Notes*, as well as a critically acclaimed fiction series, The Principles of Love. She is co-editor of *Before: Short Stories about Pregnancy from Our Top Writers* and *After: Short Stories about Parenting from Our Top Writers* and editor of the forthcoming collection *Eight Nights: Chanukah Essays*. Her young adult novel, *The Other Half of Me*, will be published by Random House in 2007. Her work has appeared in *The Boston Globe* and the *Mississippi Review*, among others.

Having spent her twenties roaming the United States and hiking across Iceland and India, she now lives near Boston with her husband and three young children.

About the Contributors

JULIANNA BAGGOTT's fourth novel, *Which Brings Me to You: A Novel in Confessions* (cowritten with Steve Almond), was published in 2005, as was her second collection of poems, *Lizzie Borden in Love: Poems in Women's Voices*, and her third novel for younger readers, *The Somebodies*, under the pen name N. E. Bode. Having moved on from the glorious work of her twenties—teaching ballroom dancing and English to Spanish pilots, and running a boardinghouse for Koreans—she now teaches in the creative writing program at Florida State University, in Tallahassee, where she lives with the subject of her essay, David G. W. Scott, and their three children.

LAURA CALDWELL, who lives in Chicago with her husband, left a successful career as a trial attorney to become a novelist. She is the author of *Burning the Map, A Clean Slate, The Year of Living Famously, The Night I Got Lucky*, and a novel of suspense, *Look Closely*. She is a contributing editor at *Lake* magazine and an adjunct professor of law at Loyola University Chicago School of Law.

Caprice Crane is a screenwriter and the author of *Stupid and Contagious* and *Forget About It*, which is being made into a movie at New Line Cinema, starring Scarlett Johansson. She's spent most of her twenties writing for MTV and deftly juggling best-friendships with males alongside a series of hopelessly/haplessly romantic relationships. Her longest cohabitation with one male is with her shih tzu, Max: six years. So there's that. You can visit her at www.capricecrane.com.

Megan Crane is the author of *Everyone Else's Girl* and *English as a Second Language*. She graduated from Vassar College, received her MA and Ph.D. in literature from the University of York in England, and has yet to take "detail-oriented" off her résumé. She currently lives in Los Angeles. You can visit her at www.megancrane.com.

Donna Freitas is an assistant professor of religious studies, a freelance writer, and the author of *Becoming a Goddess of Inner Poise: Spirituality for the Bridget Jones in All of Us*. It took only five years for Donna to obtain her Ph.D. in 2002 from Catholic University in Washington, D.C., and don those fancy robes on graduation day, but a full six years of living among hundreds of college first-years in residence halls before she could finally break her habit of signing up for the apartments that came with the jobs. She now lives in Brooklyn with her husband and occasionally takes the subway into Manhattan to look longingly at the Union Square apartment where she once lived (for free).

Hollis Gillespie, a *Writer's Digest* Breakout Author of the Year, is an award-winning, syndicated humor columnist and NPR commentator. Her books are *Bleachy-Haired Honky Bitch*, *Tales from a Bad Neighborhood*, and *Confessions of a Recovering Slut and Other Love Stories*. Her column, "Mood Swing," appears weekly in *Cre-*

ative Loafing, a system of major alternative newspapers published throughout the Southeast. Gillespie lives in Atlanta, Georgia, with two cats, one incontinent pit bull, and one adorable, incredibly well-adjusted, above-average five-year-old daughter. You can visit her at www.hollisgillespie.com.

LAURIE GRAFF is an actor and writer living in Manhattan. She is the author of the best-selling *You Have to Kiss a Lot of Frogs*, *Looking for Mr. Goodfrog*, and *Scenes from a Holiday*. Her monologues appear in *The Best Men's Stage Monologues of 1999* and *New Monologues for Women by Women*. Her acting credits include Broadway, Off-Broadway, and commercials. In her twenties, she worked as a coat-check girl, waitress, dog walker, cat feeder, house sitter, and office temp. Her most humiliating moment was in her thirties, shooting a commercial as an alien dressed head to toe in latex, and zapping people in Times Square. She grew up in Queens and spent a few years in Los Angeles, returning to New York when a relationship ended because she wasn't a good enough driver. Now in her forties, she acts and writes lives and loves like in her twenties but wiser. She'd love to hear from you at www.lauriegraff.com.

Born-and-bred New Yorker **ANNA JANE GROSSMAN** is a freelance writer whose work has appeared in *The New York Times*, *The Washington Post*, Salon.com, *Elle*, *Modern Bride*, *Marie Claire*, and *Seventeen*, among others. Since entering her twenties, she has also found employment as a nanny, a rock-climbing instructor, a tutor, an editorial assistant, a fact checker, a dog walker, a face painter, a copywriter, a blogger, a gossip columnist, a wedding columnist, and a staff writer at both *The New York Observer* and the *New York Post*. When not working, she's been a girlfriend, a heartbreaker, a heartbreakee, an "other woman," a psycho-ex, and a commitment phobe. Anna Jane is cowriter of *It's Not*

Me, It's You: The Ultimate Breakup Book and cofounder of the site Breakupnews.com.

KRISTIN HARMEL is the author of the novels *How to Sleep with a Movie Star* and *The Blonde Theory*. She is also a frequent contributor to *People* magazine and a freelance writer whose work has appeared in *Glamour, Health, Modern Bride, American Baby, Woman's Day, YM, Men's Health, Teen People, People en Español, Who* magazine (Australia), the *St. Petersburg Times*, and dozens of other magazines and newspapers. She appears monthly as "The Lit Chick" on the nationally syndicated TV morning show *The Daily Buzz*, which airs in more than 150 markets coast-to-coast. In her twenties alone, she has lived in Paris, New York, Tampa Bay, and Miami. She currently lives in Orlando and is working on her third novel. She has an admittedly unhealthy obsession with *Sex and the City*, and, much like the fictional Carrie Bradshaw, she's still trying to figure out what she's doing when it comes to dating. Visit her or drop her an e-mail at www.kristinharmel .com. If she doesn't write back right away, she's probably out shoe shopping.

JILL KARGMAN is a writer based in New York City who is deathly afraid of clowns. After graduating from Yale in three years, she learned she still needed to start as a Xerox whore at the bottom of the magazine totem pole. After languishing in the trenches of assistant life, she and her writing partner, Carrie Karasyov, wrote the 2000 Sundance film *Intern*, about their struggles. Their two novels, *The Right Address* and *Wolves in Chic Clothing*, were national best sellers and published in eight languages; in addition, they wrote a young-adult book, *Bittersweet Sixteen*. Jill's freelance work includes more than ten shows for MTV, including episodes of *MTV: Ultrasound* and *So Five Minutes Ago*. She has written more than a hundred articles that have appeared in magazines, including *Vogue*, *Harper's Bazaar*, *Interview*, *Town & Country*, *British GQ*, *Elle*, *Teen Vogue*, and *Travel + Leisure*, as well as her weekly column for *W* magazine online, "EyeSpy" at Style.com. Her new novel, *Momzillas*, is about a scary sect of type-A competitive mothers on New York's Upper East Side. But no matter what dangers lurk in the shark-infested mommy waters, she never, ever would trade them to be back in her twenties.

ERICA KENNEDY is the author of *Bling*, a hip-hop Pygmalion tale about a win-at-all-costs rap impresario who is determined to turn a beautiful small-town singer into a crossover megastar. She has written for *Vibe*, *Us Weekly*, *Teen Vogue*, and *InStyle*. She has also published essays in *The New York Observer* and *Newsweek*.

DEANNA KIZIS'S first novel, *How to Meet Cute Boys*, got rave reviews from *Kirkus*, *Booklist*, *People* (three stars) and *Us Weekly* ("hot pick"), among others. Her new novel, *Finishing Touches*, about an aspiring interior designer who falls in love with her best friend's widower, was released in May 2006. Deanna has also been the West Coast editor of *Elle* and a contributor at *Harper's Bazaar*. Her feature stories have appeared in *Allure*, *Details*, *Cosmopolitan*, *Elle Decor*, *Interior Design*, *O at Home*, *Elle Girl*, *Nylon*, *Entertainment Weekly*, *Los Angeles*, *Domino*, *Lucky*, and *Women's Health*. Some other, less fortunate, facts: Number of ex-boyfriends: nine (it's shocking how long it took her to calculate this). Number of crappy apartments: three. Number of crappy dates: unfathomable. Number of dream dates: one, with her husband—the very patient, gentlemanly Julian—whom she married in September 2006.

BETH LISICK is the author of *Monkey Girl*, *This Too Can Be Yours*, and *Everybody into the Pool*. She also does some acting, makes short films, and organizes the monthly Porchlight Storytelling Series in San Francisco.

CARA LOCKWOOD is the author of *I Do (But I Don't)*, which was made into a Lifetime original movie, as well as *Pink Slip Party* and *Dixieland Sushi*. She was born in Dallas, Texas, and earned a bachelor's degree in English from the University of Pennsylvania. She has worked as a journalist in Austin and is now married and living in Chicago. She ended all but one of her codependent relationships with MasterCard, Visa, and American Express. She pays her balances in full (almost) every month.

ANNA MAXTED is a freelance writer and author of the international best sellers *Getting Over It, Running in Heels, Behaving Like Adults*, and *Being Committed*. Her latest novel is *A Tale of Two Sisters*. She lives in London with her husband and their two sons. Anna finally moved out of her parents' house at age twenty-two, after her dear friend—and homeowner—Caren offered her a room to rent. A year later, Caren politely asked Anna to leave on account of her being far too annoying to live with.

MEGAN MCCAFFERTY is the author of the comic novels *Sloppy Firsts, Second Helpings*, and *Charmed Thirds*, which chronicle Jessica Darling's life from her sixteenth birthday through her college graduation. The next book in the series, *Fourth Comings*, is about her tumultuous early twenties. Megan also maintains a (retro) blog via www.meganmccafferty.com, on which she posts pages from her old journals. For most of her twenties, Megan lived in New York City, worked in magazines, and ate way too much frozen yogurt. She currently resides in Princeton, New Jersey, with her husband and young son. Megan is happy to report that her ass looks better in her thirties than it did in her twenties, but acknowledges that this might be an optical illusion created by her ability to afford more flattering jeans.

JENNIFER O'CONNELL'S books, *Off the Record*, *Dress Rehearsal*, and *Bachelorette #1*, have been called "decadent fun" by *Kirkus Reviews*, declared "chick Lit at its most fun" by the *Denver Post*, and selected a "hot pick" by *Us Weekly*. With the valuable skills she learned in her twenties, including the art of swirling soft-serve yogurt on a cone and how to blend a perfect chocolate-Oreo milk shake, Jennifer is thankful to have a fallback career if this writing thing doesn't work out. And her kids are thankful they have a mother who doesn't balk at the idea of ice cream and rainbow sprinkles for breakfast. She received her BA from Smith College and her MBA from the University of Chicago. She can be reached at www.jenniferoconnell.com.

SHANNON O'KEEFE is an agent with the Park Literary Group. She received her BA and MFA from the University of Notre Dame, and also worked in football recruiting and fund-raising for the university. After finally extracting herself from the Midwest, Shannon ran off to New York in pursuit of book publishing, fine dining on the cheap, sample sales, and errant sports bars. At some point, Shannon started referring to Pittsburgh as the place where she grew up and Brooklyn as home.

ALISON PACE is the author of the novels *If Andy Warhol Had a Girlfriend* and *Pug Hill*. She lives in New York City, where she is at work on another novel. In her twenties, Alison was an art gallery assistant, a sales associate, an advertising sales assistant, a graduate student, a researcher, and a manager of an art gallery. Novelist, hands down, is the best job she's ever had. Visit her website at www.alisonpace.com.

PAMELA RIBON writes a lot. Like, a lot. Seriously. When she's not writing novels or working in film and television, she's clicking away at her personal site, www.pamie.com. That's where she met her husband, which sounds creepy, but it's not. No, for real! In her twenties, she held a number of bizarre jobs that led to fun, fantastic adventures like death threats from crackheads, strangers eating oysters off of her toes, and seeing her novel, *Why Girls Are Weird*, published by Downtown Press. She currently lives in Los Angeles but spent much of her twenties in Austin, Texas—the perfect city in which to have your Quarterlife Crisis.

ALEXANDRA ROBBINS is a *New York Times* bestselling author who lectures frequently to university students, young adults, and professionals working with those groups. She regularly appears in the national media and has written for several publications, including *Vanity Fair*, *The New Yorker*, *The Atlantic Monthly*, *The Washington Post*, and *Cosmopolitan*. She can be contacted at www.alexandrarobbins.com.

MELISSA SENATE spent her twentysomething years not writing a word. Instead, she edited other people's words while working for a publisher of romance novels. In her early thirties, she wrote her debut novel, the best-selling *See Jane Date*, kissing corporate life goodbye for good. Her latest novel (her sixth!) is *Love You to Death*, a fun, fast-paced mystery. Melissa lives on the southern coast of Maine with her husband and young son. Visit her website at www.melissasenate.com.

LEANNE SHEAR and **TRACEY TOOMEY** coauthored the novel *The Perfect Manhattan*. Still in their twenties, they use their expertise as bar behaviorists (and best friends) to dispense advice to clueless bar patrons everywhere as the "Whisky Chicks." In addition to bartending, they've done everything from stalking celeb-rities undercover for tabloid magazines to playing a slutty nurse on *All My Children*. Visit them at www.whiskychicks.com or www.theperfectmanhattan.com.

LEAH STEWART is the author of the novels *Body of a Girl* and *The Myth of You and Me*. She spent much of her twenties wor-rying that she was wasting her twenties by not living in New York City, going out every night, and wearing more fabulous clothes. Now happily settled into her thirties, she lives outside of Chapel Hill with her husband and daughter. Visit her at www.leahstewart.com.

After spending her mid-to-late twenties sponging off the Japa-nese government while teaching English as a second language to de-spondent middle-schoolers, HEATHER SWAIN settled in New York City with her husband. In 1999 her short story "Sushi" was chosen as one of twenty winners in a national contest for new young writ-ers and appeared in the book *Virgin Fiction 2*. She has written two novels published by Downtown Press/Simon & Schuster, *Eliot's Ba-nana* and *Luscious Lemon* (which was shortlisted by *Romantic Times* as the Best Chick Lit Book of the Year and awarded the Best Fic-tion Novel of 2005 by the Indiana State Library's Center for the Book). She is also the author of a novella, several short stories, per-sonal essays, and nonfiction articles that have appeared in antholo-gies, online, in literary journals, and magazines such as Salon.com, *American Baby*, and *Other Voices*. She now lives in a crooked house in Brooklyn with her husband, their children, and a dog.

REBECCA TRAISTER is a staff writer at Salon.com. She has also written for *The New York Observer*, *Vogue*, *Elle*, *The New York Times*, and *New York* magazine. She lives in Brooklyn.

GISELLE ZADO WASFIE is the author of *So Fly*, a coming-of-age love story set in New York City's hip-hop music industry. She is happy that her twenties are at last call and hopes that her thirties won't feel like one long hangover. For more information, check out www.gisellezadowasfie.com.

Five Things You Must Be Armed with as You Go Through Your Twenties:

1.

A Magic 8-Ball. You're sick of feeling overwhelmed and just can't face making another decision on your own.

2.

Twenty dollars that you hid in your jacket pocket last winter. You're poor. And, well, life feels a little boring. But now you're twenty dollars richer and—what do you know— things are looking up.

3.

A sleep mask. Let's face it, you've got a lot on your mind, and you can't afford to sacrifice your beauty rest.

4.

A best friend, whether she's downtown or miles away, one with whom you can complain, find comfort, and laugh.

5.

Your best heels. You'll want to look stylish and poised, and feel comfortable and confident as you walk all over your twenties.

Permissions